Mutiny in the Danish Atlantic World

Mutiny in the Danish Atlantic World

Convicts, Sailors and a Dissonant Empire

Johan Heinsen

BLOOMSBURY ACADEMIC
LONDON • NEW YORK • OXFORD • NEW DELHI • SYDNEY

BLOOMSBURY ACADEMIC
Bloomsbury Publishing Plc
50 Bedford Square, London, WC1B 3DP, UK
1385 Broadway, New York, NY 10018, USA

BLOOMSBURY, BLOOMSBURY ACADEMIC and the Diana logo are
trademarks of Bloomsbury Publishing Plc

First published in Great Britain 2017
Paperback edition published 2019

Cover image: Jan von Gent, 1683 © Det Kongelige Bibliotek | The Royal Library

A catalogue record for this book is available from the British Library.

ISBN: HB: 978-1-3500-2736-7
PB: 978-1-3501-0925-4
ePDF: 978-1-3500-2735-0
eBook: 978-1-3500-2737-4

Names: Heinsen, Johan, author.
Title: Mutiny in the Danish Atlantic world : convicts, sailors and a
dissonant empire/ Johan Heinsen.
Description: London ; New York : Bloomsbury Academic, an imprint of
Bloomsbury Publishing Plc, [2017] | Includes bibliographical references
and index.
Identifiers: LCCN 2017012288| ISBN 9781350027367 (hb) |ISBN 9781350027374 (epub)
Subjects: LCSH: Havmanden (Frigate)–History. |Mutiny–Denmark–Case
studies. |Rumor–Case studies. | Discourse analysis, Narrative–Denmark.
|Sailors–Denmark–Social conditions–17th century. | Convict
labor–Denmark–Social conditions–17th century. |
Denmark–Colonies–Caribbean Area–Social conditions–17th century. |
Sailors–Denmark–History–17th century. | Merchant
marine–Denmark–History–17th century. | Denmark–History, Naval–17th
century.
Classification: LCC VB860 .H45 2017 | DDC 359.1/334–dc23LC record available at
https://lccn.loc.gov/2017012288

Typeset by RefineCatch Limited, Bungay, Suffolk

To find out more about our authors and books visit
www.bloomsbury.com and sign up for our newsletters.

Contents

Illustrations

Acknowledgements

The research presented in this book was made possible by a two-year grant from the Danish Council for Independent Research (FKK).

Along the way, I've enjoyed the comments and suggestions of a great number of scholars – too many to name here. I would like to thank them all for their suggestions and encouragement. The organizers of the 'Carceral Archipelago' conference in Leicester and the workshop 'Runaways: Desertion and Mobility in Global Labor History, c. 1650–1850' in Amsterdam deserve special mention. Both events helped me formulate and think through ideas explored in this book. My editor, Emma Goode, has also been exceptionally helpful in making this book a reality.

Special thanks go to Sara Pinto, who helped me search through Portuguese parish registers and translated several Portuguese sources used in the book, and to Kathrine Funding Højgaard, who helped me dig up manuscripts in the Royal Library in Copenhagen. I also want to thank a few of my great colleagues at Aalborg University, especially Bo Poulsen, Torben Kjersgaard Nielsen, Lars Andersen and Will Kynan-Wilson, all of whom have discussed sources with me or provided feedback on chapters. Another good colleague, Carsten Hjort Lange, did not read any of it, but our daily discussions about Italian football have been just as valuable.

I would like to dedicate this book to my family: to my father, who made me love the docks; to my mother; who made me love books; and to my girlfriend, for her seemingly endless patience.

Introduction

In late October 1684, a Danish traveller was on the last leg of a long return voyage from East Asia when he witnessed a deplorable scene. He had been in the service of the Dutch East India Company for almost two decades, but had quit in order to return, via Amsterdam, to his native Denmark. En route to Copenhagen, the ship sailed dangerously close to the Swedish coast just south of the town of Marstrand, not far from Gothenburg. Strong currents and anxieties about the shoals around the island Læsø forced the ship, the *Sankt Jørgen*, towards the Swedish coast. In his journal, the traveller, Jens Mortensen Sveigaard, lamented the long October nights and the dangers of the rocky skerries. To his relief, they at last managed to anchor. It was then that the crew spied 'the wrecked and deserted West India Man called the Seaman'.[1]

This ship's story was terrifying. As Sveigaard had been in Asia for decades, he had probably not heard it before. However, the crew of the ship knew the tale, despite misremembering the name. The vessel was called the *Havmanden* ('The Merman' in Danish). Most of the thirty-gun frigate was under water, but the masts still stood 'tall and dry'.[2] It was a naval ship, but had been in the charge of the Danish West India and Guinea Company and headed for the young Danish colony of St Thomas in the Caribbean when it was taken off its intended course in early 1683 after the most violent mutiny in Danish history. About 200 people had been on board, roughly half of whom were convicts. At the time of the *Havmanden*'s wrecking, in late March 1683, a convict by the name of Jokum Gulliksen had been its captain for two and half months. He was among the nine men executed at the north-eastern gate of Copenhagen in early July 1683. This spectacle of exemplary terror was reportedly witnessed by 'thousands'.[3] It involved a performance of penitence followed by prolonged torture. The German boatswain's mate who had been singled out by the court as the ringleader had his 'arms, thighs and legs broken' first, before he was 'placed on the wheel at which point he was granted Royal mercy and strangled'.[4] He was supposed to have lain there until he died. The torture and execution of the other eight followed. The

Figure 0.1 Illustration made for second mate Jan von Gent's 1683 leaflet on the events on the *Havmanden*. It depicts three important stages in the story. The artist is unknown. Many details align well with other sources on the mutiny. Jan von Gent, *Dette er en Grundelig Beretning* (Copenhagen: 1683). Image rights: The Royal Library, Copenhagen.

entire scene was printed with a ghastly illustration (Figure 0.1) accompanied by a short narrative of the disastrous voyage written by the ship's second mate.[5] The crime that warranted such a spectacle was 'rebellion' – a term revealing the political timbre that many heard in the story.

This execution captivated contemporaries as well as later historians. However, it also obscured part of the story. Seventeenth- and eighteenth-century accounts accentuated the theme of penitence inherent to early modern executions and turned the story of the mutiny into an affirmative tale about men who had lost their way, but whom the priest managed to bring to their senses just before their justified end. One observer described them as 'hardened and of different religions', but assured his readers that the diligent work of the priests, aided by God, at last made them 'go to their deaths in happiness'.[6] To posterity, the story of the mutiny became the story of the execution – whether the violence of the scene was emplotted as triumph or, as several nineteenth- and twentieth-century accounts had it, as a signifier of a brutal past.[7] Thus, as the story was told and retold, it became one with a moral: power always wins.

This book tells the story differently. It brings the sailors and convicts into the history of the Danish Atlantic World as actors, but perhaps most importantly as storytellers whose words and actions changed the history of the empire. This book centres the story of the early Danish Atlantic World on them. After all, they built the empire, then almost unmade it. Thus, it tells the story of the empire as a story of *dissonance*. By this term, I mean to signify incommensurable and antagonistic perspectives that exist within a shared world, but do not add up.[8] Much of the dynamic and instability of the early Danish Atlantic World owes to the cacophony as such perspectives clashed.

Fragmented empire

The empire-builders of the conglomerate state of Denmark-Norway have recently been conceived of as 'small time agents in a global arena'.[9] The efforts of scholars at placing these agents within the framework of the wider emergence of the Atlantic world have added to a general understanding of the many connections and conflicts that defined Atlantic history. They have, however, centred on the eighteenth and nineteenth centuries exclusively.[10] In a sense, the beginnings of the empire have come to lack a meaningful narrative. As an example, a recent work on slavery in the nineteenth century summarized the seventeenth-century Danish Atlantic World through a set of negatives: 'a lack of leadership and failing connections with Denmark.'[11] This summary is correct, yet the unexplored question is how this state of failure came about. Clearly it was not the intention of the Danish West India and Guinea Company. The mutiny, and as such the agency of lower-class actors, forms a crucial part of the answer.

The Danish colonial empire was long in the making. Its beginnings go back to the start of the seventeenth century when the Danish king, Christian IV, held ambitions for the Danish-Norwegian state to become a European superpower. This included following in the slipstreams of English and Dutch seafarers. Thus, in the 1610s, plans materialized to establish a colony in East India. Dutch knowledge, personnel and capital figured heavily in the plan and eventually a Danish East Indian trading company modelled on Dutch blueprints was established. It sent its first expedition from Copenhagen in 1618 which, ultimately, established a trading colony at Tharangambadi on the Coromandel Coast of the Indian subcontinent.

These years were important to the story told in this book in another way as well. In the same period, the ambitions of the early modern Danish state also materialized in the opening of a new penal institution called *Trunken* at the naval dockyard of Copenhagen (Bremerholmen). There, felons from the entire conglomerate state and its scattered, thinly populated territories were to toil in the service of the increasingly militarized state and its navy. The hard, physical labour they performed helped build the ships that were key to the ambitions of Danish rulers, and they also helped establish the military infrastructure necessary to make Copenhagen a military stronghold. This institution had been preceded by the building of a prison workhouse, again in the Dutch mould, that functioned in the same way but this time for female offenders. The proto-industrial workhouse was one of the earliest experiments in large-scale manufacture on Danish soil.[12] Thus, at the same time as the state sought to throw hooks into the global economy, it also reformed its penal system, instituting a flow that saw convicts from the entire realm become coerced workers of the state and its experiments in armament and new modes of production in Copenhagen. Eventually, they would become colonial labourers as well.

Danish colonial ambition stalled after a costly attempt at intervening in the Thirty Years War (1618–48) in 1625–29. This also brought to an end plans of westward colonization. Soon, the Danish East India colony was left to its own devices, and by the 1640s colonial aspirations had been more or less abandoned. However, in the following decades Danish merchants continued to partake in the burgeoning Atlantic trade. In the middle of the 1650s, serious plans emerged to add a Caribbean colony to the empire, and a West India Company was established with a base in Copenhagen. A further rekindling of Danish ambitions came as war between Denmark and Sweden spread to the Atlantic theatre and a Swedish slave-trading fortress on the Gold Coast (modern-day Ghana) was conquered by a Swedish privateer in Danish service. It was handed over to the Danes in 1658 and a trading company for African trade was established, operating out of Glückstadt (now in Germany, but formerly Danish) on the Elbe River, where several well-connected foreign merchants were based.[13] Across the Atlantic, the first real push came in 1665 when an expedition arrived at the small volcanic island of St Thomas in the Leeward Islands, hoping to turn its steep slopes and ancient forest into a Danish plantation colony.[14] The initial attempt failed, but in 1671 a new West India Company (heavily subsidized by the king) was established in Copenhagen and two ships left the Danish capital heading for the Leewards. They arrived in the spring of 1672, and successfully settled at St Thomas. Around the same time, contact was re-established with the outpost on the Coromandel Coast, which was – incredibly – still Danish.

The Company colony of St Thomas was conceived as a tightly controlled plantation complex built on the coerced labour of indentured servants and convicts. Underpinning its establishment was a vision of a closed loop of goods and people circulating between metropole and colony to the dual benefit of Company investors and the state. The use of convicts might have been prompted by the fact that the right to slave trading was at the time held by the African Company in Glückstadt. Thus, the West India Company needed other avenues of coerced labour. Indentured servants helped build to the English Caribbean colonies that appear to have been a model for the Danish; thus, it is logical that they were considered a first option.[15] However, the unwillingness of the urban and rural poor to migrate led authorities to conceive of the above-mentioned penal institutions as reservoirs of labour. Thus, in the Company's charter the king granted them access to 'as many [men] of those who are convicted to our irons and prison as [the Company directors] find useful, and of women as many as they desire among those who are brought to serve in the prison workhouse or other places due to their unseemly living'.[16] Such convicts were envisioned as the Company's labourers in its attempts to reap a profit from the production of cotton, indigo, tobacco and sugar, but first they were to help establish the necessary colonial infrastructure in the Caribbean – clearing forests, hauling building materials and erecting a fortress. Such labour was not unlike that which convicts at the dockyard prison already performed. A recent collection of essays conceives of such work as 'the reproductive labor of empire'.[17] In these ways, the use of convicts in the early Danish Atlantic World must be understood in relation to the market of coerced or semi-coerced labour in general and to already established models for the exploitation of criminals in the service of the state.[18]

This use of convicts was also part of a larger trend in early modern colonial empires.[19] The Portuguese had been trailblazers in this respect, shaping their system of convict transportation on Roman law and its notion of exile. Thus, the convict was not unfree in the colony itself, only restricted from going back to Europe.[20] A 1615 law allowed the English to follow suit, enabling their courts to sentence criminals to exile overseas – although it did not become commonplace until the Transportation Act of 1718. English practices were modelled on indenture, so upon arrival the convict was usually sold to the private sector for a set amount of years. This also meant that in the colony they were indistinguishable from the indentured.[21] The Swedes then emulated the English, creating a similar scheme of convicts-as-indentured servants in 1640.[22] The Dutch dabbled only briefly in Atlantic convict transportation in the 1680s, but operated a major circulation of convicts between their Indian Ocean colonies.[23] The French used convicts as early as the Atlantic expeditions of the 1540s, but institutionalized the practice only at the beginning of the eighteenth century, when convicts were used on a large scale in North America.[24] Meanwhile, the Spanish transported considerable numbers of convicts to act as soldiers or workers in their fortresses in North Africa, Central and South America and the Pacific.[25] Yet despite all of these parallels, the Danish model in which a trading company was given the right to recruit convict labourers appears to be without foreign precedent. Further, a unique feature of the Danish system was the fact that whereas convicts in other empires were conceived of as either banished people or as a form of indentured labourers, Danish convicts, widely referred to as 'thralls' or 'slaves', were conceived of as colonial workers for life.

The use of inexpensive, coerced labour was key to realizing the feverish dream that drew in investors. However, the history of the Danish Atlantic World is not one of monopolistic control, but rather one of open inter-imperial trade. St Thomas was transformed into a polyglot slave trading and smuggling entrepôt centred on an open harbour, heavily influenced not by Danish, but by local Dutch and English interests. Part of this transformation was due to structural drivers ranging from a lack of risk-willing capital to the climate in the newly founded colony, which was conducive to rampant disease, but it owed just as much – if not more – to the manifold practices and resistances of an array of actors. Mistakenly, the convicts had been assumed to be docile workers. The mutiny on the *Havmanden* was the most important in this series of events. It struck the Company at a crucial juncture: while it had managed to send yearly expeditions with fresh supplies and workers to the colony in the first part of the 1670s, it struggled economically. The state helped partly cover the losses and assisted the Company with sailors and materiel, but when the Scanian War broke out in 1675, pitting Danes against Swedes in a battle for control of the Baltic, resources were diverted elsewhere. Thus, for the next five years, the governor, Jørgen Iversen, struggled to keep control of the colony as it began to spin out of control. The death rates among Company workers meant that it failed to reap substantial harvests. Instead, other economic interest had taken hold. The second Anglo-Dutch War of 1672–74 had prompted the arrival of a number of migrants from the nearby Dutch and English islands. They became planters. Some of them brought their own enslaved workers, and their influence increased in the absence of Company ships. They challenged the Company's plan of a monopoly, though Iversen worked hard to keep them in check. However, there was nothing he could do: St Thomas was taking on the characteristics of the 'empire without dominion' that were to define its history.[26] Then in 1680, after war had ended, the Company scrambled to regain control. A reorganization of it and an influx of new investors, some of whom were partly forced by the state, followed. Iversen, however, was weary and returned to Copenhagen, leaving the colony to his successor, Nicholas Esmit, who arrived via a Dutch ship and took charge of the island and its 300–400 inhabitants. The Company managed to send out a small ship that autumn with fresh supplies and a new merchant for the colony. However, when the ship returned the following summer, it was with reports from said merchant that the new governor was not acting in the interest of the Company. Rumour circulated that he dabbled in piracy. Thus, to the horror of the Company's directors, the colony was becoming increasingly embedded in the regional economy rather than profiting the business and its investors.

The directors worked hard to regain control of the colony. Iversen was brought back in, and he was key to the plans of resettling the colony with Danish subjects. However, the recruitment of indentured servants remained slow, so the Company again opted for convicts. At this point, the rights to slave trade had been transferred to the Company, but its two attempts at supplying the colony with enslaved Africans had failed: the first, in 1674, because of a shipwreck; the other, in 1680, because diseases had ravished the crew upon arrival on the Gold Coast. Convicts remained the Company's only steady supply of coerced workers. Thus, the disastrous voyage of the *Havmanden* can be read as the last desperate gasp of a Company that was already drowning.

Preparations for the voyage had followed on the heels of a tumultuous spring of 1682, when new directors had taken charge. They were forced to sell their only vessel, the small ship *Den Kronede Grif*, which had made the 1680 voyage to St Thomas, in order to fit out the voyage.[27] They lacked funds: many investors had failed to pay what they owed, and so had the king himself, who had agreed to pay for the upkeep of the African holdings. Apparently, part of what was owed came in the form of victuals for the *Havmanden* voyage.[28] The directors had fashioned a supplication to the king, explaining the necessity of borrowing ships. The argument was thoroughly mercantilist: the Caribbean island was of great importance to the kingdom's economic future both as a source of colonial goods and as a recipient of Denmark's agricultural produce. The supplication, however, was painfully realistic in one respect: it was explicitly clear that the Company was too weak to carry the burden of colonization by itself. They needed two ships (one for the West Indies and one for an African voyage) and help in fitting them out with both men and victuals.[29] They only received one, the *Havmanden*, forcing them to conjure up a phantasmagorical four-legged itinerary of going to the Caribbean with as many Danish subjects as possible, then to the Gold Coast and back with 300 enslaved Africans, before bringing colonial goods back to Copenhagen.

Securing whatever funds they could, the Company directors outfitted the ship. Slowly the Company received goods from all over the Danish conglomerate state: rye from Jutland, wheat and peas from the island of Lolland, beef from Zealand, wood from Norway.[30] There was flax cloth from merchants in Northern Jutland[31]; casks of mutton came all the way from Iceland.[32] The beer was brewed locally on Christianshavn while the pork was brought from Amager.[33] Further, there was French brandy bought via Hamburg to serve the Company merchants in Africa.[34] (There was ordinary Danish brandy for the sailors and locals on St Thomas.) Via Amsterdam they bought East Indian goods such as silk cloth and corals as well as brass and copper trinkets and bars of iron, all intended for trade in Africa.[35]

The ship left on 6 November 1682. It was to begin a new era that never came. 200 people were on board, including about 100 convicts, some of whom had their families with them. As many people as possible had been recruited, and the ship was tightly packed. Iversen's family and Company officials appear to have filled the cabins. The officers, or at least the petty ones, seem to have been placed in the forecastle, while the convicts and indentured servants were to live below deck. Where the common sailors fit in, is somewhat unclear, though the sources hint that they lived on the lower deck as well. Upon entry in the North Sea later that month, the ship experienced the first of many storms. Soon, the drinking water turned foul. Then, on 20 January 1683, the *Havmanden* was taken over by a large group of convicts allied with a band of angry German, English, Danish and Norwegian sailors. They killed the ship's Dutch captain, Governor Iversen and a handful of their loyal men. They wished to take the ship to Ireland and share the spoils equally among all who took part in the mutiny. It was an act of piratical seizure underpinned by egalitarian conceptions echoing Atlantic piracy. However, their unity collapsed in the following weeks, and a large contingent of its passengers were set ashore on an island in the Azores, before the convict-captain decided to try and take the ship back to Denmark. However, by late March, the ship was caught in a storm, and wrecked on the Swedish coast.

This was a devastating blow for the Company. The voyage was to bring enough Danish subjects to cement Company power and Danish domination, as well as a governor determined to fulfil Danish colonial fantasies. It was also meant to bring in enough bonded Africans to begin large-scale sugar production on

St Thomas, and to bring the Company an immediate influx of cash. Hope was lost when news from Marstrand arrived. In a letter to their African officers on the Gold Coast, the directors lamented how 'the company's compass [had been] quite dislocated' by the mutiny. The ship was insured in Amsterdam, but the case drew out for years. The mutiny also appears to have further deterred investors from investing in the Company. For the next few years, its internal correspondence reads like a prolonged meditation on powerlessness. Meanwhile, cut off from Copenhagen, the Caribbean colony found other ways of maintaining itself, even profiting by maintaining an open harbour for inter-imperial trade and piracy. While the Company sent out several ships in the second half of the 1680s they were all much smaller than hitherto, bringing only small batches of coerced labourers. The rights to the slave trade were leased to private merchants, as were the rights to trade to and from St Thomas. Further, the king agreed to let a group of foreign merchants under the Brandenburg flag establish a trading outpost on the island.[36] Their operations made St Thomas one of the most important regional slave markets. In the meantime, the Company was dormant and only in 1697 did it re-emerge properly, and by then it was with a different vision of empire – one heavily centred on the slave trade. At that point, the Company, as explored in the Conclusion to this book, actively argued against ideas of using convicts as colonial labourers.

At its core, the floundering of the West India and Guinea Company in the 1680s and 1690s was not determined by economic constraints on the part of merchants and capitalists in Copenhagen. While the West Indian business nearly dissolved, the Danish East India Company gained momentum, ushering in what has been termed a 'great age' (from 1687 to 1704) by scholars.[37] Had the West India and Guinea Company not been so troubled, it seems likely that investors would have invested in the Company, rather than seeking to take over its rights. Instead of structural limitations, it was the blow of the *Havmanden* mutiny and its subsequent shipwreck that definitively side-lined the Company and allowed its Atlantic enterprise to become so profoundly embedded in the chaotic exchanges of the maritime Caribbean.

The meanings of mutiny

This book is about two things: first, the making of Denmark's Atlantic empire, and in particular the role of coerced labour in its making; second, the way in which lower-class storytelling and traditions of resistance shook this empire. It centres on the days of the mutiny and posits this event as a saturation point at which a host of different factors and traditions came together and enabled singularly powerful action that brought a crisis to the dual (and often intertwined to the point of being indistinguishable) projects of capital accumulation and state-driven empire-building. By extension, this is also a book about *how* to study such events.

Not only was this mutiny key in shaping the early Danish Atlantic, but it is also among the best documented of its time across empires. As already noted, several short accounts in print exist. We also have letters from those involved and the detailed sentence pronounced on the mutineers, specifying who had done what on board. However, the following chapters lean most heavily on a journal produced by the ship's supercargo and Company assistant, Simon Braad.[38] On the face of it, Braad's account is a typical, straightforward journal: each day's entry has navigational information on winds, currents and sails. However, as will be demonstrated in detail in Chapters 1 and 2, it sometimes takes a form that suggests that it was written with retrospective knowledge of events. Braad also imparts knowledge that he admits having gleaned from others on board, most likely at a later date. Another problem with its production is how Braad goes to great lengths to describe the ship post-mutiny as governed by a pack of thieves ruling through terror. Yet at the same time, he quotes their words in ways that would have compromised his safety. Having been evicted from the cabins, he could only have written such remarks in the crowd on the decks. This would surely have been impossible. Yet we do know that the text was not written long after the events it describes. It existed when Braad was examined by the Company authorities in Copenhagen at some point in mid-April 1683. He references it several times in his answers and some of his formulations are almost verbatim, suggesting that he had it with him and/or that he had used it to rehearse. This window implies that the account is a most likely rewrite adding to a pre-existing barebones journal kept on the ship itself. This rewrite can be deduced to have taken place in the five or so days from when Braad left the ship at Marstrand and before he arrived in Copenhagen. It would seem that the journal was produced in an effort to account for the voyage in expectance of a confrontation with the Company authorities in Copenhagen. There are several hints of the 'intended' audience throughout. The most important is the way Braad references a now lost letter sent to the Company directors on 9 November at Elsinore: 'as I reported to the high and noble directors . . .'[39] Clearly, he assumes that his reader knows the contents of this letter.

The text he presented to them is about 16,000 words long. The interrogation is, approximately, another 5,000 words. Together they form the most detailed account of a seventeenth-century mutiny in the Atlantic, and probably the most detailed of any extant account of a shipboard mutiny before the second half of the eighteenth century.[40] At its core, the journal presents an attempt to explain the mutiny as a result of failed authority on the part of the ship's Dutch captain (a plot explored in Chapter 2). Thus, it played off of common tropes about power and how it was supposed to be exercised. As a performance of Braad's own accountability, it served him well. As one of the few of those who came back, Braad was never charged with anything, and the Company even trusted him enough to later send him back to Marstrand where he helped salvage the goods from the wreck.

Yet despite its careful attempt at constructing a recognizable plot that might serve as a demonstration of Braad's innocence and ability, the journal also provides many details extraneous to this narrative. Much of it testifies to, or stems from, stories circulating within the ship after the mutiny. This can be explained by his anticipation of a legal aftermath in which authorities would be eager to establish who had authored the conspiracy below deck. Thus, the text is intensely preoccupied with what was said and rumoured. Braad knew that words or exchanges picked up might be of importance in court. However, this extraneous information allows for other readings than the one he might have intended. It introduces dissonance to his story which comes to contain reverberations and echoes of lower-deck discourses. The first part of this book hinges on re-emplotting such traces of a different world of discourse taking place just of out of earshot of the authorities.[41] Thus, the text can we worked to reveal the ship itself as a complicated, many-layered social sphere ripe with antagonistic perspectives and voices.

As I explore Braad's accounts, as well as a host of other sources, in order to understand the processes of mutiny, I wrestle with how historians have interpreted mutiny. I would argue that it is possible to divide much of the existing international literature on early modern maritime unrest into three categories based on their way of explaining such events. I propose to call the three (often overlapping) models they apply: first, the 'visceral' model; second, the 'theatre' model; and third, the 'class struggle' model.[42]

The 'visceral' model for explaining mutinies hinges on a notion that the acts of lower-class subjects were driven by instinct. This atomizes history, as it results in a disregard of the social dynamics inherent to such events. Instead, mutinies become the result of gut reactions or simple criminal dispositions. Such a mode of causation is on full display in the accounts of the few Danish historians who have touched on the mutiny since the nineteenth century. Their accounts have emphasized the destitution experienced by the mutineers, but have also placed a heavy emphasis on the stereotypically depraved character of the ringleaders in order to explain the violence of the event.[43] Of course, while such a way of explanation remains intellectually unsatisfying, the visceral model, has one thing going for it. Indeed, hunger and thirst was a defining part of life on the ship in the months leading up to the mutiny, as well as an important driver in other actions of the social groups involved (discussed in Chapters 4 and 5). However, its atomizing tendency runs counter to the sources which continually hint that the mutiny was a collective effort premeditated by weeks of deliberation below deck. Thus, while it can point to a causal trigger (though it was far from the only one), it cannot explain why the mutiny happened *the way it happened*.

More is to be gained from dealing with the second model – what I propose to call the 'theatre model'. Its most famous proponent was historical anthropologist Greg Dening, who used it in his iconic study of the mutiny on the *Bounty*, but it is congruent with a much older way of explaining shipboard unrest, in fact such a model acts as the structure of Braad's journal. Dening puts great emphasis on the culture of life at sea, arguing that the ship and its greatly ritualized world was akin to theatre. Ritual or 'ceremony' produced 'efficiency' in 'moving a large number of men with the least idiosyncrasy on their part and without the distraction of conflict with one another'.[44] It did so by turning the order of deference and regularity into something 'socially real'.[45] In this way, the 'theatre' of shipboard life made order, even hegemony, a reality through its continuous performance of 'unambivalent spaces'.[46] The *Havmanden* was replete with attempts at performance. Indeed, post-mutiny, one of the first actions of the new leaders was a highly ritualized oath-taking ceremony, explored in chapter three. From such a premise, Dening deduces that mutinies happen when ceremony fails, unsettling a host of relationships as the authorities no longer act their part in the script. This lack is seen as opening up a space of improvisation in which subordinates begin to renegotiate their part.[47]

While Dening's model stresses the importance of the culture and social world of life at sea, it is unfortunate that it hinges on a tight correlation between what happened in the cabin and what transpired on the decks: implicitly this means that lower-class subjects become actors of history when the performances of their superiors fail.[48] Yet a failure of the authorities to act their parts is certainly part of Braad's way of conceiving the mutiny. Thus, as I argue in Chapter 2, it forms part of the explanation, though far from all of it. The main problem for applying it directly on the *Havmanden* is, however, rather obvious: most of the mutineers were not mariners, and they were not used to living in the highly ritualized world of the ship. To stay loyal to Dening's metaphor, we might say that they did not know the script.

In a response to the work of social historian Marcus Rediker, Dening stated that he did not believe that 'political ideology was the cause of the mutiny'.[49] This is the same as saying that the mutiny was not caused by traditions of the lower deck, but by a failure of those in the cabin. Opening a path for a maritime history from below, Rediker (and the many scholars who have in recent years followed in his trail) has argued for the centrality of such traditions in maritime social life. The ships that helped build Atlantic capitalism, Rediker argues, were like factories, and the sailors were their proletariat who slowly, but steadily, developed practices that allowed them to contest their exploitation.[50] In this view, shipboard unrest becomes meaningful as a form of class struggle, and the traditions of lower class egalitarianism help explain the radical appeal of phenomena such as Atlantic piracy which had its heyday in the 1710s and 20s as well as sailors' role in the age of revolution. Rediker's assertion came first in a study of the social worlds of English merchant sailors and pirates in the eighteenth century, but it has since been transposed to help interpret and explain the struggles of many other lower class and subaltern actors. Thus, scholars have used the frame of class struggle to explain conflict on naval and slave ships, as well as in colonies, ports, plantations and garrisons all around the early modern Atlantic World.[51] It has also been used by scholars of the Indian Ocean World.[52] The analysis in this book would have been unthinkable without the many fruitful discussions this turn has prompted.[53]

In the context of this book, the main strength of the model is its analytical re-centring which calls for in-depth reflections on the specifics of how shipboard unrest came about and was played out from the vantage point of the lower deck. Thus, it helps us to think through what Rediker calls 'the process of shipboard revolt'.[54] I wish to add to our understanding of such processes by zooming in as much as possible, applying the methodologies proposed by micro-historians. They help tease out the complexity of such processes.[55] Thus, the mutiny on the *Havmanden* was catalyzed by a host of factors including immediate destitution, the material deterioration of the ship itself, rumours about the hardships of colonial servitude, class-based resentments against the officers, dreams of spoils echoing Atlantic piracy, abusive superiors, long-standing traditions of flight on the part of convicts, equally long-standing traditions of resistance on the part of maritime workers, anti-Dutch resentments, notions of faulty authority and more, and its furthering was aided by many different types of relationships, some which formed in the voyage itself and some which predated it.[56]

However, perhaps most importantly, this close scale reveals the importance of storytelling and rumour in acts of lower-class resistance. While such storytelling is rarely found in archives, its imprints are almost always there. Like dark matter, we cannot observe it, but we can observe its gravitational pull.[57] This pull should alert us to its ability to shape history. Even if there is no 'unproblematically authentic' voice to be encountered in the archives, subaltern groups such as convicts spoke and their words did hold power to shape the course of history.[58]

Stories and rumour

At the heart of this book is an attempt to show how the telling of stories and the transmission of rumour transformed the social worlds of ships (as well as colonies and prisons).[59] In order to think through and contextualize such practices of speech, I have attempted to think of ships in terms of sound and listening. Life at sea was, for the most part, life in a space which according to philosopher Sir Francis Bacon contained 'nothing to be seen but sky and sea'.[60] Instead, ships were experienced by the ear. They were soundscapes of loudness and muteness, the former being a privilege as well as a tool of authorities and the latter being the reality of subordinates. In turn, we need to think of the process of *listening* as different groups and actors construed the noises of others.[61] A ship contained many different spaces for listening, interpretation and narration and each space was tied to different traditions and dynamics.

The importance of such spaces reflects in the sources and their intense concern with speech. Scholars have argued that conflicts over speech were frequent in young and threatened colonial communities.[62] This was the case with the ship specifically and with the Danish Atlantic in general.[63] The archive of the *West India and Guinea Company* abounds with reports of what had been heard and rumoured: uneasy narratives full of echoes. They tell of a world of broken oaths, unruly tongues and disobedient utterances – instances of captured speech whose complex dissonance reveals the social world constituted by empire-building.[64]

As the writings of early modern voyagers amply testify, ships were full of words and noises, some authoritarian, others egalitarian.[65] Sailors and passengers filled the lulls of voyaging with stories, often touching on subjects that were not seen as befitting of such actors by their superiors.[66] For instance, in his early-eighteenth-century diary, a Norwegian sailor recorded a rhyme about the tongue of 'Jan Hagel' (a commonly used synonym of the common sailor): 'do not take heed of Jan Hagel's stories, they often speak of what they cannot know.'[67] The rhyming is lost in translation, but the idea is clear: sailors' tongues spoke too much and out of turn. Of course, the irony is bountiful, as this was recorded by a man who was a 'Jan Hagel' himself and whose stories, explored in Chapter 4, speak indiscriminately of a great many subjects including a great deal about struggles at sea.

This is not the time or place to theorize storytelling or rumour.[68] My aim is not to deal in abstracts, but to study specific practices in order to show the power of words and their speaking in transforming social relations in the early modern Atlantic world. However, from the theories of others it may be helpful to draw out some rudimentary features of the type of acts that I propose to focus on.

Lower-deck discourse took place among people who were, in a sense, equals, literally in the same boat.[69] That is not to say that there were not important divisions amongst them. Not only were ships intensely stratified, but the *Havmanden* contained even more divisions than usual, perhaps most importantly that between free and unfree. Storytelling effaced this division, as argued in Chapter 2, where I explore the physical and social space in which such exchanges took place and how they developed in the course of the voyage. Most importantly, in this regard, the unusually crammed confines of the ship was a world of many listeners. This social context also meant that stories evolved as they were often expressed by many tongues, not in concert, but in exchange, one tongue picking up where another left off.[70] As argued by cultural historians, stories told by early modern lower-class storytellers riffed dexterously on a wide range of themes within a somewhat shared culture, whereby they got much of its power to move their audiences.[71] This also means that different actors might not hear, and, by extension retell a story in exactly the same way.[72] Such exchanges and the drift they imply made them polyphonic, somewhat open-ended, constantly shifting as new narrators took the stories told in new directions.[73] While we can rarely trace such shifts directly, they are key to understanding how stories and rumour travelled.

Despite storytelling and the spreading of rumour being a shared experience, it could often not afford to be completely open as superiors (as explored in Chapters 3 and 4) listened carefully to the words exchanged by their subordinates. Thus, much of the storytelling analysed in this book can be conceptualized as part of what anthropologist James C. Scott has labelled 'hidden transcripts'.[74] Because of the stakes involved it hinged on secrecy, and on controlling who picked it up. As we think about the social conditions under which stories were told this is a key consideration. While the notion of a hidden transcript has received considerable criticism for the way that it conceptually dichotomizes the discourses of the powerful and those of subalterns,[75] it remains absolutely vital to any close study of processes of class struggle to consider how muteness and loudness was negotiated and how the necessary trust for the telling of transgressive stories within a given community was built. These processes and the way they changed throughout the voyage are explored throughout the first part of this book. Further, they play a part in the later chapters as well, in which they are explored in a wider setting.

The social character of such exchanges is a key feature in the context of this book. By social, I mean two things: first, that storytelling and rumour was informed by the material conditions and power dynamics shaping a given historical context; and second, that they created a relationship or even a community between the speaker and the listener. By extension, they hold the potential to transform said social situation. Storytelling shaped such communities by allowing for an exchange of experiences, though obviously not necessarily one's own.[76] In turn, the social dynamics of storytelling means that what is narrated becomes 'the experience of those who are listening'.[77] Thus, storytelling is a form of sharing that is tied to specific social spaces.

Storytelling has often been asserted to thrive in places of boredom and manual labour. Few places were more clearly defined by these characteristics than the voyaging ship. Rediker has identified the yarns of sailors as taking place around the tedious manual work such as that of picking oakum.[78] Similarly, in his discussion of storytelling in the memoirs of soldiers and sailors in eighteenth- and nineteenth-century France, David Hopkin notes how locations such as ships 'brought large numbers of men together and forced them to live in intimacy with each other'.[79] In turn, the 'long periods of enforced idleness associated with such environments turned storytelling into a valued activity'.[80] On the *Havmanden*, boredom and the constant churn of work and rest experienced by the sailors was, paradoxically, matched with a physical threat of hunger, disease and an uncertain future that the convicts especially had to cope with. Scholars have often asserted how uncertainty bred rumour, which can be understood as a way to gain agency through interpretation in times of distress.[81] Thus, both of these intertwined forms of subversive exchange had almost ideal conditions on the lower deck of the *Havmanden*, as they did on many ships traversing early modern oceans.[82]

All of this hints that the story offers something 'useful' to its listeners – again a point that requires us to pay careful attention to the specifics of the social conditions in which stories were told and heard.[83] Stories could contain a moral, practical advice, proverbs etc. Similarly, rumour could relate news from afar. Employing a very old term, we might say that stories have a 'poetics.' Aristotle defined poetics as a mode of storytelling countering the contingencies of history. He argued that while history simply told things as they happened, poetics took on the more noble task of narrating according to 'likelihood and necessity'.[84] In this way, the poetics of storytellers deals in knowledge of what 'a certain kind of person tends to say or do'.[85] This means we can learn from stories – a practical dimension that connects the past with the future. Thus, stories become models for potential actions. Hopkin points towards this dimension as well, when he remarks how storytelling 'gave soldiers and sailors the fantasy of revenge over their officers, but it also allowed them to explore avenues of resistance, such as desertion, and the consequences that might flow from such acts'.[86] As he argues, this means that 'stories could mobilize individuals to action'.[87] From Braad's journal (itself poetical in this sense, as I discuss in Chapter 2) as well as other sources we sense how stories in this regard become transformational of the social settings that foster them; thus, the solidarities that formed on the lower deck of the *Havmanden* owed much to stories of past experiences providing intelligence of what lay in store for those about to become part of Denmark's colonial empire, but also to stories about potential ways to get out of this bind. In this way, the story of an event becomes inseparable from the event itself.[88] Throughout this book, we will come to see how this was the case in many of the types of acts through which lower class actors challenged the powerful.

* * *

The book is divided into two parts. The first, The Noises of Mutiny, explores the processes of the mutiny on the *Havmanden* and its dissonances. Chapter 1, The Promises of a Seller-of-souls, takes us into the thick of the mutiny. It considers how the governor acted in the lead-up to the mutiny, and attempts to answer the question of how the convicts and sailors interpreted the promises he made to them. While we have no direct access to their discussions, the stories and rumours which had circulated in the first ten years of the Company empire provide a sense of what might have been spoken, and helps explain what earned him the dramatic slur 'seller-of-souls' uttered moments before his death.[89] Chapter 2, Echoes, provides a meditation on the causes and processes of mutiny. It offers a close reading of Braad's journal, revealing the many dissonant echoes of the world below deck which he picked up in his own attempt to fashion a plot about failed authority out of the confusing events of the ship. Deconstructing Braad's elite narrative, the chapter attempts to use the extraneous fragments he provides to construct an alternative narrative of the lower deck and the storytelling that preceded the mutiny. Finally, Chapter 3, *Ways of Listening*, traces the attempts at recreating order within the ship post-mutiny by the mutineers themselves. It explores how shipboard order and ritual worked to inculcate certain ways of listening, and re-emerged as an order of eavesdropping and informing. Evicted from his place in the cabins, Braad described the experience of being subjected to such an order and the anxieties it provoked. The chapter ends with the breakdown of the coalition behind the mutiny and its violent aftermath which brought the ship back into Danish waters before its wreck.

Whereas Part I focuses on the ship and its complicated social world of rumours, plots and thresholds, Part II, A Social History of Dissonance, situates the mutiny in a wider context of lower class traditions and struggles. Chapter 4, Jan Hagel's Stories, examines traditions of conflict and resistance among Danish seafarers throughout the early modern period. It does so from a comparative perspective and in light of recent research on maritime culture and radicalism. It looks especially at the unique writings of maritime workers in the Danish empire themselves as they reveal a culture in which stories of transgressions and resistance circulated. This is followed up in Chapter 5, Birds in Cages, by an exploration of the traditions of resistance of convicts, both in the institutions from whence the convicts on the *Havmanden* had come, but also in the colony where they had been headed. It focuses particularly on collective attempts at running away – an act that shared many features with mutiny and often began with acts of storytelling. The last chapter, Dissonant Empire, explores the maritime culture that flourished in the absence of Company intervention on St Thomas. As the mutiny on the *Havmanden* left the island isolated, other actors such as smugglers and pirates filled the void.[90] By exploring the histories of the pirate crews that used St Thomas as a harbour in the period, the chapter demonstrates how this phenomenon itself was driven by both rumour and legend.

A note on translations: Translating seventeenth-century Danish into modern English can make for some awkward prose. Instead of masking this inelegance, I have opted to be as true to the originals as possible. The one systematic exception is punctuation. Seventeenth-century Danes rarely used full stops and generally wrote incredibly long sentences. In order to be as close to the original as possible, I have also retained the Danish spellings of foreign names.

Part One

The Noises of Mutiny

1

The Promises of a Seller-of-souls

In some circumstances, a promise can be heard as a threat. Such ambivalent words had sounded on 19 January 1683, in the evening before the mutiny. They had been spoken by the governor of St Thomas, Jørgen Iversen, and had evoked his power over the lives of his subalterns. He had uttered them on the deck of the *Havmanden* to a group comprising mostly of convicts. The uneasy resonances that they are likely to have heard in his words stemmed from a decade of discordant empire-building in the Danish Atlantic in which he had played a major part. Now this history of conflict echoed in a single speech act and inflected upon its reception. Thus, Iversen's words that night tunes us into that space of interpretation that was emerging below deck as well as the dissonance of the early Danish Atlantic world in general.

Iversen had already retired for the evening when the ship's Dutch captain, Jan Blom, had sought his help. In itself, this marked the gravity of the situation as the two men had clashed over questions of provisions and authority from the moment the ship embarked in early November.[1] Iversen had been insulted by Blom's unwillingness to treat him like his equal, while Blom seems to have been annoyed at the governor's meddling in the running of the ship.[2] At the time in question, the two had argued intensely for days, loudly enough that the people living below deck got wind of their discussions. Despite having been at sea for two-and-a-half months, the ship had only just recently entered the English Channel and was at this point somewhere southeast of Plymouth. They were running out of drinkable water, but Blom wanted to press on, apparently hoping to stop at Cape Verde, while Iversen wished to seek an English harbour right away. However, now they were forced to join forces; at night Blom had furled the sails because of fears that the ship would run upon shoals in the dark when a group of convicts (and likely a few sailors) had forced him off the deck and reset the sails.[3]

According to Simon Braad, the ship's 23-year-old supercargo and Company assistant, Iversen took a lamp and ventured out on to the deck 'to learn who the

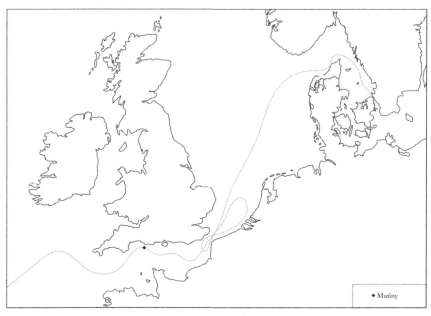

Figure 1.1 A reconstruction of the itinerary of the *Havmanden*, based on Simon Braad's recordings and sightings. Copyright © the author.

authors of this work might be'.[4] Braad was likely right there with him, as he seems to have acted as Iversen's right-hand man.[5] The governor was a veteran of colonization in the West Indies. Born in 1638, he had travelled from Denmark to the British Caribbean as a youth. There he had toiled as an indentured servant. Later, he became a merchant.[6] Such experience appears to have been the reason that the Company chose him to be the first governor of the Danish colony of St Thomas (1672–1680). Now he was returning to resume that task for a second term.[7] Along with him was his family, including his son from his first marriage (he was a widower), his sister and her family, and his second wife, the niece of Copenhagen's mayor, whom he had recently married. She was visibly pregnant at embarkation.[8] This time he hoped to stay on St Thomas, which he had left in the summer of 1680 after having struggled for years with disobedient Company servants and the equally troublesome Dutch planters. Thus, he had confronted angry men before, but his usual hard-line approach would not serve him well this time. His motive of singling out an author (the first step in producing exemplary punishment) was frustrated: Thus, 'he did not learn it, as one would not rob the other'.[9]

Faced with solidarity, Iversen changed tactics. He engaged in a dialogue in order to quell the crowd before him, asking them why they were acting in this way. In his journal, Braad allows them to produce a reasonable answer: not only could they not endure the starvation that had befallen them, but they also protested continuing at sea because of 'the great leak' of the ship. They wanted instead to seek harbour right away. They had 'sensed' Blom's intentions 'to continue our voyage at sea'; whether they had simply overheard the men in the cabin fighting or it had been related to them by way of the sailors or petty officers is unclear, but in any case, they had listened to and interpreted the words reverberating through the spaces of the ships.[10]

At this point, Braad shows Iversen masterfully quelling the crowd by appeasing them:

> then the governor asked them to be content until tomorrow as the Captain would do his utmost with the help of God to go to Plymouth (...) that same place to get them what they requested. Hearing this they were satisfied and so the governor fetched a bottle of French brandy to pour them, then sat inside the castle and personally poured each one of them [a drink] from the bottle, and there said to the convicts that he expected them to behave as good people, then they should not doubt that with the help of God as they reach St Thomas in the West Indies he would treat them in a manner that would please them. Then, after they had said, yes Mr. Governor, we will behave as is proper, each one went to their usual place below deck.[11]

The scene ends as each person returns to their proper place within the shipboard geography. This is how power is enacted, Braad seems to say: a masterful performance of linguistic intervention.

However, Iversen's words and his promises to the convicts were ambiguous. He was implicitly reminding the subalterns of his eventual power over their lives in the colony. And when the mutiny erupted the morning after, it was obvious that Iversen's performance had not produced an orderly ship: no one had returned to their proper places. In fact, it appears only to have been what Rediker has termed a 'catalytic event'[12]: the convicts and sailors had been drinking through the night, swearing each other allegiance and conjuring other futures than one at Iversen's mercy.[13] Thus, as an exemplary speech act creating order, Iversen's performance that night was distinctly ineffectual.

In a sense, Iversen's assurances of a harbour *had* met his audience's demands, and we might have expected them not to mutiny, but to simply side with the governor in his conflict with the captain. He had, at least according to Braad, spoken up in the face of the hardships they had suffered at sea. Instead of siding with him, though, they killed him without hesitation the next morning. The key to understanding this paradox and the discrepancies it forces upon Braad's account, lies in a difference in perspective – in the ship's dissonance. Simply put: while *Braad* heard the words as the timely and exemplary intervention of a true authority – and one that he knew his readers in the Company office to admire – the convicts, indentured servants and sailors to whom Iversen spoke heard him differently. Therefore, the key question is: how did they interpret the governor's promise about life in the colony?

We are not privy to the discourses below deck that night. Braad lived in the cabins. He picked up fragments, but never overheard the hushed discussions taking place below deck. However, this should not lead us to abandon the task altogether. Paradoxically, Iversen's own writings can provide us with a sense of what kind of stories might have informed the space of interpretation that emerged below deck. Thus, in answering how the crowd heard Iversen's words, we must interrogate these writings and read them against their grain in order to construct an outline of the rumours that circulated about his reign.

The poems of poisonous tongues

To the Company directors, as to Braad, Iversen's word had been a lantern in a pitch-black night. While their economy crumbled, he had kept the island of St Thomas afloat financially, even when, during the Scanian War, the Company failed to provide the nascent colony with provisions for more than half a decade. His writings provided the directors with most of their knowledge of their investment. When Braad aligned himself with the governor and made his words symbols of true authority, he did so in part because he knew the esteem that his readers in the Company office held for Iversen. But the convicts and sailors are likely to have known other stories about the man and his colony, prompting them to listen differently. In fact, in a sense, these stories and their circulation were the reason that the ship was crowded with convicts instead of free labourers or indentured servants. When, in early July 1682, the directors of the Company had written to the king asking for convicts for their Caribbean colony, they had lamented their difficulties, as 'nobody freely signs on to go there to serve as indentured servants'. This forced the directors to ask for as 'many of Holmen's convicts that might be fit for it; similarly, from Børnehuset twenty women to send them to the West Indies to populate the country'.[14] 'Holmen' was shorthand for Bremerholmen, the naval dockyard where convicts from all over the Danish-Norwegian empire toiled in the service of the state. *Børnehuset* (the Children's House) was another name for the prison workhouse were women and children were coerced into labouring in manufacture. The Company would have preferred voluntary labour, but had been forced to apply for 'iron convicts' – a labour pool they had been granted access to in their 1671 charter and which they had tapped into each time a ship left Copenhagen until this point.[15]

This admission of futility which brought the need for convict labour to replace indentured servants reads as a scar that can be historicized; the original wound had been inflicted by stories incised into the colonial narrative by the empire's Atlantic subalterns. The blade itself is gone, bereft of archival directness, but the suture attesting to its sharpness remains a powerful testimony. These subaltern stories had circulated widely.[16] It was a storytelling that was as old as the Company empire itself. In a sense, it even preceded it. In the Company archive is a chronological minute book going all the way back to the first outbound voyage in 1671–72. It was written by Iversen and, in many ways, demonstrates his power as it records his dealings with the people. However, the first entry is prompted by subversive speech that had interrupted this authorial monologue even before it had begun.[17] Thus, this anxious self-recording begins: 'Since it has been found that some of those who are in the service of the chartered West India Company do not fulfil their promises which they have confirmed by oath …'[18] Effectively, Iversen could be referencing either the sailors, the indentured servants or the around three scores of convicts on board. In either case the crime was one of speech.

Iversen had sought to counter lower-deck discourse with orders that nobody except the very ill were allowed to disobey; all must come to service whenever the ship's bell rang; and everyone was to do so willingly, not 'letting themselves be driven to fear God in the way that an ox is driven to the plough'. A 'love of God' was necessary for the success of the voyage, but on board ship Iversen had experienced how God was 'daily disgraced by sinful acts especially cursing and swearing which is the reason […] that he does not bless the progress of our voyage'. As would be the case with the *Havmanden*, the voyagers of this initial expedition had suffered in the North Sea. No 'swearing by God, or his holy death and sufferings or other bloody oaths by which God's holy name is dishonoured' was to be heard and anybody uttering such words was to be beaten at the mast. So was anybody who overheard such swearing and did not report it. In this way, the ship was a space of listening, in which the authorities sought to make sure that no ear could be trusted. Everyone was to listen for signs of the social order unravelling, and any person that 'begins any mutiny or lets any improper words slip from their mouth that can cause any disagreement among the people against their superior will be punished without mercy.' Overhearing such 'improper talk or speech' without revealing it made the listener a punishable oath-breaker. Collective complaining was also prohibited.[19] In this way, Iversen took on the role as a speaker whose words claimed the ability to constitute the social in a way that counters any speech that was not attuned to the conception of the whole that he articulated. He would act in the same way ten years later. In the interim, he also attempted such authoritarian performances in the Caribbean.

Initially, the importance vested in the word varied within the empire's uneven geography. While speech was perceived to carry tremendous force (both authoritarian and subversive) by the actors on board the ship in 1672, a letter from the Company directors in Copenhagen reveals how such intensities resonated differently elsewhere. Referring to the conflicts between Iversen and the mariners in the voyage, the directors advised Iversen to pay no regard of the mariners'words or talk'.[20] To Iversen, continually confronted with disobedient workers on board ship and in the colony, such a politics of disregard seems to have been unimaginable. From their office in the Stock Exchange in Copenhagen, the directors also quickly came to realize the subversive force of maritime voices and their critiques of authorities. In a letter to Iversen from 1673, we note how the illicit speeches had migrated from the ship to the public in Copenhagen. In response to the staggering number of deaths from diseases in the colony, the directors wrote that it was:

> unpleasant to hear that of all the people sent out only few were still alive, which was not good for the company since everybody here [Copenhagen] dread going there [St Thomas], especially since the mariners that have come here have declared that you let people starve and thirst so that they die from it. But as we know that it is the slander of evil people and your enemies we have, whenever possible, brought people to other thoughts. But so that people might have more desire to go there we think that you should immediately start feeding the people in a Danish manner, giving them as much as they would like, since our Danish people are used to being full.[21]

Stories were circulated by mariners, and they did not speak well of either colonial life or the authorities governing it. Further, the stories spread so that it was later reported that 'among the common people our colony is so badly spoken of that they think that as they come to serve in the West Indies they are worse off than in serving in Barbary'.[22] Indentured servitude was counted as equal to being a 'thrall or slave'.[23] Such circulation was what forced the Company into an uneasy reliance on convict labour.

This unwillingness to migrate has been interpreted as linked to the tropical diseases that ravaged the colony.[24] No doubt, diseases were a major deterrent for migration. About three out of four convicts died within a year after embarking the ships of the first half of the 1670s and the indentured did not fare much better.[25] Such stories about disease were known to the people on the *Havmanden* as well. In their largely unsuccessful recruitment campaign of 1682, the Company directors had taken diligent care of countering stories about rampant diseases, demonstrating, in turn, that they still resounded.[26] However, careful reading of the letters to and from St Thomas indicates that there was more to the stories circulating than fear of disease. The stories stuck specifically to Iversen and his excessive authority.

In the Caribbean, Iversen had asserted his authority aggressively over all rungs of the small colonial society. He had been tasked with building a castle and establishing a plantation economy on the tiny uninhabited volcanic island shooting out of the sea between the Spanish island of Puerto Rico and the British Virgin Islands. The male convicts – as well as the enslaved he was able to buy locally – worked for him, clearing the ancient forests and hauling building materials. They also performed whatever tasks the Company required, such as quarrying limestone and harvesting salt. The construction work was especially tough and there is no reason to doubt that this regime of work, combined with malnutrition, contributed to the staggering death rates reported (as I will discuss in Chapter 5, many convicts were in a parlous physical state even before they arrived on St Thomas). Those who survived heard Iversen's tongue assert itself over and over again. However, the polyglot community that came to constitute the colony proved difficult to keep in check.

Planters had come from all across the region, especially the Dutch islands of Curaçao and St. Eustatius, to settle St Thomas and formed an elite within the island's small community of a few hundred people. Likely they were motivated by the Anglo-Dutch conflicts marring life in the Dutch Atlantic. They carried local knowledge and enslaved persons with them, although not in great numbers, building modest plantations for a variety of crops on the slopes. While they were made to swear oaths of fidelity to the Company, they slowly grew bolder in their challenges of Iversen's authority. From the middle of the decade, a Dutch planter had kept an inn selling kildevil, a drink made from the slim sugar harvests that the soil produced, to planters and servants alike.[27] Iversen lamented how the drinking took place at night making it impossible to enforce 'silence'.[28] Drink made the small community under Iversen's command into 'the devil's house as they [the Company servants] themselves wanted to be master'.[29] At one point, the Company smith got so drunk that he first gave 'improper words' then broke into the fort. During the trial, he was unable to answer why he had done so, as he explained that he simply could not remember.[30] During another such incidence in 1677, Iversen himself had a physical altercation with one of his soldiers who had become drunk and missed Iversen's own religious service in the fort. Iversen was devout, but some of his servants did not share his enthusiasm. The soldier in question was found cursing outside and when confronted a fight ensued. In the end, he was locked up.[31]

To Iversen such incidents were an affront not only to himself, but also to God. He had been forced to keep a lenient policy towards different religious creeds, but insisted that people should attend service of one kind or another. During Easter 1679, however, he had found that there were more 'Germans' (a term which Iversen used to include the Dutch) drinking kildevil in the inn than attending the reformed church. A few days later some guards got so drunk that one failed to 'tame his tongue' and another had 'forgotten how to speak truth' while a third ran about 'as a fool'. A planter's wife at one point wished Iversen to the Devil and gave 'other defiant words'.[32] Iversen kept locking up disobedient subjects, but never managed to maintain order. While inebriated, the people disregarded his pronouncements as though 'a dog had barked at them'.[33] Thus, the power vested in his speech was thoroughly challenged. At one point, he brought the planter-turned-innkeeper to trial.[34] Not even this brought peace, and indeed may have gained Iversen a few enemies.

The image Iversen paints of colonial social relations is one of a constant struggle between his own actions and words and those of his idle subjects who 'sat and wasted their time with talk'. It was a colony of dissonance, and in both his day-to-day relations and in his letters, Iversen carefully policed what such speaking out of turn might mean.[35] According to him, the people had continually broken their oaths by 'affronting' him with 'unseemly requests and words which can cause dispute and disagreement among us'. In 1678, this made Iversen dictate that 'if after this day anybody affronts me with unseemly requests and disgraceful words then they will be punished as disobedient and rebellious people that seek to disturb that agreement and peace that should exist between us'. This effectively turned any sign of disrespect into mutiny.[36]

Thus, in his writings, Iversen's voice comes to signify the only source of truth, hierarchy and religion within the otherwise eroding speech community. Such is the burden that makes his authoritarian ways appear both heroic and ambivalent (in that he never really succeeds). In this way, his depiction of colonial authority hinges on governing what can hardly be governed, to keep chattering tongues pinned down for as much time as possible. In one of his frustrated letters, Iversen went as far as to fashion a taxonomy of disobedience in which he ranked almost all of the colony's men into five different tiers from the 'most pious' to 'ringleaders'.[37]

When Iversen initially left the island in the afternoon of 20 September 1680, he left on bad terms with many of the colony's inhabitants. Among his adversaries were several of the planters, including one who that same morning had tried to make Iversen declare him an honest man. Iversen refused.[38] The man, Pieter Jansen, was ranked worst in Iversen's taxonomy. Coming from Curaçao, he had brought a distilling pan for making kildevil.[39] He had also refused to take his oath.[40] Jansen and Iversen had been fighting for more than two years, culminating in a brawl in 1679 when Jansen had interfered with Iversen's recording of church attendance. When Iversen fined a woman for skipping church, Jansen had reportedly stated that the women were better off spending Sundays doing domestic labour in the house.[41] Iversen read this speech as a sign of disobedience. Punches were exchanged and the incident resulted in the planter being incarcerated until the arrival of Iversen's successor.[42] From his prison, Jansen – according to Iversen – kept breeding discontent among the people. So did his wife, whom Iversen at one point found speaking to the servants at the fort. Iversen called her and her husband 'rebels' and she replied by affronting his honour by calling him a 'rogue'. This prompted Iversen to lash her.[43]

Such conflicts lend credibility to Iversen's remark that 'a part of [the people] were happy, as I came away from the country, and if they could bar me from coming back, their joy would be even greater'.[44] In fact, they made the attempt. Not only did the above-mentioned planter write the directors demanding satisfaction, but the new governor, Nicholas Esmit, teamed up with both the innkeeper and many others and wrote up a set of accusations. Thus, in the autumn of 1681, a set of twenty-two brief attestations against Iversen arrived in Copenhagen. In a letter, Esmit explained that these were only an excerpt of the complaints that sounded against Iversen; if recorded in full, they would take up 'an entire volume'.[45] Among them were grave accusations of rape, drunkenness, embezzlement and at least six murders of 'Christians' as well as the unwarranted killing of five enslaved Africans.[46]

Iversen accepted what he seems to have perceived as a challenge. He appears less worried about his neck than his reputation, suggesting his solid standing with the directors of the Company who had vested his voice with so much truth and power. In two letters totalling fifty densely written pages, he rebutted the complaints one at a time.[47] Hints suggest that he wrote them up in the Company office.[48] He fashioned himself as a master of linguistic performance, claiming for himself a sphere of truth against the 'poems' of 'poisonous tongues'. The very archive he had brought home with him – his journals, minutes and the meticulously kept books – formed part of this self-representation as a carrier of truth as he references them throughout. They served to prove that he had always acted in the Company's interest, and that his 'haters' were only venting 'slander'.[49]

Yet while the letters present a carefully constructed performance they also offer glimpses of colonial conflicts resonating in fragments of captured speech. This allows us to read them against their grain. Further, the letters' construction of authority produces several interlocked paradoxes that, like the captured speeches and the gaps in Braad's account, hint at a dissonant colonial reality. Thus, as a source to conflicts in the colony, the two letters are (if read very slowly) unmatched by any other document in the vast, but distorting, Company archive. This is, paradoxically, where we most clearly hear both the power Iversen's voice was vested with and the tongues of subalterns dislocating such a soundscape.

Iversen attempted to displace the polyphony entirely. Although many different strata of St Thomas were represented in the accusations, Iversen claimed they were all being orchestrated by Esmit, who was seeking to undo him.[50] From this sure-footed foundation in his own writing, Iversen carefully turned suspicion against his successor who had opened up trade at St Thomas to foreign nations.[51] To Iversen, colonization was an agricultural enterprise tied to a national mercantilist project; Esmit's moves instead made St Thomas a node in the maritime Caribbean (as discussed in Chapter 6). Stories circulated that Esmit had been a pirate with the English. Iversen subtly references these stories and continually linked Esmit to theft: Esmit was attempting to rob Iversen of his honour and would surely go on to rob the Company of its profits. Thus, the accusations were turned on their head as they only testified to the character of Iversen's adversary. Iversen even used wit to drive home the point and most of the twenty-two rebuttals were accompanied by their own snarky proverb. One illustrates the overall structure of Iversen's portrayal of his opponent: 'he who shears the pig gets much screaming and little wool.' Esmit had raised a great noise by committing rumours to paper, but would get nothing from it.[52]

But the argument wavers. At times Iversen averts the accusations and defers. While he had no difficulty in rebutting the accusations of embezzlement and theft (using his own books as evidence), his response to the accusations concerning his troubles with the lowest ranks of colonial society are shot through with unease.[53]

One of the complaints involving Iversen's sexual licence concerned a convict by the name of Hans Wadskye. He had come from the naval dockyard prison with the first ship. According to Iversen, Wadskye was a 'foolish human who had done me much harm'. Perhaps, Iversen was hinting of Wadskye's love of drink. In a journal, Iversen notes two instances when Wadskye had been drunk and disorderly: on the first occasion, Wadskye had been involved in a fight; and after the second, Iversen got word from three enslaved Africans that Wadskye had said that if the French from nearby St Croix were to invade, he would abandon Iversen's command. Wadskye was promptly bolted up, though later released.[54] Now he haunted Iversen in another way. In his rebuttal, Iversen explains that Wadskye had been in love with another colonist, Sara Tømmermands, who was a Company servant (although it is unclear if she was a convict as well or rather an indentured servant). Wadskye had been protective of her and jealous of any potential suitors. He had approached Iversen several times to ask for her hand, but Iversen claimed that she did not return Wadskye's affections and therefore he was unwilling to arrange the marriage against her will. Apparently Wadskye took offence with the decision, 'so he has said that it was my fault that she did not want to be his wife and that I wanted to keep her as my whore'. Then, however, the story turns as Iversen is forced to recognize that he had misspoken: he admits to having said that 'it was better if she was my whore than his wife'. Iversen makes this remark read as an offhanded joke, but in a text that is otherwise vehement in the construction of Iversen's words, it seems jarringly out of place. Iversen quickly turns attention away from the issue. Having committed Wadskye's story to paper was itself a crime on the part of Esmit who had thus enforced such a 'slanderous complaint'.[55] The words issued by subalterns like Wadskye did not belong on paper, even if they had a disconcerting resonance to them.

In part, the unease felt in the passage reads as intentional. In referring to a level of crude everyday talk and exchanges that was not normally committed to paper, Iversen subtly hints that Esmit's accusations belong to this level, rendering them scandalous even on principle. Thus, he gives a glimpse of such fraught discourse in order to play off of the notion that this talk cannot be taken seriously. However, at the same time the passage presents Iversen's tongue as uneasily embroiled in scandalous exchanges turning the argument dialogical, allowing for echoes of colonial conflicts and rumours.

This uneasy structure in which Iversen admits to excesses in the everyday relations of the colony in order to strengthen his overall argument repeats itself in the accusations concerning deaths of Company servants, including convicts and indentured servants. According to the accusations, several Company workers (both indentured servants and convicts) had died shortly after having been violently assaulted by Iversen.[56] In all cases Iversen excuses himself: the servants had died from diseases, not from the beatings. However, he did not deny having punished the deceased, but argued that they had all suffered from dropsy which they had brought on themselves. According to Iversen dropsy was 'the idleness disease'. Thus, his beatings are turned into attempts at extracting labour, but also at saving the dying from their own destructive proclivities, animating the otherwise lethargic. One servant had been found lying on the ground, unwilling to move. Iversen admits having hit the man with 'a twig or stick' because he 'was not willing, in my opinion, to strive towards saving his life'. Iversen's punishment of a boy by the name of Jens Sørensen was a similar case. Jens had been of 'evil wit', although others had called him 'simple' and Iversen admits to having let all his other servants birch the boy on his backside after the discovery of several accounts of theft. This collective punishment was meant to be a 'mirror' to the other servants, and echoes collective modes of punishment used in ships, armies and prisons. Sørensen died shortly thereafter, but Iversen assured that he had died from diseases contracted while having run away after his last theft; sleeping in the 'bushes' (always a transgressive location in Iversen's writings) he had brought the disease upon himself.[57]

Other deceased people had run away as well. In 1672, four Company servants, two indentured servants and two convicts, had deserted with a Company boat. They had stolen gunpowder and several guns and gone for St Croix (I discuss such runaways at length in Chapter 5). One of them, Kresten Mortensen, had been caught and later died in his confinement. This was a difficult case to narrate, as putting a dying man in shackles would have been incriminating. Instead, Iversen claims that Mortensen was at the time so well that he had to be locked up as he would otherwise run away again. Instead, it was Iversen himself who was sick. He still had an injured hand to show for it. From his sick bed, he had been unaware that Mortensen had fallen ill and that the people who were supposed to feed him were failing to do so. He denied that worms had been crawling from Mortensen's body when he was found dead. He even deflected blame for Mortensen having been buried covered in 'shit'. This was, in fact, the blame of Mads Hansen, the planter who had made the very accusation.[58]

The Company directors had previously demonstrated that they shared this conception of the destructive idleness of the people. Upon receiving news of the initial voyage, they had written to Iversen, lamenting that they had heard of how 'some of the people due to idleness will not keep clean and have great problems with the vermin and worms of the country'.[59] Naturally, they had an interest in keeping everyone healthy and, by extension, productive. Thus, Iversen's argument and its depiction of the social world of the colony, although seeming crude to modern readers, fit his audience.

In other passages of his defence, the odium that Iversen rebutted was that he himself had been personally involved in physical punishment. The particular engagement of the authority made it look like personal revenge and in general it was seen as improper for a sovereign to carry out punishments himself. In fact, the act of punishing as such carried a stigma. Corporal punishment was the job of provosts or the dreaded hangman and often counted as a dishonest profession, thus Iversen had acted in an unbefitting manner on several levels.[60] This was the case in the death of Gabriel Sax, a convict and 'an idle rogue and thief of days that I could not get to work'. Because of his laziness, Iversen made him herd cattle. This was a job Iversen thought appropriately easy, but Sax 'lied down under one or another bush to sleep and let the cattle tend themselves because of which they found their way to the sugar cane'. The damages were severe and 'therefore, I could not neglect beating his back, since I had many times warned him and said that I would beat his shirt if he did not tend the cattle well'. This led Iversen to reflect on the difficulties of punishments: 'as one company servant would not obey my commands to punish the other for their disobedience and other unseemly acts and [because] I did not want to use a negro to beat a Christian, then I had to do it myself'.[61] When he commanded them to beat someone they refused stating they 'were not provosts' and when he asked them to bolt someone up 'they answered me that they were not hired as executioners'.[62] Yet in spite of such difficulties, punishments were necessary as 'I have had there a party of handed-over bodies to toil with who took heed of neither good words or threats, and therefore I myself had to beat them ... if I wanted them to do what I with good words asked of them'. Language and punishments were means to the same end: extracting labour. Iversen's emphasis on his proper use of speech serves to legitimise his use of violence. Instead of appearing to be excessive, his violence becomes instead the only logical response as his subjects contravened the order that his tongue had attempted to constitute.[63]

Yet there are paradoxical, logical fallacies at play in Iversen's argument. For instance, punishment was dealt because the convicts resisted being punished. This becomes clear as Iversen turned even more defensive. He refused that he had 'stepped on [Sax's] stomach and throat', but accepted that he might have 'given him a blow with my foot, when he like a rogue has let himself fall, which manner a party of them had learned from the negroes to throw themselves on the ground when they were to be punished'.[64] The convicts were learning the tricks of the enslaved, but without the benefit of their productivity. Sax was punished because he had thrown himself on the ground in order to resist being punished. This unseemly mimicry was an act of resistance, and the use of power was, therefore, justified. Despite the difficulties in carrying out punishments, Iversen argued that they were strictly necessary if he wanted to 'keep order among such ungodly bodies'.[65] Without the beatings the people would 'without a doubt' have thought themselves 'master' or have run away causing great damage to the Company, he argued.[66]

Thus, the convicts and the indentured were in a sense too mobile (when running away), yet also too static (when idly refusing to work, or resisting punishment). Iversen refers to these paradoxical, unruly subjects as 'bodies'. He uses this phrase three times in the rebuttal; twice, when explicitly discussing convicts. Both times he calls them '*offuergiffne kroppe*' which translates awkwardly to 'handed-over bodies', but also connotes something given up and abandoned. The convicts had been given to Iversen not as people, but as a form of lives already lost; it was his task to render them productive. In this way, the convicts are constructed as devoid of any positive distinction or capacity except one: labour. Yet this conception of the convict as a body also renders Iversen's self-representation ambivalent in a way that is analogous to the discrepancy marking Braad's account and its portrayal of Iversen's exemplary speech act that works, yet does not work. The last of the three mentions of 'bodies' highlights this paradox. This was the case of the Norwegian convict Anders Pedersen. Iversen laments the affronts that he had been dealt by 'handed-over bodies that neither Holmen nor the punishments of the prison workhouse could turn good'. This lamentation was the end of a short biographical narrative of Pedersen, who had come from Bergen after being imprisoned on charges of theft and murder. Iversen had promised him that if he behaved, he would after a time become a free man, yet again, the promise was futile: Pedersen soon ran away with another convict. One night they emerged from the woods and broke into the Company stores, stealing a casket of meat and some beer. The companion was caught, but Pedersen returned to the woods where he stayed for another nine days until, one morning, two planters hunting pigeons came upon him. They tried apprehending the convict, but he attacked them with an axe. The hunters then retreated and approached Iversen, asking for assistance in catching the man. Iversen allowed it and explained that if Pedersen resisted, they should shoot him in his leg. When the runaway was found, he attacked once more. The planters fired at him, and hit him in the face with a load full of shot. He continued resisting, so he was shot again, this time with a bullet through the leg. Then they 'took him to the fort where he confessed that he had no other reason for running away, but that the

Devil rode him.' Twelve days later, he died from his wounds. Iversen's promises and commands had been wholly ineffectual.[67]

This encapsulates what is perhaps the most resonant paradox of Iversen's defence, which alerts us to an antagonistic colonial reality in which authority was continually contested by workers and planters alike. While Iversen's defence rests on a construction of his own power (linguistic and corporal) as a strict necessity producing both labour and docility in the service of a greater good, no such production is in fact made visible. Thus, the term 'bodies' is rendered ambivalent as the body in question transforms from a potential source of labour into either the inert body of the collapsed servant, or the dead body of a runaway convict shot dead on account of his 'roguish resistance'.[68] As a performance of Iversen's ability as both author and authority, the letters stumble over the bodies that prove an oppositional force in both everyday power relations and the narratives he crafted. Thus, the agency of these indentured servants and convicts expresses itself in the limits on both Iversen's tongue and his pen. And as the subjects of rumour circulating within the empire, they would do him even worse.

Colonial heroics and systemic violence

Iversen's self-representation found a surer footing in his defence concerning his handling of the enslaved, although it came with other discrepancies. Here, he had products to show, and argued that his reign of terror had actually made them productive. When defending himself against the accusation of having used Company slave labour on his own plantation, he again turns the question on its head by asserting how he had used seven of his own enslaved workers in hauling wood for the fort until they had 'blown themselves so that they have hernia and cannot be used for hard work'. Unlike convicts, the enslaved could be animated to work to the point of breaking, and in the context of precarious empire-building, such a firm power over human life turned into a point of pride and a demonstration of competence.[69]

However, the enslaved Africans' running away caused fear and several plots had been discovered, even though Iversen had taken great care in limiting subalterns' access to vessels.[70] He also explicitly referenced stories he had heard from St Eustatius and Barbados where, he explained, maroons had sought to murder all Christians and make the islands their own.[71] While Iversen had been accused of killing several runaways, he denied the charges. Their deaths were a fact, but he gave a different cause: during the punishments of the enslaved, Iversen insisted, they had on several occasions held their breath for prolonged periods, thereby taking their own life.[72] He also argued that they were prone to suicide because they believed that 'when they die they go to their country again which they also say themselves, when I die, I run to my country'. However, so as not to deprive the law of its spectacular terror, Iversen had the bodies cut into pieces and hung near the houses where the enslaved lived.[73] Again, the punished were to serve as mirrors – which, in contrast to the beatings of convicts, are shown to have worked. For a time, they were quiet. In this strategic assertion, the rebuttal is turned into a demonstration of colonial authority. In a particularly unsympathetic twist, Iversen claimed that one needed to use fire during punishments, the flames being a remedy as it forced 'such hard-hearted dogs' to inhale. Thus, Iversen turns an accusation of excessive violence into a demonstration of colonial know-how.[74] Apparently, no-one in the Company office questioned if this method of suicide was even physically possible and even modern historians have reproduced the notion that the enslaved were capable of killing themselves by holding their breath.[75]

While all these strange concessions, paradoxes and gaps are meaningful to us as they point towards the dissonant speech community and brutal social relations in the colony, and strongly hint at the contents of the type of stories that mariners circulated about Iversen and life in his colony, they seem to have had little effect on the Company directors. Our attempts at tracing the reception of his letters are made difficult by the loss of that year's minute book.[76] At the same time, the Company was itself in disarray. The directors continually lamented the fact that they did not know 'the foundation' of the business. Participants had not provided the funds promised and old accounts had yet to be settled.[77] In this chaos, Iversen's pen offered accountability.[78] In stressing the value of the many volumes he had brought home, Iversen referenced something almost sacred. This chaotic state seems to have enforced a state of exception that made arbitrary violence and its uneasy ambivalences appear like structural necessities. Iversen played an integral part in the business of the Company throughout 1682, and he was central to the preparations of the voyage from start to finish.[79] The minutes of the chaotic preparations make no mention of conflicts, abuse or death concerning subalterns.[80] Neither do the orders and instructions for him. Whereas his dealings with the planters were detailed at some length, the convicts and indentured servants are mentioned only in passing as a resource to dispose of as he saw fit.[81] Through such a politics of disregard, Iversen's instructions constitute him in a way that is analogue to his own figuration of the relationship between him as sovereign and the forced labourer as a mere body.[82]

The Company's esteem for Iversen has been mirrored by historians. They have not denied his propensity to violence, but his part as a heroic protagonist in traditional narratives of Danish colonialism has made for some awkward excuses. He has been portrayed as the singular reason the colony did not disintegrate. On several occasions, historians have reproduced the notion of necessity outlined above.[83] Further, Iversen's violence has repeatedly been interpreted as the result of a personal breakdown caused by the continual stress upon a man who was otherwise of a solid disposition.[84] I find this interpretation unlikely. Iversen's letters are coherent all the way through and their deployment of wit does not suggest a man who is unable to cope with the situation at hand. More disconcertingly, such an interpretation glosses over the fact that Iversen's violence was in fact fully congruent with this prevailing configuration of subjects such as indentured servants, convicts and the enslaved, and the way their lives were tied to such structures of exception.

The majority of the convicts who embarked ships for St Thomas were chosen among the inmates of *Trunken*, the dockyard prison on Bremerholmen in Copenhagen. There, male convicts from all over Denmark-Norway laboured for the state. From what we can tell from the sources, those sent to the colony were almost exclusively drawn from the cohort carrying life sentences. Most appear to have been either thieves or poachers, and most would have been branded or otherwise disfigured, having received physical punishments before entering prison. Prior to embarkation, they had performed intense physical labour in the service of the navy. They wore chains and were nicknamed 'iron prisoners'. The work was very demanding. Such practices of displacement and exploitation were brutally coercive, but to seventeenth-century elites they made perfect sense. This was due to the stigma suffered by the groups of convicts singled out for transportation. Honour and its obverse played a major part in how early modern Scandinavians understood punishment. All prisoners whose corporal punishments had in this way involved an executioner or the public display afforded by the pillory were counted as 'dishonoured'. This was a serious matter; these forms of punishments were seen as defiling, marking the punished as living outside of civic society for the rest of his or her life. Honour was intricately linked to 'honesty' and so the dishonoured were also seen as dishonest, unable to speak the truth and to bear witness.[85] A dishonoured man could no longer enter into military or naval service. Nor could the dishonoured become citizens.[86] They were, largely, considered unpardonable. Thus, losing one's honour had very real consequences.

In a way, dishonour signalled the perpetual loss of one's belonging to community. In this way, it can be likened to the social death that scholars have seen as marking the life of the enslaved. Scholars have argued that what distinguishes the enslaved from other forced labourers was the fact that the enslaved were effectively seen as non-subjects – as having no social life outside of the relations of domination that they were subjected to. Enslavement was 'a substitute for death, usually violent death'.[87] Such an existence of non-subjectivity and 'conditional commutation' was also exactly what characterized the dishonoured convicts carrying life sentences. Further, the extraction of penal labour and subsequent transportation of convicts were driven by many of the same economic and political forces that created and sustained Atlantic slavery; as subaltern labourers, they were more or less interchangeable.

Contemporaries certainly saw this likeness as well. Convicts doing time in *Trunken* were widely referred to as 'slaves' and by the eighteenth century 'slavery' had become a punishment that persisted in Denmark-Norway until the 1850s.[88] In his summation of natural law, eighteenth-century scholar Ludvig Holberg drew the analogy in a remark on the dishonoured: 'in this way Slaves are thought not to be proper members of a city'.[89] To become a dishonoured convict labourer was to cease having a part in the political body. Tellingly, the earliest instance of the term 'slave' used about convicts in Denmark-Norway that I have seen is from 1682 and regards a group of convicts dispatched on a Company ship from Bergen in Norway (where several vessels stopped along the way, suffering desertions and then taking on more convicts to fill the ranks) to St Thomas. It was written by the Company bookkeeper.[90] Thus, the term was employed by people who knew full well the difference, had it mattered to them. The term was used, although rarely, by authorities in the colony as well.[91] On at least one occasion (explored in Chapter 5), those authorities sentenced runaway convicts in the colony to sale. While the systems of criminal justice on the island itself were from the beginning differentiated according to race, the category of dishonour even blurred such lines as it cut across races. This was not only the case with transported convicts. When white military personnel in the Danish West Indies committed offences, they were also at times convicted of hard labour in chains which was also referred to as 'slavery', and at least one text explicitly likened this to the conditions of 'another dishonoured slave or negro'.[92]

Elites saw the dishonoured subjects as ideal colonial labourers exactly because they were already lives lost. This also meant that Iversen's admissions of violence toward the convicts, like that towards the enslaved, were not particularly difficult to swallow for the Company directors. In a very real sense, they were socially dead, alive only for their properties as workers. They had been spared their lives, so as to work. While, in theory, the indentured merited more attention, the fact that they were recruited among the poorest classes of society, many being boys and girls from the prison workhouses, meant that their subject status was also challenged at best. Such systemic violence is overlooked in the way historians have treated Iversen and his excesses by resorting to psychology. The key to understanding his casual admissions of violence lies in the construction of colonial power and labour. Thus, no matter the causes, the deaths of subalterns were not really a scandal to the men in Copenhagen's Stock Exchange. Iversen's ability to turn the argument on its head demonstrates this. Rather, the scandal was on Esmit's part, having perpetuated slander (no matter its truthfulness). He had confused colonial labourers with subjects. A body may have a tongue and make noise, but it has no voice. Iversen's adversaries had confused the two. In this way, these deaths were more problematic as stories, than as facts. To the Company directors, Iversen's letters did not testify to an excessive violence, but to what was both necessary and proper in order to succeed in their venture.

However, the circulation of such stories about colonial life contributed to history in another way. While we have no sure way of knowing how much of this human misery the convicts heard in Iversen's promises in the evening of 19 January 1683 when he asserted his authority over their fates in the colony, the existence of such stories and the persistent trouble that rumour about Iversen's reign brought the Company go a long way in helping us explain the actions of the mutineers towards a man, who at times appears to have acted on their behalf.[93] Certainly, only a fragment would have been enough for the convicts to hear his promises as the veiled threats of an excessive and abusive authority; he had implicitly reminded them of the power they were being subjected to. Their interpretation of this power is most likely to have been influenced by the narratives and rumours that his reign was worse than 'Barbary', and that Iversen's reign brought only starvation and death as had been reported in the maritime Copenhagen where many of both sailors and convicts had lived. Thus, where Braad had heard the promises of a true political authority who in a timely fashion countered impending anarchy, the mariners and convicts who had turned the lower deck into a site of storytelling, rumour and interpretation might, therefore (and with reason), have heard the veiled threats of a murderer. Subtly, the words uttered in the morning when Iversen was killed support such an interpretation.

The meaning of a slur

In the chaotic lead-up to Iversen's killing, Braad had, as on the night before, been in his company. Once again, the governor had carried himself with paternal authority. According to Braad, the two had encountered the captain on the quarterdeck at sunrise. Blom was at a loss; he told them that his sailors were sitting below deck alongside the convicts, drinking brandy. At this point, Iversen took charge.

Below deck, Iversen and Braad found the German boatswain's mate Hans Biermand and several common sailors among the convicts. Biermand seems to have struck the governor as the one most out of place in this unseemly party. He probably lived among the petty officers in the forecastle, whereas the other sailors in the party most likely lived on the lower deck (although the living arrangements of the ship appear somewhat unclear as the presence of the large contingents of passengers and convicts on this otherwise naval ship must have prompted some improvisation). According to Braad, Iversen asked Biermand, 'what the meaning was behind him sitting here below with the convicts drinking with them as this is not his place to sit, but in the forecastle?' Biermand replied sharply: 'shut up, I have no business with you!' Thus, Biermand played off of the bifurcated power structure of the ship, as Iversen was formally only in charge of passengers and convicts, while captain Blom held sole authority over the mariners. This was when Braad, as he himself reported, interjected himself into the scene, asking what kind of brandy the party was drinking. It proved to be the costly French kind that did not figure in the daily rations, but had been shipped only as cargo for the distressed servants in the Company's Gold Coast castles.[94] From this, Braad deduced that the party had stolen it from the hold.[95]

Then things escalated fast. Biermand got angry at the quick-witted Braad and exclaimed in 'an angry way in his own tongue' that '*der Teufel sal euch im Hertz fahren, so viel als ihr Zeit*'. The syntax is muddled (possibly hinting that Braad's German was not particularly strong), but it might translate into a curse along the lines of 'may the Devil go in your heart for the rest of your days'.[96] No matter its specific meaning, the curse made Braad and Iversen back off. Iversen went upstairs and into his cabin while Braad went to tell the captain of 'such hard words'. However, upon them leaving the lower deck, the angry party got up and followed them, so Braad chose instead first to keep at a distance and then, when he saw his chance, to hide among the convict women in their quarters deeper within the lower deck.[97]

Therefore, Braad did not hear for himself what happened next. He had it told to him in detail at an unknown later date by a passenger by the name of Junker Friberg, a royal page who had ventured on board at the impetus of the king in order to learn matters of navigation.[98] Friberg had witnessed Biermand and a group of convicts as they confronted the captain on the quarterdeck where he stood with several of his officers. The mutineers were at this point armed with knives and cutlasses. Braad reports the words that he learned had been exchanged on the occasion as direct speech. Likely, he knew that his journal would be read in a legal context upon his homecoming, in which it would be crucial to find out who the 'author' of the crime was. This put an added stress on singling out those who stimulated others to action through speech. As reported by Braad, Blom had made concessions to the angry mutineers. He promised that:

> If we cannot get to Plymouth and we have to go to sea with this favourable wind, I will give each man one pot [just under a litre] of water a day, and sometimes when we cannot get to the water, [I will] give each in its place 1 pot of beer as well as occasionally a bottle of wine for each mess, and moreover [I will give] good food. More I cannot give you.[99]

Biermand stumped the plea by asking the obvious: 'how he [Blom] could now claim such a thing, as they had until this point suffered such great thirst and, furthermore, he [Blom] had himself said that if we do not immediately reach harbour it would go absolutely horribly because of the water.' Here, we sense how the state of necessity had, in the preceding weeks, turned the ship into a space of fraught relations in which every word was carefully interpreted. Biermand's apt reply put the captain further on the defensive and forced him to excuse himself as, 'he had, thank God, enough water in the ship to get to the adjacent islands'. Presumably he was referring to the Azores, though the formulation makes it unclear. However, Biermand continued with 'his growling and proud words'.[100]

In this confusion, someone called for Iversen in the cabin. He showed himself, but on his way to the poop deck he was confronted by another group of mutineers headed the same way. He asked them, 'where they were going, and [said that] if they have something to say they could say it [to him] under the stairs'. The poop deck was, in a sense, a reserved space, the territory of authority, and perhaps Iversen was defending its honour. Or perhaps, he simply did not want to have to deal with an even bigger group of people. At this point, Biermand shouted in German from above that the people should throw the governor overboard. Braad reports that this 'happened promptly after he had prayed much for his life as he clung to the starboard [railing] by the mizzen shroud'. Braad's slightly contradictory words hint that Iversen fought his attackers. Soon, however, he was gone in the waves.

Braad's lengthy description is in line with the much shorter narrative of the Dutch second mate Jan von Gent. He witnessed the scene first hand, but says little about it. His is a 1,500-word account printed on one dense sheet of paper as the type of exemplary, cautionary crime tale so well-known by scholars of early modern Europe. In its detailed print, you can actually see Iversen clinging to the railing.[101]

The general congruence gives us some reason to believe that Braad's account is accurate. Constructed in anticipation of a court martial, he knew that any inaccuracy was bound to be revealed by the testimony of others, so he had a strong incentive to give as accurate an account of the event as he could. The sentence itself also puts Biermand in charge of these vital minutes. However, the verbatim dialogue reported by Braad does seem somewhat stilted, even a little awkward. It is a little *too* orderly, and too centred on Biermand, considering the mob he had at his side. Whether this hints at a conscious distortion on the part of Braad or how Friberg had told him the words, is impossible to tell. Here the archive itself is laced with storytelling. However, this awkwardness should prompt caution at taking the exact words at face value.

And yet one part of Braad's report subtly breaks apart this stilted pattern and its implicit silencing. In a story of small, at times almost imperceptible, shocks that slowly disjoint the whole, this is perhaps the most significant, at least in the context of Iversen and the way the men below deck interpreted his words. When Biermand called for the mutineers to kill Iversen, Braad claims that he spoke German and that he had shouted: 'grab the governor and throw that rogue and seller-of-souls overboard.'[102] The term seller-of-souls ('*Siæle forkiöbere*') is significant and something of a mystery. It is not a common Danish term, nor was it at the time. '*Siæle*' means souls, but '*forkiöbere*' makes no real sense in Danish. It is, however, reminiscent of the German word '*Verkaufer*' meaning 'seller'. Thus, Biermand, reportedly a native of Hamburg, is likely to have called Iversen a '*Seeleverkaufer*' which Braad had then translated, awkwardly, to the point of rendering his account almost meaningless.

The term seller-of-souls actually had Dutch origins. In Dutch, we find the derogatory term '*zielverkoper*' – meaning also seller-of-souls. This term signified a group of recruitment agents operating in all major Dutch ports. In the Dutch empire (and the German territories where they also operated) the '*zielverkoper*' was an infamous figure. Maritime historian Jaap Bruijn has called them 'wholesalers of personnel'.[103] They worked as intermediaries between newly recruited sailors (often Germans) and their major employers: the Dutch navy and the East India Company (VOC) in particular. They also supplied the recruits with lodgings in boarding houses and food while they awaited the next ship to sail. Thus, the sailors lived under their roofs and did so on credit. This allowed for great abuses as the sailors got locked into spirals of debt. The *zielverkoper* thus came to hold great power over the recruits. Often conditions in their boarding houses were terrible, even prison-like as leaving was forbidden. The *zielverkoper* lent the sailors money 'in return for an I O U (*transportbrief*) entitling the crimp to recover the cost of the recruit's accommodation and subsistence through monthly deductions from the man's pay when it became due.'[104] Such IOUs could then be sold on. As Bruijn has remarked, the name had originally meant 'seller-of-letters of conveyance but [had been] corrupted to seller-of-souls'.[105] There are examples of Dutch sailors attacking the boarding houses of *zielverkopers*.[106]

The term is, however, very rare in Danish sources. *Zielverkopers* had no real Danish equivalent. The Danish naval recruitment worked in ways different from the Dutch, and the trading companies did not demand large contingents of personnel. Therefore, the term mainly appears in Danish in comments from people who travelled to Dutch territories. For instance, speaking about the Norwegian and German sailors he met at the Cape, a Danish East India traveller, ship's chaplain Hans Mesler, remarked how the ungodly ways of life on board Dutch ships made the German and Norwegian sailors curse 'the day they had come among the Dutch and had been seduced and tricked by the seller-of-souls in Amsterdam'.[107] Here the notoriety accorded by Bruijn was in full effect.

On the *Havmanden*, however, the term's meaning seems strangely incongruous. Biermand had not been recruited by Iversen. It is unlikely that he had ever been in the hands of a *zielverkoper* on Danish soil. We do not know how this German mariner, reported by Braad as being from the city of Hamburg, ended up on the *Havmanden*, but it is most likely that he was initially recruited for the Danish navy as a sailor during the Scanian Wars in which the navy and army sought personnel from Northern Germany as well as from Amsterdam. Many of the foreign mariners on the ship, including the officers, appear to have been recruited in this way during the war. Biermand's name, or that of a namesake, figures in a list of recruits from 1678, although this lists him as recruited not from Hamburg, but from the duchy of Holstein, ruled by the Danish king.[108] He is likely to have been hired for the voyage in the same way as everyone else: by having responded to a note posted on the door of Copenhagen's Stock Exchange advertising for 'some seafaring people who desire to serve the Company to take on a voyage to the West Indies and from there to Guinea and then home again'.[109] Thus, the literal meaning of a crimp can hardly be what Biermand was referring to. Iversen was across the Atlantic at the time of Biermand's recruitment for the navy, and the advertisement for the *Havmanden*'s voyage had asked interested parties to contact Blom, not Iversen. Instead the term seems out of its original context; a stubborn, confusing knot that unsettles the flow of Braad's otherwise exemplary yarn.

While the exact words recorded seem somewhat constructed, the term '*zielverkoper*' makes little sense in Braad's narrative. It is out of place in his story; too ambivalent in its need of interpretation to be a strategic construction. In this it stands in marked contrast to the stilted exchanges between Blom and Biermand. Possibly, Braad did not even know its precise meaning; his somewhat strange translation hints at this possibility. He might have noted it because Biermand had reportedly uttered it in a command to his accomplices, making him the author of the murder of Iversen. In this way, the very utterance, not its specific meaning, signalled his guilt and merited accurate transcription. However, its meaning (or lack thereof in Braad's mangled translation) complicates Braad's story.[110]

Thus, we can interpret this specific term and its incongruity as a moment when the disruptive event of the mutiny and its social world forces itself into the narrative structure opening it up to interpretation. Simply put: if Braad were placing words in the mouth of Biermand, he would have picked different words – words more evidently meaningful to both him and his readers in the Company office. The dissonance that the term brings to Braad's narrative reveals another origin and marks the text as dialogical. In this way, it represents what is perhaps the clearest trace of the discussions that had taken place below deck in the weeks preceding the mutiny, connecting us, in uncertain ways, to a site of discourse that Braad neither fully understood (having not experienced it first hand, as he lived in the cabin), nor allowed his readers to know. Thus, it reveals a reality more complex than what Braad's otherwise tightly policed narrative suggests.

So how should we interpret this fragment? I would suggest that the importance of the term is precisely in the detached quality of its meaning. Its denotation of the abuses of colonial and maritime power relations had been transferred from one context to another; from a Dutch context, in which it had a very specific meaning, to a Danish one in which such a meaning was absent, but in which it instead signals how colonial processes bound people in ways they themselves recognized as abusive. This hints that in the nights below deck, the actions that the mutineers had first fantasized about and then swore to make reality were, to them, placed in the larger context of maritime and colonial conflicts and even something which we might think of as traditions of radicalism. Thus, this minuscule fragment relates the story of the *Havmanden* to a larger Atlantic history of maritime conflict and struggle.[111] In their own situation, and in what they knew from rumour to face in the colony, the mutineers identified the workings of power relations that were paralleled elsewhere. In turn, the term hints at a powerful space of interpretation having formed below deck across the cultural, social and legal divides that had existed among the people for whom it had for two-and-a-half months been their living quarters – a space in which antagonisms could blend together.

In a way, Biermand was speaking on someone else's behalf. Just minutes before, he had claimed to have no conflict with Iversen, but now he suddenly called for his apprehension with a very specific term of abuse signifying Iversen's role as man who held an unjust power over others. What made Biermand attribute the term to Iversen? He might have had many different things in mind; the most obvious possibility could have been Iversen's role in the recruitment of the small contingent of indentured servants.[112] However, this possibility is contested by the fact that none of the indentured appear to have played a prominent part in the mutiny itself. I find it more likely that Biermand was simply referring to the convicts themselves. After all, the group to which he yelled the command was made up mostly of convicts, who therefore must have known its meaning or at least its insinuation of abuse – possibly from the discourses that had preceded the events. In a way, this fragment speaks on their behalf. It speaks of a score that was theirs to settle, but which the sailors now took part in.

In turn, this confirms that the killing of Iversen was premeditated by storytelling about him. The widely circulating rumours about his brutal reign explain why these discussions resulted in his death. Thus, while Braad, the Company directors as well as later historians have seen Iversen as a colonial hero, the convicts, indentured servants and sailors deliberating below deck read him differently. We cannot fully know what they spoke of, but this stubborn echo, seller-of-souls, indicates that they knew full well what to make of the governor's promises and the power he evoked over their lives.

2

Echoes

The noise was terrible. A loud hammering; violent, shattering bangs, a few seconds' interval between each hit, set against a backdrop of shuffling feet, muffled voices and unnerving clamours. Captain Blom had barricaded himself inside his cabin after having been assaulted by Biermand and his fellow mutineers. The source of the noise was a wooden boom which the angry men on the outside used as a makeshift ram, each hit forcing the door ever more open.

Moments earlier, Blom had still been on top of the castle where he and Biermand had fought. Reportedly, Biermand had called Blom a 'dog' and a 'rogue' and asked 'why do you refuse to seek harbour?' Then he yelled to his co-mutineers, 'get him and throw him overboard', which made the captain plead for his life. Again, Braad reports the interaction as direct speech. Blom had exclaimed: 'my dear Hans, sure I am old enough to die, but for God's and my dear wife's and small children's sake, let me keep my life, and I will give you 100 Rix-dollars and what [you want] to have.' Blom had been given the exact sum of 100 Rix-dollars (a relatively modest sum as the Company was hard pressed for capital) in cash to be used in the case of having to enter a foreign port due to an emergency.[1] However, despite Blom's begging Biermand was merciless and replied: 'It is too late, you should have done that earlier. There is no mercy with me, but with God there is mercy.' Then punches where exchanged. Blom proved strong; Biermand was injured and the captain managed to jump from the poop deck and to get into the cabin before the mutineers could stop him.[2] Quickly, he constructed a makeshift barricade.

Realizing that his assailants were breaking through, Blom fired a gun through the half-broken door, injuring one of the convicts outside. Seconds later, the mutineers breached through and flooded the cabin. However, their adversary had vanished into thin air. At last, through a storm-shattered window, they spotted him desperately clinging to the ship's stern in an attempt to crawl into the gun-room below. The Irish convict named in the sources as Mikkel

Thomassen (probably Michael Thompson in English) then grabbed a rifle, likely Blom's own, and put an end to whatever desperate plan the captain had devised.[3]

From his hiding place among the convict women and children below deck in the front of the ship, Braad could hear the reverberations of the ominous percussive hits of the ram and the guns fired. The noise must have sounded disorienting to those who, like him, had not been privy to the discussions that had unfolded below deck in the weeks before. Yet in his journal, Braad tried to make sense of it all, crafting a tale that implies a clear cause to the event. In a sense, this plot rendered the noise of the mutiny as the inevitable culmination of a slow crescendo of destitution, misfortune and, most importantly, failed authority on the part of the captain.

It had been a troubled voyage from the beginning. The *Havmanden* had limped through the foggy *Kattegat* – the shallow sea that run from the northern tip of Jutland to the southern part of Scania, separating the open North Sea from the Baltic – aided by a smaller naval pilot ship. On 15 November, they saw the island of Anholt, two miles west. Its shoals were infamous. That night they sailed 'in dark weather and hard winds'. In the morning, it was foggy. They heard cannons from ships they could not see.[4] However, they crawled on. The pilot left them on 19 November, having helped them pass the northernmost tip of Jutland. This was when the real trial began. Facing the open North Sea, the weather turned bad and the next day the ship was engulfed in the first in a series of storms that would mar the voyage.

The rough westerly winds on 20 November forced the ship towards the coast of northern Jutland and its dangerous sandy shoals. Braad provides glimpses of panic: at midnight, they had 'driven so close to land that we had not above 25 or 26 fathoms of water'. Their fears of running aground prompted action, 'accordingly the Captain had the anchors readied'. This was sensible, but his next move was more dubious to the Company official, as Blom 'started to let people sense that he wanted some of the goods [thrown] overboard'. Thankfully, it cleared up at daybreak.[5]

There is a subtle distance in this portrayal of Blom – one that is symptomatic of Braad's journal at large: Blom is too silent. If the supercargo had wished to show his captain as an authority, a storm would have been an ideal occasion for Blom to speak, animate and encourage. This muteness of Blom recurs as a subtle theme throughout Braad's journal. It is a play on expectations that afforded Braad a way to implicitly criticize the deceased captain by drawing on the tropes of voyage narratives and conceptions of proper authority. Generally, storms were seen as events where leaders should animate their people and make them work in unison.[6] Theirs was the task of communicating courage.

We find such ideals in many contemporary voyage narratives of travellers from the Danish-Norwegian empire as well as other Atlantic empires.[7] For instance, one East India traveller caught in a storm describes how: 'our captain, as a brave naval hero, commanded us not to abandon our courage, but to think of how the all-mighty God would look upon our distress with mercy. He would at least save our lives, we should simply pray and work, then everything would end well.'[8] Praying and working were the tasks of the people in distress, but those actions were predicated upon the courageous words of authorities. Other voyagers described the necessity of a firm command in such situations as the crew would often murmur. As an example, traveller Hans Mesler remarked how during a storm, his captain heroically 'hindered the [people's] evil and rebellious business'. He did so with threats 'as he immediately fetched his sword of command and let them know that he would immediately cut off and maim the first hand that wanted to start to untie the boat and longboat to save themselves without attending to the common good'.[9] Storms called for firm action and authoritative speech. Mesler, however, later grew weary of his captain and his officers whom he accused of depriving his people of victuals and treating anybody speaking up on their behalf violently. This results in a change in Mesler's portrayal of his captain who during a fierce storm later in his journal is described as 'timid'.[10] Storms were moments for political and religious speech acts and implying muteness was a form of critique. Throughout his journal, Braad plays on these ideals of men of speech and action in order to subtly fault Blom with improper command.

They were lost after the initial storm. Rations were then cut short as the weather kept the ship from making progress. Repeatedly, the crew hailed fishermen to get word on their position.[11] By the middle of December they finally made some progress, but then the weather turned for the worse once more. The air was 'thick' for three days. During the night between 19 and 20 December, Blom anchored as he insisted that he had seen glimpses from an English light. In the morning, they could see nothing as the fogs had again enveloped the ship. They lay there for days. The sea was shallow so they knew they were close to some coast, but not which one. Slowly, the ship crawled south-west. They hailed a Swedish merchantman headed for Lisbon, but without success. Then the winds died down, and the next day they hardly moved. Finally, at midday on 23 December, the fogs lifted, revealing the cliffs of Dover to their right and Calais to their left.[12]

At this point, Braad interrupts his chronological descriptions of the ship's navigation in order to meditate on what he saw as the intertwined state of deteriorating shipboard social relations and material conditions. In a note inserted between the entries of 23 and 24 December, he provides a detailed picture of 'the misery that the people, one with the other, until this day, have had for some weeks concerning their food'. Most meals consisted only of dry bread, and the scanty hot meals were boiled in sea water. A mess of seven was served only enough for four.[13] There was only water to drink, and far from enough of it. Everyone – even those who messed in the cabin – were served only 'one cup of rotten water a day, so that it was a great pity with us miserable people that we were so badly treated here in the cold North Sea'.[14]

Blom's decision to shorten the rations might have had some sense to it. The sources suggest that the Company had not shipped sufficient provisions. In the archive, there is an account of the provisions acquired for the voyage. In it, they make an estimate of food for 100 people for five months and forty people in 10 months.[15] The latter are specified to be the seafarers who needed double the provisions in order to complete the next leg. However, there were approximately 200 people on board. To add further incentive, several of the Company's transatlantic crossings had taken longer than five months. For instance, the first expedition had taken a total of seven months. Blom also had first-hand experience that an Atlantic crossing might take longer. As the supercargo, Braad would have known that the rations were insufficient, but considering that the Company directors were the audience for his journal, it makes sense that he put the blame solely on Blom.

Besides, things were aggravated by the fact that there were several other stores of food on board. In the hold were provisions shipped for the Company servants on St Thomas and on the Gold Coast. Perhaps most importantly there was the food brought privately by the captain, with which he treated his inner circle. Braad frames this contrast by remarking how 'things were more joyful among those who had something nice with which to help themselves'. Implicitly, he faults Blom for not having listened to the people's distress in his own state of plenty. Their 'hunger and thirst was often brought before the captain both by the governor and by the rest of us, but to no avail'. Blom would simply excuse himself deferring all complaints to the steward.[16] However, Braad had already indicated that the steward was untrustworthy. He was not the man chosen by the Company for the job. Early in the voyage, Blom had deposed the original steward and sent him back to Copenhagen with the pilot ship. On that occasion, Braad tells us that Blom 'accused [the steward] of being inept in the role given to him by the company'. In his place, he installed one of the free people, a Dutchman called Jan Pietersen Peis.[17] Thus, Braad's readers are not surprised to learn that complaining to the new steward met only with 'evil and unpleasant answers, so that it was sensed that the Captain and the steward were accomplices and would unfortunately not allow people their right.' This sense of a 'right' was further attacked when anyone tried reasoning with Peis. In such situations 'the Captain defended him and sometimes had those the steward complained about beaten'.[18] Iversen's word, which Braad vested with proper authority, was fully disregarded by Blom who always did 'just opposite of what the Governor asked of him'. There was friction all around. In general, Blom and his officers 'put up such an unseemly house on board'. Thus, those 'who were to be a good example unto the rest' instead fought continually 'so that even though they had been ordered to dine together in the cabin, they ate, out of mutual hatred, one party in the cabin and another in the forecastle'.[19] How Iversen fits into these messy relations is somewhat unclear, as Braad seems unwilling to cast dispersions on him and instead centres the focus directly on Blom. However, in his interrogation, Braad gave further details, as he explained that Jacob van Bronckhorst, the ship's Dutch merchant, had been on the side of Blom against Iversen. On one occasion when Iversen had spoken up against the infringement on the people's rights, the merchant Bronckhorst had even attacked him physically, beating his 'mouth and nose bloody in the presence of the Captain'. No punishment ensued.[20]

Implicitly, Blom's inability to speak and to listen becomes a way for Braad to explain the mutiny. Braad's phrase 'an unseemly house' is telling. In early modern Europe, the household was considered to be the base unit of society. Living in a household meant to live in an ordered hierarchy of patriarchal relations; a metaphor for society in general.[21] As far back as Aristotle, the house had been the opposite of anarchic political communities. In the household, Aristotle had argued, natural relations among man and wife, parent and child, master and servant ruled uncontested.[22] Such naturalness was at odds with the always sliding and antagonistic political negotiation that was at the heart of the city and its political community where people would speak about things far beyond their station and knowledge. Braad draws on such conceptions as they were intrinsic to the general notion of the ship as a place that should not have a space of negotiation within them.[23] By not acting in accordance to their natural positions, the authorities, but mainly Blom, had disjointed the ship. He had failed to perform in a way as to become both feared and loved and this had cursed the ship with politics – with speech out of place and with divisions. An 'unseemly house' was a state in which contingencies would unfold. Braad was foreshadowing what was to come.

Over Christmas, the ship passed the Strait of Dover. Powerful winds drove them close to the French shore and they used every opportunity to head towards more open waters.[24] Then, on 30 December, they got caught in a 'mighty storm'. Again, Braad interrupts his remarks on the navigation to tell us how the boatswain, the constable, the carpenter and the cook had appealed, reasonably, to Blom that they would 'not be able to endure any longer'.[25] At this point, the ship's council, including Iversen, was summoned. They decided for a change in plans; the ship was to head for Norway. This was common practice for Company ships struggling in Kattegat or the North Sea. Blom had also done so before in a previous Company voyage and Iversen's first expedition had prompted a similar move.[26] They turned around, but by then the winds had 'multiplied'. On 1 January, the sea rose high enough that the waves 'broke the cabin windows to pieces'.[27] The following days were terrifying as the waves kept towering. They even took away 'those things that were on the top of the castle'. This provoked dire thoughts, 'so that at this time we thought about that which would surely have happened if another wave had come'. Once more, with the people in need of courage, Blom is silent. However, God was still merciful, 'as he heard our devoted prayers, and showed his two children great mercy, and did not want the water to be their grave'.[28]

As the weather cleared up, the crew found themselves guessing that they had made a great headway towards Norway. Unfortunately, now the winds were contrary. This sparked new discussions and 'it was decided to seek the Channel again'.[29] A plan had formed of seeking a harbour in Holland, but they were lost. On Sunday 7 January, Blom tried hailing a fisherman to act as a pilot. He did not respond to the signals. Two days later, the lookout spotted a small fleet of Dutch ships in the distance that 'were guessed to have come out of Texel'. At noon, the following day, they made contact with a ship from Middelburg which gave them news that they had Nieuwpoort to the southeast, but also warned them of a nearby shoal of only three fathoms. That night they fired 'upwards of 20 shots, [to get] a pilot who could lead us to a good road in Zeeland'. Braad implicitly underlines the incompetency of Blom and his mates when slyly remarking: 'and if God had not been as merciful as he was, it would have cost not only the ship and the goods, but also all the souls to be found on board.'[30] Blom was still mute.

On the morning of 11 January, they seemed to catch a break. Two French fishermen came on board and promised to pilot the *Havmanden* to Zeeland. However, they demanded a steep price for the task and Blom had only a small sum at his disposal. Over the next days, the crew worked the ship to follow the fishermen's hookers through fogs, hail showers and shoals. There were several meetings between the parties. At one point, the fishermen decided not to take them further until they were paid, but one of the mates managed to appease them. The following day, however, they came on board again saying that the winds could no longer take them to Zeeland, and instead offered to pilot the ship to Ostend, 'to which the Captain replied no, because there is no good harbour to lie in'. At that point, the fishermen left them for good.[31] A new plan was hatched of anchoring at the Isle of Wight to get 'some provisions for both the sick and the healthy on board and to get some fresh water and [to have] reparations done to the ship, which was very leaky'. According to Braad, they had twenty-six sick in total. It is unclear when the leak had sprung and if it was caused by the storms or simply the gradual wear and tear on the ship.[32] Its actual severity might also be questioned, since the ship continued for months at sea afterwards, at times with a diminished crew. However, a leaky ship meant that the crew would be put to the hard labour of pumping. Symptomatically, Braad never mentions this labour; to him, the question of the leak is solely a question of anxiety.

Rotten water, violent storms and, worst of all, a captain unable to cope with the situation: this is how Braad explains the violence that erupts over the following pages of his journal. It was merely a reaction, he seems to say. He was right in stressing the material conditions of the ship and the way they threatened the lives of those on board. The convicts below must have felt this acutely as their previous stays in Copenhagen's prisons meant that they arrived on board in an already deteriorated state. In the immediate aftermath of the mutiny, Braad quotes one of the convicts saying that, 'after this time none should suffer such hunger as previously'.[33] The demands of the convicts in the night before the mutiny also centred squarely on the destitution they experienced below deck. However, other ships had seen similar destitution without it prompting mutiny. In fact, in earlier voyages there had been many more sick and dead. During Iversen's first expedition to St Thomas in 1671–72, four out of about sixty convicts had already died before this point in the voyage. A total of twenty-seven convicts died in that voyage.[34] This places even greater importance on the second part of Braad's explanation: the notion that Blom's failed authority was, ultimately, to blame.

We have reason to believe that Braad's account provides a reliable picture of conditions on board. There is nothing that disputes it. Second mate von Gent provides only a brief remark on the material conditions when noting that by the time they entered the Channel, they were 'suffering from great lack of water, each man getting only half a cup of water a day'.[35] He offers nothing that negates Braad's claims in any way. At the same time, Braad's account of Blom matches fully with a letter that Iversen sent home with the pilot ship in November. In it, Iversen wrote to the Company bookkeeper to complain. He began by referencing a fight he and Blom had in the days before embarkation – something which had prompted the Company directors to venture on board to try and mediate. According to Iversen, it stemmed from Blom wanting Iversen to live 'on his mercy as a boy'. Now Iversen wrote to tell them that this was exactly what was happening on board: 'since I sailed as a common hand, I have not had as bad meals, than I have had until the 17 [November] in this ship, so that there has been only a slight difference between my food and that of the convicts'. He felt sick, which he attributed to 'the bad and thick beer'. It was also a matter of honour and status as Iversen was 'unwilling to beg'. Iversen explained that Blom and his few select men themselves had 'no desire to eat that which is eaten in the cabin when they are not themselves seated'. He even reasoned that 'the cabin boy Jan Simonsen is treated much better than I am'.[36] Clearly, Iversen felt deprived of a marker of his status and that Blom ran the ship with a small clique.

Perhaps most importantly Braad's account of Blom echoes accounts of how the captain had comported himself in a previous voyage in the service of the Company. After having joined the Danish navy in 1678, he was picked out to serve the West India and Guinea Company in 1680 for the first expedition to the colonies after their war-time hiatus.[37] This was the voyage of the much smaller ship, the *Kronede Grif* (Crowned Griffin), which left Copenhagen in late August 1680 with supplies as well as a new merchant, a priest and a few convicts and servants for the colony. During this voyage, reports from the merchant, Hans Jonsen, and others suggest that Blom had behaved himself in much the same way as he would two years later. Two months in, they had anchored in Norway after having been 'driven back and forth' in the North Sea.[38] Having anchored, Blom refused to sail for weeks, despite the winds being good. At this point, the priest and a lieutenant, Christopher Heins (who later became governor of St Thomas), wrote to the Company, exposing Blom. Apparently, he had decided that he was the sole authority on the ship. Like Iversen, Jonsen had been deprived of authority, which made the priest remark how 'it does not seem good that one person alone has such an absolute command'. Even in absolutist Denmark, the ideal of government was one in which leaders took heed of advice. According to the priest, Jonsen had attempted to take care of Company interests, but had been 'shamefully and coarsely spoken to, without any cause'. Subsequently, he was stripped of 'all command so that he cannot get anything done unless he wants to be ostracized from the cabin, something he has often been threatened with'. The only reason that the priest and the other Company officers had not spoken up to Blom was due to fears of getting the same treatment. Instead they chose 'silence'.[39]

Eventually, however, the ship did leave Norway. By March 1681, it reached St Thomas, more than six months after having left Copenhagen. Four people had died en route. According to Jonsen, the ship had been close to foundering because of 'mad navigation'. Blom had mistreated the priest, expelling him from the cabins. Jonsen speculated that this was because Blom wanted to manipulate the ship's journal. Except for the first mate and 'one or two others' everyone was treated badly, even violently. A passenger, listed as a 'joiner' in the crew list, was beaten in the head 'so that he has been confused in his mind ever since'.[40] This violence is mentioned only once in the correspondence, but a later complaint found in the Company archive from the brother of the joiner lends credibility to the claim. Apparently, Blom had claimed that the injured man had wanted to run away and had then hit him in the head with a cane causing him to drop to the floor where Blom continued hitting him. The man's brother, a tailor, was also part of the voyage and had witnessed the beating first hand.[41] Seemingly, Blom did not fear the Company authorities. He belonged to a different order: 'he also dared to say that he had no business with the Company, and that he was subject to Admiralty jurisdiction'.[42] Along with his select few, he feasted while everyone starved. As was the case on the *Havmanden*, Blom had brought along plenty of brandy, and at one time he had been so drunk that he was unable to find the altitude of the sun. He and his cronies had also consumed some of the Company's own liquors from the hold, along with a pig that Jonsen had brought along for the people.[43]

The Company should have reacted to such reports. Unfortunately for them, they read Jonsen's complaints in light of a scandal he himself became embroiled in when he let a female servant sleep in his cabin. This brought him in conflict with the priest, who then changed sides and mended his conflict with Blom. The priest had attacked the servant in his sermons on board on the grounds that 'she was a whore and was to receive a whore's pay'.[44] Arriving in the colony, both Blom and the priest joined with the governor, Nicholas Esmit, who had his own reasons for wanting to side-line Jonsen who carried orders to close the harbour which Esmit had opened to foreign traders, making a profit for himself. They put the girl on trial, sentencing her to public absolution for her sins, which Esmit, in a letter, argued had caused great contention among the sailors. Most importantly, this latter conflict made the priest rescind his comments about Blom in a second letter to the Company in which he argued that the issues around Blom had only really been a minor quarrel, and that he had been spurred to write about them by Jonsen.[45] In this way, this unrelated case influenced how the Company evaluated Jonsen's portrayal of Blom. Thus, in November 1681, they concluded the case by admonishing the merchant, telling him to give up his grievances and repent his sinful ways.[46]

We hear a strong echo in Braad's portrayal of events two years later, especially Blom's combination of reclusiveness and abuse. However, we should not then jump to the conclusion that this ring of truthfulness means that Braad's way of constructing the meaning of the mutiny provides a satisfactorily full explanation of its cause. The logic followed by his narrative is similar to that proposed by Greg Dening, who suggested that mutinies could be prompted by a failure in the performance of proper authority. Certainly, Blom's conduct might have spurned the hatred that the mutineers seem to have had of him. Like the convicts did not trust Iversen, Biermand's attack on Blom in the morning of the mutiny clearly shows that the mutineers did not trust the captain. Yet there is nothing in the sources to suggest that the men and women below deck longed for authority. Their dealings with Iversen, whom Braad depicts as Blom's polar opposite, suggests this more than anything. As we have seen, Iversen was killed with as much determination, even though he had, according to Braad, carried himself with authority and fairness. Thus, Braad's explanation becomes internally discrepant. There are other problems with this model as an explanation as well: while some of the naval mariners on board might have been put off by the fact that life on the *Havmanden* did not happen according to its regular routine, the major part of the mutineers were men and women to whom such order was alien in the first place. In a sense, if its explanatory force is to be accepted, the model hinges on them knowing the script of the performance, which they did not.

Instead we should read the plot that Braad constructs in the light of the audience he wrote for: his employers in the Company office. Ann Laura Stoler has remarked how 'proof of competence and good judgment was demonstrated in no small part by configuring events into familiar and recognisable plots'.[47] This is very much what Braad's account of Blom is: a recognizable plot, which lends its writer accountability – something he needed, as everyone returning was, naturally, suspected of having been part of the mutiny itself.

Yet in places, Braad's journal and subsequent examination contains hints at a complexity that the logic imparted by his way of explanation rules out. Part of this character comes from the fact that he himself was also spinning yarns (for instance incorporating the words of Friberg or things he overheard long after the mutiny itself during events discussed in the next chapter). Through such appropriations his story becomes dialogic, at times disjointing the structure it imparts. Ultimately a composite construction crafted from fragments, Braad's tale contains a surplus of meaning that brings it ever so slightly out of tune with itself. As was the case with the incongruous phrase 'seller-of-souls', whose possible meanings were explored in the previous chapter, these extraneous elements hint that there was much more to the mutiny than simply the roaring of stomachs and an authority who failed to act as such.

Thus, instead of either accepting the logic Braad infers on the event or abandoning his journal outright as a source, we can begin to read for the gaps and dissonances in the plot that he crafts – sifting through the scraps for subtle clues to help us build a more complicated story. We can also relate such findings to other sources besides Braad's words in our efforts to glean meaning. Doing so, we move into much more perilous territory in which our uncertainty and the need for interpretation becomes much greater, yet we are rewarded with a sense of how this lower-deck community had emerged.

Under the cover of noise

Before we can begin this line of enquiry, however, we should consider the very space in which such discourses resonated. Events recorded by Braad hint how it had been oppressive. On the day after the mutiny, all chests within the ship were sorted through; anything deemed valuable was kept, and everything else thrown overboard. To the supercargo, this represented utter wastefulness and he remarked on several of the costly things, principally cloth, hurled into the waves. According to him this happened for the mutineers 'to be masters of much more space'.[48] However, it might have been only a sensible response to the experiences of those who had lived in the crammed confines below.

We do not know the exact measurements of the *Havmanden*, but ships of this type tended to range from between twenty-two and thirty metres in length and upwards of seven and a half metres in width.[49] We do know that fully manned as a naval ship, the *Havmanden* had held 150 men.[50] Fully packed as a slaver the directors had estimated that it would hold 300 people in total, yet this might have hinged on the construction of temporary decks. At the time of embarkation in November, about 200 people were on board – in addition to a hold full of Company goods, most of which were to be unloaded at St Thomas. No doubt the spatial arrangements needed for gender separation had eaten up space as well. The presence of considerable numbers of women and children must have greatly complicated the living arrangements under the decks and in the cabin, although the sources are unclear as to how this was dealt with in practice. It seems that three groups inhabited the lower deck, living separately: common sailors; male convicts; and female convicts (where the score of indentured servants fit into this schematic is unclear). Braad repeatedly hints such a spatial layout with phrases like 'among the convicts', or 'among the women and children'.[51] However, it is also possible that at least some of the sailors lived in the forecastle where the officers seem to have had their quarters, in lieu of space in the cabins. What we can say with certainty is that space on the *Havmanden* was at an absolute premium. Such density risked creating an amoebic disease environment that might prove deadly. It also gave rise to an oppressive atmosphere, in which eavesdropping would have been rife.

In such a large crowd, speaking up would have entailed a remarkable danger. Scholars have pointed to two circumstances under which individuals are atomized to such a degree that hiding a transcript becomes virtually impossible: situations in which there is enough vertical mobility for subjects to have a reasonable expectation of becoming the elite; and situations in which surveillance creates a social situation in which there is no space in which to speak.[52] It is the latter that concerns us here. The *Havmanden* can be conceived as such a space of surveillance, although it worked in an aural and not a visual way. The very density of people on the ship would have enhanced the atomization of the individuals in the shipboard community as there was simply no safe place to speak due to the large number of ears within earshot. There was no a priori social site where the dominated could count on their words not being picked up by people who might seek to feather their own nest.

Yet a site of discourse did form. Therefore, we must read the mutiny as the result of the creation of such a space, a transformation of its dense, oppressive community through incremental, uneven steps in which solidarities formed across this tightly packed lower deck and the social groups that inhabited it; the making of a space in which to speak and listen which overcame the density and the limits it might have imposed on careful speakers.

At the same time that they worked against it, the material conditions no doubt also aided this formation. First of all, they levelled the divides among the different groups of subalterns: on board convicts and common sailors appear to have dressed the same; they ate the same food (though rations were probably differentiated, as they were in the colony[53]); they shared the same demoralizing experience of seeing their rations diminish and their beer and water turn foul; and, during the nights in the tight confines of their shared living quarters on the lower deck, they had the same paradoxical experience of hearing the noises of their roaring stomachs mix with the tell-tale sounds of merriment resonating from the cabin.

Yet this space worked to facilitate discourse in some unexpected ways as well. While the storms would no doubt cause a great deal of anxiety, especially among those on board who were not used to seafaring, they also offered a sort of sonic cover. An early modern wooden ship caught in a rough sea was an extremely noisy place. Not only did the assault of the waves create a constant roaring within; the ship itself also began making noise. One Danish eighteenth-century traveller described how one of the most 'disconcerting' things during storms was the ship's 'creaking and roaring [...] in the timber as well as by the cannons. It seems that the planks and beams are about to jump from one another. The cannons squeal, howl and appear to want to tear themselves loose.' All of this 'makes a disconcerting music and a horrible noise in the ship. In the middle of the ship, the mast does its own work and makes a peculiar uproar. All of this only creates fear.'[54] Others heard such shipboard noises as part of a religious soundscape: 'every plank in the ship gave in and twisted itself, every nail and spike wrenched and wriggled, so that inside the ship it was as if many organs had been playing loudly.'[55] Such cacophony provoked deep anxieties, but also countered eavesdropping to a degree by affording sonic cover, because sounds would no longer travel. A whisper would have been audible only to those very close by. The nervous bustle created by so many people might also have added a sonic cover for illicit exchanges, muffling sounds that otherwise would have echoed through the hollow resonator of the hull. Thus, at certain times conditions for speaking were suboptimal, but at other times almost ideal.

To the men and women living below deck, this dynamic of veiled words and curious ears was a defining characteristic of social life. As we shall see in the next chapter, Braad experienced this himself after the mutiny, when he was evicted from the cabins. Up until the mutiny, however, we get only rare glimpses. The first of these comes as Braad, three weeks into the voyage, describes how, 'a notice was read to all the people in which it was ordered that they should come willingly to prayers and sermon whenever the bell rang, and that nobody were to swear and curse to the resentment of God and the offence of others, which unfortunately have happened to this day'.[56] While we do not know who spoke the disruptive words, we do know that such irreverent speech was a widely recognized trait of sailors. Across oceans, the sailors of European maritime empires were reviled for their blaspheming ways.[57] The strong link between blasphemy and ships' crews might be owing to the consequences that such foul language might have occurred at sea. Not only could blasphemy provoke God's punishment of the entire shipboard community, but due to its character as a 'speech of provocation' it was also seen to be potentially upsetting to the fragile social order by igniting 'simmering disgruntlement'.[58] Thus, blasphemy was a language in which hidden discourse could get a veiled public expression. Like the Danes, authorities in other empires tried stifling such unruly tongues.[59]

Many Danish travellers encountered such voices. In the context explored here, the scene on the *Havmanden* reads almost as a repetition of the events in the first voyage of 1671–72 discussed in the previous chapter. Incidents concerning blasphemy also abound in Danish voyage narratives. Often they were recounted as moral lessons in order to serve as 'a mirror to all blasphemers'.[60] They also hint at the social dynamics of such speech. The traveller Sveigaard, mentioned in the Introduction, told a story of common hands at work. During their most laborious tasks, he overheard how 'Jan Hagel started mutually to curse and spew many bloody oaths from their throats; though they dared not let any of the officers hear it because a beating would ensue'.[61] Sveigaard's remark is interesting; not only because it attributes blasphemy to presumably low-born sailors, colloquially known as 'Jan Hagel', but because it shows the reflexivity with which the utterance of such words could be imbued. Sailors used foul language to signify their dissatisfaction knowing that they could not do so in the presence of their superiors due to the consequences that would entail.[62] Blasphemy was an expression of a form of courageous daring and masculinity in the face of hierarchy. It might also have served to test bonds. If a sailor or convict blasphemed among his peers and none winced, objected or told, it signalled complicity and a certain enclosed space of uninhibited discourse. It created bonds of trust (or if failing: distrust), thereby performing the useful task of demarcating the social site of the hidden transcript to its speakers.[63]

Recalcitrant discourse makes itself felt implicitly in other instances early in the voyage. In the morning of Sunday 3 December, someone from the cabin sensed that something was not as it should be. Perhaps the words sounding from the convicts' quarters deep within the dark lower deck came off as merrier than usual. A group of convicts were found to be drunk – a state they surely could not reach on the meagre rations of spoilt beer. Instead, they had been drinking brandy all night; albeit quietly, so as not to be discovered. It took until the afternoon for the liberators of the stolen spirits to be uncovered. What transpired in the meantime is unclear, although it seems likely, in light of their strategies on 19 January, that the convicts were unwilling to rat each other out. In the end, however, the silence was broken and it was discovered that three convicts, Jørgen Pohinske, Anders Berger and Friderich Beniche, had managed to steal the brandy 'the last time that water was taken from the hold'. How they had succeeded in accomplishing this cunning act is also unclear, but the circumstances suggest that some of the sailors were in on the plan. The spoils had been great: a cask of brandy.[64]

In order to appreciate the meaning of such a feat we must consider its collective character. Not only was it a response to a state of scarcity shared among all and whose severity Braad's account underlines at every opportunity, but within the tight confines of the lower deck, the very act took on a social dynamic. Even if the act itself could be done without anybody finding out, knowledge of the act of consuming the stolen would surely spread. However, a thief could of course 'buy' the complicity of others with loot. Through this process, the act became collective, just as listening to blasphemy without objecting made it a social act. In this way, theft also created and then tested a bond between the perpetrators and the witnesses. If this bond failed, the crime would have become public. This was the case in a voyage detailed by Mesler when a boy (who had come on board in secret) confessed that two sailors had ingeniously 'drilled a hole in the shutters or partitions from boards, and through it into one of the Company's casks of wine, from which they drank using a quill'.[65] On the *Havmanden*, the plot was perhaps less ingenious, but the conspiracy seems to have been stronger, hinting that at this point there had formed a site for everyday forms of resistance on the lower deck. It was this site that would be the grounds for the building of the mutinous coalition.

The three offenders were shackled for twenty-one days.[66] We do not know if such acts of law were accompanied by readings of the articles, as was protocol. This was practiced in other voyages, but Braad is silent on the matter – perhaps because it would in fact have portrayed Blom as an exemplary captain carrying out the word of the law, which ran counter to Braad's otherwise negative representation of his captain. If this ritual was indeed carried out, the ceremony proved futile. Later in the voyage, several more acts of theft came to light. On the night of the mutiny, the mutineers broke into the hold once more. At least two other such instances of pilfering from the hold were discovered after the mutiny – one perpetrated by convicts, another by sailors – and both involved stealing brandy. It seems highly unlikely that these were the only pilfering to take place below deck in the voyage. Most likely, they were simply the ones discovered. Among the convicts was a man named Christopher Dichmand, who according to rumours circulating within the ship, was able to 'open all locks on board, without a key'.[67] No doubt Dichmand's skill represented a valuable competency on a ship that for most of its members became defined by the paradoxical experience of scarcity amidst abundance.

There are clear signs that the people below deck sensed the merriment that resonated from the cabin. The cheers that reverberated from Blom's quarters and the scent of alcohol on the breath of members of his clique would have sharpened the feeling of being justified in acts of theft. As remarked by sound scholar Brandon LaBelle: 'sound imparts flexibility, and uncertainty, to the stability of space. Sound disregards the particular visual and material delineations of spatial arrangements, displacing and replacing the lines between inside and out, above and below'.[68] While the convicts had to hide their intoxication and keep their voices low, Blom's clique did not have to trouble themselves to do the same.

The sounds echoing through the hull seem to have spurred the imagination. In the murky aftermath of the mutiny, it was claimed that one of the mutineers, Jan Sanders, a common sailor of English descent, had originally conceived of a plan for a mutiny to be carried out on Christmas Eve: 'when the best opportunity would present itself as was sensed that the authorities and the other officers were drunk'.[69] This plot was neither discovered nor carried out at the time. It is unclear why the plan did not come to fruition, as Braad picked up on it only much later. However, its very existence attests to how, by late December, plans of mutiny were being mooted. The very fact that it was not given up (hence, Braad's and, in turn, our lack of knowledge) shows how a space for discussion in which radical ideas floated had at that point formed below deck. At some unknown point Sanders also went so far as to steal six cutlasses from the gunroom which he hid, and which were later used in the mutiny – something Braad picked up in the flurry of stories that circulated after the event.[70] In this way, Braad's journal provides subtle hints that while the men in the cabins fought over authority, the men and women crammed below deck, and bound together through a shared experience of destitution and acts of everyday resistance, began to envision and discuss possibilities of deposing of such authorities altogether.

Fantasies of retribution

In the heat of the mutiny, Biermand's words and curses had sounded vicious – or at least so Braad had been told from people who had heard the words uttered in the flurry of activity. Biermand and the convicts 'stood there and growled at [Blom]'.[71] One imagines a pack of dogs and sounds of violent animality. However, the word had other interlocked meanings as well: growls are described by a Danish dictionary from 1686 as 'evil words by a human who is angry'.[72] This is one of the many ways in which Braad signifies an atmosphere of rage; the air was thick with abusive terms echoing through the narrow confines of the ship. As argued in the previous chapter, this anger was partly the result of the way the men below deck had discussed those in the cabin. Thus, it connects what happened in the chaotic minutes of the mutiny to what had taken place in the long drawn out days and nights that preceded it. In certain passages, Braad even hints at such a connection himself: in both his journal and interrogation, Braad argues that there had existed some sort of a list as to who were to be killed. He believed that he had himself been among the people singled out, but was saved for reasons that I discuss at length in Chapter 3.[73] The existence of such a list is indirectly confirmed by the violence itself as it appears directed at the people closest to Blom. The steward Peis suffered 'the most miserable death, not only being badly beaten as he lay on the deck, but even getting so many holes in his body from bayonets'.[74] Thus, they not only killed him, but also defiled his body in a way that Braad suggested was highly symbolic. The mutineers also killed the ship's master, Christopher Hysing, who also appears to have been part of Blom's clique, as well as a man named Jan Simonsen, a sailor described also as Blom's 'cabin watchman'.[75] In his interrogation Braad described the latter as the 'Captain's nephew' and he was the person Iversen claimed had a much better standard of living than him.[76] We have already explored the possible meanings of the resentments held towards Iversen. These acts of violence were not acted out against whomever simply came in the way of the mutineers. Instead, there was a sense of retribution to them.[77]

Thus, while the words themselves come off as unintelligible growling, we sense a social logic behind them. As noted by James C. Scott, fantasies of vengeance were often key to the discourses of subalterns: 'The frustration, tension, and control necessary in public give way to unbridled retaliation in a safer setting, where the accounts of reciprocity are symbolically at least, finally balanced', he argues.[78] Sailors had a long, although opaque, tradition of telling stories about superiors and injustices, explored in length in Chapter 4. Such stories often rotated around ways in which a higher justice manifested itself. As Scott remarks: 'Fantasy life among dominated groups is also likely to take the forms of schadenfreude: joy at the misfortunes of others. This represents a wish for negative reciprocity, a settling of scores when the high shall be brought low and the last shall be first'.[79] It is also in the context of such fantasies that we must place the discussions which the mutineers had about Iversen and the colonial empire many of them were forced to take part in.

While the anger directed at the upper echelons in the shipboard hierarchy is perhaps not difficult to understand in light of the material conditions reigning on board, Braad's journal provides what might be indications that there was some surprising complexity to it. The first such instance is an event during the mutiny which Braad records, but which appears strangely meaningless. On 30 November, Iversen's wife had given birth to a daughter. This was an unusual event on an early modern European ship and must have caused some hubbub. The baby daughter survived only for six days. On Tuesday 5 December, Braad tells us that, 'at night during the first shift, the Governor's small daughter, after having been baptized by him [Iversen] and called Else only a little earlier, was called to the Lord'.[80] Her body was placed in a small coffin located in Iversen's part of the cabins, awaiting a proper burial when they arrived at St Thomas. On similar ships, dead children of upper-class passengers were at times buried temporarily in the ballast, then laid to rest properly whenever the vessel made landfall.[81]

A month and a half later, in the tumult of the mutiny, the mutineers searched the cabins after having shot the captain. They broke into Iversen's compartment where the Irish convict, Mikkel Thomassen, Blom's killer, found Iversen's wife in her bed. He stole a gold chain from her, before she escaped below deck. He, or someone else, also found the coffin, which was promptly thrown overboard.[82] Braad appears to attribute no meaning to this action, except perhaps to highlight their recklessness, yet its resoluteness presents several possible interpretations.

Some seafarers believed that having a dead body on board ship caused bad luck. We find an example of this in the narrative of a contemporary British voyager, Lionel Wafer, who during his Pacific voyage on a pirate ship in the 1680s, encountered what he considered a noteworthy discovery on a Peruvian beach as he stumbled over bodies that looked as if they had been dead for only a week. Wafer's touch revealed that they had dried out and were light 'as a Spunge or a piece of Cork'. A local then told him that these were the bodies of a group of heroic Amerindians who had committed collective suicide as a form of resistance to Spanish tyranny. They had buried themselves alive in the sand. Wanting to document the incident (which fed into British notions of Spanish brutality), he carried the body of a boy on board the ship, but here he met with resistance, the sailors 'having a foolish Conceit, that the Compass would not traverse aright, so long as any dead Body was on board, threw him overboard, to my great Vexation'.[83] The men on board the *Havmanden* might have had similar concerns as they saw the ship's chaotic navigation.

An alternate, but somewhat related, interpretation is possible. Sailors were typically deprived of proper burials. Historian Brian J. Rouleau has remarked how: 'Far flung from the elaborate mourning rituals characteristic of the land, mariners experienced death in an unceremonious manner that in many ways reinforced their inferiority aboard the vessel.'[84] Many convicts also never received proper burial, some even being interred in unconsecrated ground. Perhaps the sailors and convicts were disgruntled that Iversen's baby received a privilege denied to them. Had the sailors, in their nightly discourses, cursed Iversen's deceased child, the bad luck she brought them, or the difference that her coffin embodied? We cannot know, and apparently neither could Braad. However, this very act prompts us to consider just how many elements there might have been to their actions.

The same goes for another event that transpired in the days following the mutiny. At this point, new flags were sown, seemingly for the purpose of camouflage. One was a Dutch flag 'from red and white bunting, and some blue canvas shirts, since they had nothing else'. Braad then remarks, 'with which flag the rebels drove about, with the firing of some pieces and said: to the health of the new flag of the Prince of Orange'.[85] Why did the mutineers toast this Dutch flag? Among the chief mutineers were several English mariners. The flag they saluted was that of William III, eventual king of post–1688 England. Perhaps they saluted a man who at this point represented a potential claim to a throne that many feared would fall into the hands of the Catholic James II? If so, the mutineers on the *Havmanden* had been discussing high politics. We should not be surprised; the writings of sailors and soldiers from the Danish navy are littered with references and remarks on the international politics in which they might themselves have been merely pawns, but which they certainly did not think themselves not worthy to discuss.

Of course, one might also read such a gesture as mockery. It would certainly have fit in the seemingly carnivalesque atmosphere that reigned for a few days after the mutiny. Nigel Worden's close study of a mutiny on a VOC-vessel in 1732 suggests that sometimes mutinies articulated antagonisms that ran along national divisions, orchestrated by factions whose ties were ethnic.[86] Were the mutineers in fact *mocking* the Dutch? It seems quite possible. While the mutinous coalition contained many nationalities, there was not a single Dutchman among them. Similar divisions marred other Danish ships. For instance, a mutiny erupted as Danish and English mariners clashed on a *West India and Guinea Company* ship in 1737 after a voyage defined by tension between the different nationalities on board.[87] On the *Havmanden*, such divisions might have been accentuated by the fact that the Dutch were mainly among the officers on board. In this way, ethnic divisions converged with class distinctions. Anti-Dutch resentments, possibly spurred by Blom's sticking to a small faction, thus appear likely to have been another factor in bringing the angry coalition behind the mutiny together.

These were elements that we should consider as we try to imagine the discourses taking place in the long nights before the mutiny. They might very well have added to the sense of unity below deck that allowed for more and more daring discourses. Both elements highlighted the myriad differences between the lower deck and the cabin, likely adding to the intense resentments that echoed in their 'growls'.

The more angry and antagonistic the discourse below deck, the stronger the unity needed to be in order to avoid such a space from spilling over, and being relayed to the ears of authorities. The most dangerous was, of course, that which entertained the possibility of turning fantasies into reality. If such matters were to be discussed, one needed as much faith in each other as possible. Early moderns had different ways of building such trust than we do today. The swearing of oaths was the most widely used device in this regard. In preparing acts of resistance, sailors (but also soldiers, convicts and other groups of colonial subalterns) were known to swear oaths and to otherwise formalize their solidarity through ritual.[88] On the *Havmanden*, we find such forms as well. At some point during the night leading up to the mutiny, a group of mutinous sailors and convicts broke into the hold; then while drinking, they each bit their thumbnails as a ritual of allegiance to the plot.[89] Such a formalization was a step in building the trust that made it possible to go from the realm of jokes, fantasies and sly critique to the realm of action. As a social, but also religious contract, the oath bound the swearer not only to what he swore, but also to God. Further, in swearing to mutiny, the ritual drew power from the law itself, as having taken part of this event would mean that you would already have committed a capital offense. Thus, from this point on there was no safe way out.

The gathering was described later as having taken place among the convicts living on the lower deck. At its centre were men whom the sources later pointed out as ringleaders: Jan Sanders, the English sailor, and Roluf Lorenzen (at times called Roluf Lybecker, hinting that he was German), a Norwegian sailor, were there 'the whole night'.[90] We must assume that another English sailor Frans Vads was as well (most likely his name was 'Francis Watts'). Claus von Kiel, a German sailor, was there too, and Peder Frandsen, the Danish sailmaker, at some point joined the Company. Biermand, who eventually received the harshest sentence of them all due to his incitement to murder the captain and the governor, seems to have been on duty, but he dropped in several times in the early morning to drink from the stolen stores with his accomplices. He bit his nail as well. The two

Irish convicts, Mikkel Thomassen and Tønnes Willumsen (likely Thomas
Williamson) were there, the former being the man who would later shoot Blom.
So were the Danish convicts Niels Jørgensen and his friend Jokum Gulliksen
who, hours later, became captain. Along with these men were a larger group of
less visible figures, principally convicts.[91]

The extent to which the convict women participated in the discourse is
unclear. When, hours later, Braad fled the scene to hide among them, he found
that they were drunk, each having their own bottle of French brandy from the
hold. He also heard them ask the male convicts 'if it was going to go well?'[92]
However, neither Braad nor the court seems to have found reason to inquire into
their participation, and none were convicted. Whether this reflected the realities
of the coalition or the law's gendered gaze is impossible to assess.

There is a telling sort of slip in Braad's account. In describing how the mutiny
was after the fact discussed among the mutineers themselves, Braad stated that
the convict Mikkel Thomassen had said that Biermand 'swore that he would be
Sanders and the other convicts faithful'.[93] But Sanders was not a convict, he was
a common sailor. The mutiny and the discourses that preceded it, for a time,
blurred the social groups of the lower deck: there, the speakers had belonged
more to a heterogeneous social site of hidden discourse and less to clear judicial
categories, ranks or classes. This is most aptly demonstrated by the convict
Jokum Gulliksen's election as captain after the mutiny. Braad was not privy to the
formation of this space and the words that were spoken in it, but I would argue
that the fragments he presents can be read as indicators that it had formed slowly
and steadily in the course of the voyage, before culminating in the discussion
during the night of the lead-up. Yet one part is still missing for us to understand
its emergence: a plan. I have already discussed the list of who were to be
murdered. There were other parts to it as well. While Iversen's and Braad's
interruption and confrontation seems to have made things escalate abruptly,
there had been a concrete plan of how to proceed beforehand. Someone, possibly
the English sailor Jan Sanders, divided the convicts into two groups. One, upon
Sanders' signal, was to break into the cabins, and the other was to storm the
gunroom. The signal was to be two stomps on the deck; the plan thus hinged on
the production of sound.[94] While this signal was never given due to the sudden
intrusion of Iversen, the party did indeed split into two. If Blom had succeeded
in his desperate plan of crawling into the gunroom, he would have been
disappointed, finding the mutineers there already.

In his discussions of what he calls 'the process of shipboard revolt', Rediker
has constructed a model of six phases that many mutinies of this type went

through. The phases, as he describes them, are: 'forming an original core of rebels [. . .]; forming a collective that would carry it out; getting out of irons (this phase would not apply to all mutinies); finding weapons; fighting the battle and seizing control of the ship; and eventually sailing the ship to freedom.'[95] Except for the optional phase three ('getting out of irons' – when and even if this happened on the *Havmanden* is unclear as the chains carried by the convicts were light enough that they did not hold them back[96]) the mutiny on the *Havmanden* followed this schematic. Such a similarity might owe to how men like Sanders knew stories of the collective actions of others, thereby enabling the transfer of knowledge – although this hypothesis cannot be tested.

Our sense of how these steps were formulated during the deliberations below deck is limited by Braad's position within the shipboard hierarchy. However, the sources allow for glimpses of how the convicts and sailors envisioned the last phase 'sailing the ship to freedom'. It hinged on relations that had formed before the voyage itself. Exploring the emergence of this plan, in turn, enables us to get a better sense of the first part – the formation of a 'core'.

Old friends and new plans

While the convicts, indentured servants and even the mariners for the most part formed an uneasy community comprised of strangers, relations among a few of them *had* existed prior to embarkation. One such nexus is of particular importance in understanding the mutiny: the friendships and family relations surrounding the naval master turned convict and eventually mutineer-captain Jokum Gulliksen, the sailmaker Peder Frandsen and the convict Niels Jørgensen. Gulliksen had strong bonds with each of these two men who proved key to the mutiny (as well as to later events explored in the next chapter). Braad explicitly calls Frandsen and Jørgensen Gulliksen 'friends' and shows them at his side at all times. However, in order to get a sense of these friendships and their meaning, we need to look elsewhere. Both friendships had existed prior to embarkation. Through their backstory of social relations in the dissonant Danish Atlantic we see the contingencies that might lead to subalternity and how the silences imposed by such status were violated by the human relations that the law could not efface, or which its punishments might even facilitate. Such relations transformed the speech community on the lower deck and were key to the formulation of the plan.

Who was the convict Gulliksen, and what ties existed between him and his fellow mutineers? Because Gulliksen had been a naval officer, it is possible to trace his backstory in great detail. Gulliksen was first brought to trial in early April 1682. His former captain, Peder Stud, a man whom he knew well from events I will discuss briefly, had served on the Low Admiralty Court before which he appeared.[97] The minutes do not report what was said on the occasion. However, from their mentions of the specifics of the case, as well as the sentence passed and various Admiralty correspondence, we get a sense of the events having led to Gulliksen's arrest. At some point that spring, Admiralty authorities seem to have realized that things were missing from the ship that Gulliksen was overseeing as interim master. The ship was no other than the *Havmanden*. Gulliksen himself had also been missing. He was suspected of having stolen from the ship's inventory.[98] We do not know what had gone missing, but from the charges it becomes clear that the navy's own guard had been sent looking for the absentee. When they found him, he evaded them. Reportedly, he had also been 'contrary' and 'obstinate'.[99] What these euphemisms entail is unclear, but they do explain why Gulliksen was also charged with disobedience. This was a serious charge, but he got off leniently. Perhaps, it was Stud who had spoken well of his abilities. Gulliksen was a skilled mariner, and Stud had relied on him at crucial hours. Or, perhaps the committee was impressed when another master, Abraham Østensen, showed up in court and spoke well of Gulliksen's character.[100] Thus, he was simply sentenced to bring back the missing inventory or pay their value, an unknown sum, in cash, and to serve for a year without pay as a common sailor.[101]

None of the missing inventory came back, nor did Gulliksen make up for them. He had only been master for a few months, having made an unlikely rise to this high rank because of an extraordinarily high number of deaths in his previous voyage – a Company voyage to Africa. Before then he had been a quartermaster. Although a petty officer, a quartermaster was paid only slightly more than a regular sailor;[102] now Gulliksen received no pay at all. He was about twenty-five years old by this point, born in 1657 to a father who was, at the time of Gulliksen's baptism, a naval quartermaster as well.[103] Thus, Gulliksen is unlikely to have had the means to pay his fine; neither did he seem willing to prove himself remorseful. He continued to absent himself, and so the case continued. By September, he was once again under arrest, probably in *Trunken* which at times served as a jail for the navy. The Admiral and famed naval hero Niels Juel penned the letter calling for the involved to meet in late September to bring the case to a close. He called for Gulliksen to be 'punished on his body' due to the 'seriousness' of his crime.[104] This would have meant a loss of honour, forever marking Gulliksen as an outsider to society.

We do not hear of any such humiliating physical punishment. Instead, an opportunity had arisen of playing on that irony which was a staple of early modern systems of punishment and their heavy-handed symbolisms. When Gulliksen was found guilty, the *Havmanden* was in the final stages of preparation for the voyage that was to end in mutiny and shipwreck. Transporting Gulliksen to a life of colonial labour in the very ship he had failed to oversee was too fitting a punishment to pass up. However, the Admiralty Court was not endowed with the power to dictate banishment to the colonies, and so they wrote to the king.

This letter exists in at least three different copies.[105] It relates Gulliksen's employment history. However, since his appointment as a second master, Gulliksen 'had not attended to his duties in any way, before he (though many gave him warnings and reminders) fully absented himself, so that the frigate had to be handed over to another master'. Because of the missing inventory, 'he has often been searched for, both night and day, and [yet] by trickery and cunning he has always escaped whenever the guard and the executioner's helpers got a hold of him, until finally he was sought out with stronger force'. Despite his first sentence, 'the person has not bettered himself at all, neither brought back the lost inventory or its value, but has instead completely absented himself from service like before, which is the reason that he is now again under arrest'. They added details on his personal life as well: 'since his return from Guinea [he had] led an evil and scandalous life, badly handled and lived with his wife, and kept the company of loose women which the neighbours and everyone who knows this person can speak of'. All of this merited punishment of 'this scandalous human being'. They suggested that to 'the disgust of others he shall be sent to the West Indies with the royal frigate now destined there'.[106]

Bundled with the letter is a scrap of paper with a few scrawled lines: 'We [are] graciously satisfied that the aforesaid Jokum Gulliksen is sent with the first ship going from here to the West Indies. Hafnia. 7 Oct. 1682. [King] Christian'. The Company had already applied for convicts as colonial labourers, so there was no reason not to transport Gulliksen as well. With the king's succinct approval, the strategic telling of Gulliksen's life fulfilled its purpose. He, and the otherwise absent story of his sexual excesses, ratty neighbours and an abusive marriage (the phrase 'badly handled' is unclear, but can be read as signifying domestic violence) becomes visible to us in a carefully policed form, as he in turn was rendered visible to the king. This is truly epistemological violence – knowledge designed to injure by way of a story that imposes an ending: transportation and a (non-)existence as a colonial subaltern. Yet while the letter depicts a man who had forfeited all meaningful social relations, the archive allows for other narratives about Gulliksen. These are stories that do not come to us fully formed with a neat beginning, a narrative arc or a suitable ending. Nor do they form a single picture of a man with a certain disposition, but instead highlight how sites of oppression were sites in which contradictory relations could form, ultimately enabling the subaltern to subvert power relations.

Studies on mutinies in the eighteenth and nineteenth century have stressed the importance of personal relations and friendships. Hamish Maxwell-Stewart has studied 'fictive kinships' on Australia-bound convict ships. He concludes that many mutinies can be traced back to a small core who often 'shared native places, or similar prior experiences'.[107] Rediker has found such fictive kinships – that is, those forged during incarceration – in his studies of mutinies on slave ships as well. He calls them 'sources of solidarity'.[108] Such relations played an important role in the mutiny on the *Havmanden*. They would have offered safe units for illicit talk. Voicing your critique of authorities to a stranger carried a heavy risk if the stranger did not harbour the same resentments. A friend or a family member was safer. Indeed, Gulliksen did not have to fear that his friends would betray him. His friendships had already survived considerable tests. In fact, they were at least partly born from them. This was the case with his relation to the sailmaker and fellow mutineer Peder Frandsen. Their backstory demonstrates that life in the dissonant Danish Atlantic could create durable bonds among the people who survived it.

Almost exactly two years earlier, in late October 1680, both men had embarked on the *Havmanden* for a slaving voyage in the service of the West India and Guinea Company. This was only the Company's second attempt at an African voyage,[109] and it came six years after the first, which had failed miserably, ending in shipwreck and a colossal financial loss.[110] Then war had suspended the Company's efforts until the peace of 1679. Economically, they were struggling, so the frigate was outfitted on the king's own account and prepared for a voyage of three legs. Gulliksen had embarked as a quartermaster. A year later, he had returned as the ship's master. However, the *Havmanden* had not crossed the Atlantic as planned. Even though the voyage to the Gold Coast was swift, trouble had presented itself: not only had the captain fought his officers on matters of navigation,[111] but he had changed the course without their consent, causing a bitter dispute with his chief mate.[112] When, in early February 1681, the ship arrived at the Danish Gold Coast castle of Frederiksberg, the lieutenant Peder Stud (mentioned above) brought the new castle superintendant on shore in the barge, finding only two Danish survivors. The lieutenant was then forced to stay there overnight. As he returned to the ship the next day, the captain stood ready with a loaded gun, furious at the delay. His officers, Gulliksen possibly among them, managed to disarm him while Stud and the mate fled to land. This led Stud to remark in his journal: 'so that I do not believe any mariner to have heard or seen such a bestial life as reigns here.'[113]

About a month later, the captain was imprisoned by the new head of the castle, Magnus Pranger. It was the crew that had pressured Pranger to change the ship's command: they had delivered an ultimatum that none would continue under the current captain.[114] It was, in effect, a mutiny, although the fact that it was successful means that it is not discussed in that way in the sources. Yet it does, in a sense, make Gulliksen and Frandsen serial mutineers.

After the mutiny, Lieutenant Stud was given command of the *Havmanden*. However, he and his crew were unable to secure more than a few enslaved Africans along the Gold Coast. During the attempt, they received news that Pranger had died, and upon their return, they found the fort in a surprising state: celebratory cannons were firing incessantly because Pranger's successor had married an African woman. Two Company officials came on board and told tales of this new commander's 'unchristian' ways.[115] He had not been sober for a single day of his short time in charge, and no trade had been conducted. Reportedly, he had 'to no purpose [...] shot off 800 lbs of powder and threatened to hang, stab to death with knives and shoot whoever approaches him'. Further he gave away gold and goods to African women and strangers, causing the local African authorities to refuse any trade.[116] This continued to the degree where 'instead of traders, one sees nothing but a fort that is daily full whores'.[117] The mariners then went on shore and seized the newlywed as they had previously seized their captain.[118]

A few days later, it was decided to abort the voyage and return to Copenhagen. Tropical diseases were thinning dramatically the ranks of the Europeans. This was a recurring problem for the Danes; the French slave trader Jean Barbot, who visited Frederiksberg castle in 1679 and 1682, described how the Danes of all the Europeans on the Gold Coast were the most susceptible to diseases. In a trenchant account, Barbot stated that this came down to bad 'government'. Good men had been 'made away, to make room for villains'. Of the two castle heads he had met, the first had been murdered, and when he visited for the second time he heard (hinting at elusive acts of storytelling) of the 'unparalleled inhumanity' of the second, who had sentenced his bookkeeper to death for 'misdemeanors' and forced him to 'make his own coffin' before he shot him.[119] Both these men had been brought to Africa in the 1680–81 voyage of the *Havmanden*. Thus, we get a glimpse of empire-building being in a state of disarray. In a letter, one of the two survivors found in Frederiksberg upon the *Havmanden*'s arrival delivered a surprising portrayal of colonial relations that turned stereotypical colonial binaries on their head: 'we had announced to the King of Fetu that we could no longer bear to watch the bestial life that was led here.'[120] 'Here' meaning among the Danes in the castle, in desperate need of the stability afforded by the African authorities.

This letter writer never made it back. Neither did the fettered newlywed. But Gulliksen and Frandsen did. The voyage home was slower than the voyage out and the human costs were staggering as both sailors and passengers died in throngs.[121] Gulliksen is almost invisible in the sources on this human disaster. He is likely to have been among the people who disarmed the captain; he probably also signed his name on the (now lost) ultimatum handed over to Pranger; and he might have been among the mariners apprehending the drunken commander. But ultimately, Gulliksen eludes us. His name figures only twice in the documents: once on a list of the crew and once on a collective written testimony in defence of Stud on behalf of the mariners delivered to the castle commander during the trial against the violent captain. Gulliksen signed with his name, revealing that he was literate.[122] Despite this anonymity he rose dramatically in rank as more and more bodies were given over to the waves. By becoming master, he crossed a divide that was rarely traversed. Common sailors often rose to the rank of quartermaster with age and experience. Their principal task in this role was to keep order among the crew, and success demanded that the quartermaster be held in respect; seasoned sailors were ideal for the task. However, quartermasters rarely rose significantly further in rank.[123] Circumstance meant that Gulliksen did, and he made a friend along the way.

I will discuss the importance of Gulliksen and Frandsen's relation shortly. However, first another person needs introduction: Niels Jørgensen, a convict with whom Gulliksen formed a bond during his short incarceration. Jørgensen had been convicted of robbery and in the records he was also described as having committed 'other unseemliness', although this is not detailed. His trial documents are now lost, so what we know is cobbled together from the daily Admiralty correspondence. Jørgensen had been convicted of robbery in the barony of Juellinge, arriving at Bremerholmen in the middle of February 1682.[124] Gulliksen had been apprehended only a few weeks later. Therefore, both were new to the institution when they met in *Trunken*. The main source on the mutinous voyage described Jørgensen as Gulliksen's 'Friend ... since the time he was also a convict'.[125] Jørgensen, like Gulliksen and Frandsen, was among the nine executed in early July 1683. Just like the experiences of being trapped in the chaotic Danish

Atlantic could foster new and durable bonds, so could the prison itself.[126] While the sources do not allow such reconstruction, it is very likely that other such cores existed among the convicts.

Jørgensen was only one among several people whom Gulliksen met in *Trunken*, and who later were part of the events on the *Havmanden*. Gulliksen is also likely to have met Mikkel Sørensen, a man sentenced to work for life for poaching and who arrived at Bremerholmen in late March.[127] Three weeks later a third convict destined to go on board the *Havmanden* and become a mutineer arrived. Unlike Jokum, Niels or Mikkel, this man's name was not a common Danish one. He went by Adolf Phillip Gorgas and in the Admiralty books he is noted to have served in the Royal Guard before being sentenced for life but pardoned for transportation.[128] Gorgas was among the mutineers as well, but was later discovered to have plotted against Gulliksen's leadership. Gulliksen's friendship with Jørgensen was stronger. What brought the two together is, however, unclear. What we do know is that post-mutiny, Jørgensen would serve as Gulliksen's provost and muscle and that the two seem to have looked after each other.[129]

These specific friendships (and likely others) worked to efface the borders between mariners and convicts. Frandsen was described by Braad as Gulliksen's 'most intimate friend'.[130] Frandsen and Gulliksen had struggled (and starved) side by side before, and now their personal bond proved stronger than the stigma of the law. In addition, Frandsen had other connections to the convicts: his sister, Karen Frandsdatter, was on board the ship as well due to her being a convict from the prison workhouse. We do not know Frandsen's sister's role in the mutiny, but her kinship would allow her to stay on the ship when, later in the voyage, most of the other female convicts were abandoned in the Azores. In a very clear way, Frandsen's connections demonstrate how convicts and sailors did not come from two separate social worlds.

Perhaps the friendship between Frandsen and Gulliksen was most important because of what it offered the discourse that developed below deck on the *Havmanden* and led to the mutiny. Firstly, their stories of dissolute empire would have enforced the convicts' dread at their future. Eight to ten of them were to be selected by Iversen to be sent on the second leg of the voyage from St Thomas to the Gold Coast, where they were to serve in the community of sin, violence and certain death so well known to Gulliksen and Frandsen.[131] Their stories of Company service would also have resonated, adding weight to the widespread rumours of colonial servitude as worse than 'Barbary'. Secondly, Frandsen's experiences with Gulliksen meant that he could vouch for Gulliksen's skills as a seaman. This was key to the last phase of the mutiny. Frandsen must have told the rest of the group about his friend's abilities and his performance in the voyage they had shared. Such a voice was necessary; otherwise it seems unlikely that the mariners would have thought a convict like Gulliksen capable of the task and elected him as captain. Frandsen gave his convict friend the credibility that his status might otherwise have deprived him of. This was crucial to the formation of the plot: someone with navigational skills was needed to take charge of the ship post-mutiny in order for the act to have any kind of viability. As remarked by David Hopkin in a study of narrative performance on the decks of nineteenth-century Atlantic vessels, storytelling was key to how seafarers established their credentials among their peers.[132] We have no reason to believe that Gulliksen did not need to do so as well, especially considering that there were free sailors and petty officers among his audience. It must have helped him that he could claim to know this particular ship in every detail as well; he was able to talk the talk.

Others talked as well. On the lower deck, Gulliksen and his friends were joined by other sets of friends. Thus, the sailors who joined them come in sets of two: two men from Northern Germany (Biermand and Claus von Kiel), and two Englishmen (Sanders and Vads) who again stuck together. However, perhaps the most important group they joined up with were a set of convicts. These were the Irishmen Mikkel Thomassen and Tønnes Willumsen, who were similarly key in the formulation of the plan.[133] Like Gulliksen, Frandsen and Jørgensen, these two appear side by side throughout the mutiny as well and after the mutiny they eventually received the charges of 'head merchant' and 'second merchant' respectively. As with Gulliksen's relations to Frandsen and Jørgensen, Braad describes these two as 'friends'.[134] Thomassen and Willumsen had come from the Stockhouse (*Stokhuset*), an institution with no surviving archive, so we have no way of figuring what had created their friendship besides this shared experience of incarceration and a shared ethnicity. Perhaps they had even known each other prior to imprisonment. Having come from an institution that seems to have functioned mainly as a military arrest in the period, a likely scenario might see them as soldiers for hire, recruited to fight in the Scanian War, though my attempts at finding the two men in the spotty military archives has yielded no results. Like the relations Gulliksen had formed in his incarceration, these two men and their story are visible only through hints in the records of the mutiny itself.

Thomassen and Willumsen were key to the mutiny in that they appear to have provided the plan of where Gulliksen was to take the ship. From Braad's description of the actions of the mutineers in the days following 20 January, we can infer that in the night leading up to the mutiny, they had collectively decided to bring the ship to Ireland and sell it, turning the mutiny into an act of piratical seizure combined with mass desertion. The two Irishmen among the mutineers appear to have played a key part in its formation, something strongly hinted by their subsequent titles. This was the plan that Frandsen would tell the other mutineers that Gulliksen, as captain, would be able to carry out.

When this plan was hatched is unclear. Its form speaks to the process having taken place on the lower deck. Braad tells us that on 21 January, the day after the mutiny, they set sail for Ireland: 'in that place the chief rebels wanted to sell the ship and goods, out of which each and every one who helped the rebellion to succeed were to get their part.'[135] The definition of 'part' was very inclusive. It included the many convicts who had taken part in the discussions below deck. In the evening after the mutiny, several convicts 'again wanted to mutiny against those who had taken over command'. However, 'the chief rebels told them that they were hereafter not to have any thirst or hunger, and assured them that they were to have as great a part in the ship and the goods, when they arrived at their destination'. This reassurance and the equality it makes audible worked, 'by which the convicts were somewhat satisfied'.[136] What had appeased them was the reassurance that the radically egalitarian plan agreed to the previous night was still in effect.

This plan echoed the distributions of plunder among Atlantic pirates. Such characters, known at the time as 'buccaneers', had become famous in Europe after their spectacular successes in depriving the Spanish of their American silver in the 1660s and 1670s. Further, they had shocked polite society by organizing themselves in ways that were democratic and egalitarian. Self-organized, they chose their captains with every crew member having a vote. If they did not like the one they had chosen, they mutinied and chose another. They also divided their spoils in a way reminiscent of the system of 'parts' used by privateers, but distributed the plunder much more equally among the crew.[137] Of course, the egalitarianism of the mutineers' Irish plan of distributing the goods equally among all was also fully appropriate as the result of yarns circulating in the dark of the lower decks, where one person's whisper blended into another's.[138] Like the yarn below deck, all had a part. Thus, the plan to go to Ireland and share the spoils might as well have been the product of the social dynamics of the act itself.

What Ireland had the mutineers, Mikkel Thomassen and Tønnes Willumsen among them, dreamt of? Possibly their yarn had been spun from the stuff of past legends. In the early seventeenth century, the Irish southwest coast had been: 'a paradise for pirates, a place of almost complete safety ..., a place where ships could be fitted out and maintained and loot spent on drink, women and all the other delights of the shore.'[139] The ports of Baltimore, Crookhaven, Youghall and Leamcon had been among the favourite pirate haunts. The crews had preyed as far away as Newfoundland. While piracy had long been endemic to these areas, it had boomed after the conclusion of the Anglo-Spanish conflict in 1603.[140] This wave of piracy had many, but not all, of the egalitarian and anarchic characteristics that were to define Atlantic piracy from the middle of the seventeenth century onwards.[141] It also benefitted from Ireland's ragged coastline, which afforded many natural hiding places.

Piracy in Ireland, however, had been if not eradicated, then at least returned to its endemic state through a long process beginning during James I's reign. Sailors turned pirates were hanged to deter anyone tempted. The English administration fought a difficult battle to cut off the land-based legs of piracy; a task complicated by the colonial history of Ireland and the difficulty of English control in Munster. The self-organized character of the trade, however, meant that gaining such control was not enough. Too weak at sea to counter the threat, James I had accepted an offer of help from the Dutch in 1611. Pardons proved a more effective way to counter the piracy threat in the end, and eventually, the English navy picked up the pace as well: by 1620, piracy had been greatly reduced. By the late seventeenth century, it had diminished 'to a trickle'.[142]

Perhaps Thomassen or Willumsen knew a safe harbour for sly operations? Or maybe it was all fantasy, the stuff of below-decks storytelling on Atlantic crossings? There is really no way of knowing. Neither can we say if such stories about piracy had circulated for weeks on the lower deck gaining in prominence over time, or if they were the product of a few inspired hours of strong drink and angry minds set on retribution. In any case, without this piratical plan, the mutiny would have seemed without an end-goal. Now it had one that could unite the mutineers; a daring plan that combined mutiny, piratical seizure, mass desertion and escape from penal labour into one package appealing to all the different groups below deck. And in Gulliksen it had a mariner who was, as Frandsen vouched, capable of fulfilling it.

* * *

Thus, in contextualizing bits and pieces picked up and included in Braad's tale, we come to get a sense of the complicated social fabric of the ship and the formation of the lower deck space of discourse and interpretation. Indeed, as implied by Braad's implicit explanation, it was a culmination of sorts, though not in the way he outlined it for his readers in the Company office. The men and women below decks were not merely reacting because their superiors failed to manage the shipboard ensemble as they should have. The one authority who *had* spoken up and acted his part was hurled into the waves along with the one whom Braad deemed too silent. Instead, the emergence of a space of interpretation and the solidarities that informed it (for a time only, as we shall see) was the product of ever-worsening material conditions, complex antagonisms in which class divisions seem to have blurred with national ones, rumours and stories about life and death in the Caribbean and on the Gold Coast as well as the character of those who ruled there, fears of imminent death due to elements and, perhaps most importantly, dreams of an escape and the riches afforded by foreign, though to most unknown, shores. Under the cover of the roaring waves all these elements blended together (though they might have had a different weight to different groups), creating a space in which to discuss concrete plans of how to take the ship and who to kill. And from the fragments picked up later by Braad, we get the sense that this space was some time in the making. Thus, the stories, rumours and plans uttered on the lowered deck came to transform the ship.

Yet while we can tease echoes of these speeches from the archival record, principally Braad's accounts, we are still left with a great deal of uncertainty. It takes a significant amount of interpretation to make these fragments reported by the elites on board speak about the life below deck. This state of unknowing stems not principally from Braad's conscious emplotment, but from below. Sailors and convicts (as implied throughout, and as discussed further in Chapters 4 and 5) knew how to conceal their words and practise camouflage, and Braad was not privy to what had happened among the inner core of mutineers. Thus, when the sources on the voyage of the *Havmanden* provide only echoes, they are not merely distorting the soundscape of the ship; the perspective that they offer is itself being distorted. Sure, their accounts are ripe with the sort of epistemological violence and silencing that scholars have come to associate with subalternity, but we should recognize and think carefully about the fact that officers and Company officials would not fully have understood the dissonances they heard in the course of the mutiny. They came from a place that was, by conscious design on the part of those below deck, foreign to them. The muted character was part of the force of such speeches, a strategic measure on the part of their speakers.[143] However, as I've attempted to show here, those speeches can nonetheless be inferred to have been shared, evolving and very powerful.

In one way, however, Braad does show us what life below deck was like. After the mutiny, he found himself evicted from the cabins, having to live with the people on the lower deck. Finding himself in this subaltern position, he suddenly found his own tongue restrained, subject to the dynamics which I have attempted to tease out here. Thus, as we follow the second half of the *Havmanden's* voyage, we get a fuller sense of the processes of lower deck discourse.

3

Ways of Listening

After the taking of the cabin, the violent noise abated. A pardon was, somehow, decided and proclaimed for all who were still alive. The accounts differ on when this pardon was given, which in turn makes it difficult to assess who might have granted it.[1] At this point, many of the people were gathered on the deck where they threw the body of the steward overboard.[2] As the noise died down, Braad ventured up on the deck as well. There he found that 'the principal rebels were in the cabin where they broke open chests and shrines and took everything important'. This was Gulliksen and those roughly ten men (about half of whom were convicts and the other half sailors, as well as the sailmaker Frandsen and boatswain's mate Biermand) who according to both Braad and the sentence were the 'chief rebels'. They had posted guards in front of the cabin.[3] Braad found that two of the three other Company assistants, Lars Tøgersen and Niels Lassen, were still alive; the third, Johan Mohr, was dead. Braad met Tøgersen and Lassen in the crowd on the deck. This is when Braad implicitly demonstrates the workings of shipboard power. He remarks how, post-mutiny, 'they could not speak to each other, but avoided each other, so as to give no pretence to the rebels, who ran about them'.[4] The three 'took leave of each other, [and] as far as possible they avoided each others' company, as they sensed that it was to the offence of the rebels, whenever they talked to each other'.[5] What they sensed were the limits imposed on subaltern discourse. Thus, in the wake of the mutiny, Braad had felt his speech restrained; now he was in the position of the subordinate who had to tame his tongue.

In his interrogation, however, Braad told something that he had slyly omitted from his journal: while he was feeling restraints on his voice, he had simultaneously played a key part in the constitution of a new imitative aural order. There, in the crowd gathered on the deck, he had conducted a prayer, which he argued he had done 'since he was used to conduct their prayers'.[6] Being a carrier of the word of God was part of how Braad fashioned his own voice. He had been conducting prayers since the beginning of the voyage, and repeatedly used this fact to explain why he had been spared. In the heat of the mutiny, when Braad had hid among the drunken convict women, several armed and angry convicts had sought him, as 'one of them wanted to break my head open with a war hammer'. However, others interceded because he had 'comforted them with the word of God'.[7] He underlines this logic by mentioning how, 'some time after this, another convict came to me and said, do you still live? Then you must stand in God's favour, since you were among those who were supposed to be thrown overboard'. However, in his journal, he tried to gloss over the fact that he had also taken this role so shortly after the mutiny itself.[8]

In a sense, this event can be seen as the beginning of a mimetic restoration of order. It may seem counterintuitive to pray to God after having just killed your superiors, but such a view is valid only if we fail to see what was now happening: the ship was being recreated by the performance of an order that was as ritualized as the one it succeeded. At this point 'a person emerged from the cabin and let the deck know who their officers were to be'.[9] The messenger pronounced that Gulliksen was the new captain, Mikkel Thomassen was lieutenant, Frans Vads was mate and Hans Biermand was master. Roluf Lorenzen seems to have become boatswain and Peder Frandsen boatswain's mate.[10] There is no mention of Niels Jørgensen, so perhaps his role as provost was not announced. As we shall see, Jan Sanders, who must have been elsewhere in the ship at the time, was not initially given a specific role. Interestingly, most of the ship's officers did not change role either: Braad remarks how 'everyone stayed in their positions'. The only exceptions were the Company officers: 'who after that point were regarded as nobody. [The rebels] took their bed sheets from them, so that they had to help themselves in whatever way they could'.[11] This meant that several of the officers, Jan von Gent among them, retained their positions. Yet now they served a convict.

The new leaders must have felt some anxiety when they emerged from the cabin to present this new leadership to the people gathered on the deck. Some might have expected a more inclusive decision-making process, perhaps even that the new officers would be elected among all, as was tradition among pirates. However, even without being allowed a vote, there seems to have been an aspect of anarchic democracy to the situation. The people had to accept these new officers and Braad's phrasing hints at grumbling: 'All the people at last let it be known that they were satisfied and then the people made an oath to be faithful to each other'.[12] This whole scene wavers strangely; it is at once born out of disruptive violence and improvisation, yet in a sense it is also faithful to the ritualized forms of shipboard power. We might say that in constituting the new hierarchy, there was a certain element of an appropriation and mutation of forms. Compared with the types of oath-taking ceremonies which this event seems to have emulated, the need for the 'acceptance' of the people was perhaps the most discordant element. Other elements were different as well: when swearing, the people itself was a different 'people' than it had been, when in early November a similar scene had unfolded. Back then, there had been an exclusion of the dishonoured among them, as the judicial and political order structuring the ceremony did not recognize them as subjects able to speak truthfully. Now this demarcation had evaporated.[13] The oath itself was also different: an oath to each other, not an oath of obedience to master.

Braad depicts the whole thing as a mockery. In the interrogation, he was asked if he had taken the oath. He answered:

> Once he heard the voice of the people he came out of the cabin [he does not explain what he was doing in there] to hear what was going on, and saw that the people were pointing their fingers upwards. And they gave off harmonious sound, but what they were shouting and if they had really taken an oath he does not know, though he sensed that it was about being loyal to each other. He himself stood with his hands in his pockets and listened and none forced him to take the oath. And as he sighed to God over such a procedure one of the Stockhouse-convicts, Joseph Hansen, heard him sighing and said to him that after this time none should suffer such hunger as previously.[14]

Braad recognized imitation in this reconstitution of the order of the ship, but the next move, however, was very different from what had previously transpired in the voyage. The new officers sent people into the hold to fetch wine and food, in order 'to make themselves merry [for] as long as it would last, sparing nothing, even the food and other things aimed at the [leaders in the] cabin and which so to speak had been none of anyone's business previously.'[15] In the new ship nothing was regarded as private.

By night 'most of the people were drunk.' However, this merry scene transformed into what is perhaps the best example of the strangely mimetic re-ordering of the *Havmanden* post-mutiny. In their drunkenness, some of the convicts grew uneasy and began to grumble about their new masters. Violence never erupted, however, as the chief rebels reassured them that they would not suffer any thirst or hunger, and that they would receive an equal share in the prize. This seems to have satisfied the convicts, who were at the times armed: 'so that some of them gave the chief rebels what guns they had.' At this point 'things grew quiet and each went to their place and slept.'[16] Echoing his description of the night before in which Iversen had intervened, the last phrase reveals how the ship post-mutiny once again became a space of power divisions; through a promise the new leaders had created order, making everyone go to their proper places. The remainder of the voyage reveals a history of how the egalitarian, collective subject that emerged in the mutiny (here still present in the promise of equal shares) became fractured, revealing its context-dependent and porous character that would eventually transform the ship as it turned into a state of terror. The dissonance in the night of 20 January 1683 is the first sign of this transition.

The ship was being recreated as a ship of thresholds and transgressions; of commands and whispers. In her analysis of mutinies among Indian Ocean convicts in the nineteenth century, Clare Anderson has argued how the close study of mutinies reveals 'that in these worlds turned upside down, convict authority structures were strongly mimetic rather than entirely anti-colonial in nature'.[17] Later in her article, she goes on to analyze how the orders established in the wake of mutinies often reintroduced power in ways that resonated with the forms preceding them – creating, again, new relations of subordination. While there are many crucial differences between her cases and the one under consideration here, there is something resonant in this notion of a mimetic recreation of hierarchy. This becomes obvious when studying the events that transpired in the hours, days and weeks after the mutiny. In her study, Anderson states that the divisions and hierarchies forming in the wake of mutinies:

> dispel simplistic notions of a single convict identity or experience of transportation. This has potentially important ramifications for readings of subaltern studies more generally, particularly in relation to interpretations of other forms of coerced labour and migration. Who was – or rather was rendered – subaltern, both by colonial authorities and their fellow men and women, and how they played out that role, moved both within and beyond supposedly common identities and experiences.[18]

Transplanted backwards two centuries and across half a globe, Anderson's remark retains all its poignancy. It also forces us to reflect on what such mimesis meant for life on board.

The order that the mutineers mimicked was an aural one; a world of drums, cannons and speech. In many ways, it had begun as a drummer marched through the streets of Copenhagen's maritime quarter of Nyboder on 19 October 1682. Many of the sailors who embarked the *Havmanden* lived here with their families. Peder Frandsen probably lived here, as did Gulliksen, before his missteps. They would have known the sharp sound of the drum dancing between the low row houses which signalled that a ship was ready to embark.[19] This was a naval ritual, but the Company had petitioned the king to be allowed to use it for its ships as well.[20] Ignoring the call to muster the ship to which one had signed on was regarded as an act of absconding.[21]

A few days later, the directors ventured on board. Shots were fired to mark their arrival. In their presence, everyone gathered onto the crammed deck. With the directors standing elevated on the poop deck, the ship's articles were read aloud. The reader stood with a small printed book in his hand proclaiming passage after passage of laws. The articles spoke authoritatively in the name of 'We Christian the Fifth, of God's mercy.'[22] The book was, however, not the West India and Guinea Company's own articles. It had been decided 'for the more authority to use the printed East India Company articles'. Instead of a handwritten document, the directors had more faith in the power vested in print and decided to alter a set of articles of the East India Company instead.[23] After the reading, some of the people took an oath of allegiance to the Company and the articles. Each person was made to point the thumb, index and middle finger of their right hand to the sky while saying the words. The fingers signified God, Son and Holy Spirit.[24]

The oath bound each person to an order instituted by the king and God. It made everyone swear and promise 'to conform obediently' to the ship's articles and to always seek the profit and advantage to the Company. This was to happen through obedience 'to our chief, the master and other officers, whom the directors have put in place to command us'.[25] Obedience was the foundation for that profit which was underlined as the end goal of this community. Further, the ship's articles specified that no person obligated to swear was to be exempt from taking the oath. However, they explicitly recognized that subjects might attempt to avoid taking the oath, but at the same time circumvented this by stating: 'If anyone hide themselves when the articles are read and the oath taken, and do not show themselves or if he is silent when the oath is read, those who do so are not to be regarded differently than if they had been present and truly had given their oath on the articles.'[26] Possibly, this condition implicitly included the convicts (and female passengers) in an asymmetrical way, meaning that they could not enter into the community and its rituals, but that the laws of such a community was nonetheless in effect for all.

The minutes of the Company remarked how everything happened 'in the customary way'.[27] We might sense what this involved from a slightly more thorough description of such beginnings on board an East India ship ten years before. There dinner proceeded 'accompanied by kettledrums and trumpets'.[28] Like the cannons, the music marked the ceremonious character of the event;

sound, thus, amplified the unequal relations signalled visually by the authorities' raised position on the quarterdeck during the reading.[29] When in early November 1682, the *Havmanden* was ready to embark, a similarly aural and festive ritual occurred. On such occasions, authorities gave speeches. In the above-mentioned description of the beginnings of an East India voyage, one of the masters performed 'an inspired oration', reminding the people of their oaths. Again, the scene was accompanied by the firing of the ship's cannons.[30]

The orders that were given to the officers stressed the need for ceremony in creating and maintaining difference as well. For instance, Blom was explicitly asked to carry himself as a 'good example'. This was a recurring phrase in the orders issued by the Company. What is special is that this performance of orderliness explicitly concerned Blom's way of comporting himself towards Iversen. This was a show 'so that others may esteem his [Iversen's] authority all the more'.[31] As we have seen, it did not work.

Both Blom and Iversen were also given copies of the ship's articles. Writing, in its materiality, was a vital technology of the production of the very ship 'as a political space'. In this way, writing was to work towards securing 'the internal social and political organisation' of the seaborne hierarchy.[32] The articles constituted both Blom and Iversen in a position to carry out law rituals as substitutes for the sovereign himself.

The *Havmanden* left Copenhagen on 6 November 1682 with drums beating and ears ringing from the salutary cannon shots. It was a sonic spectacle.[33] A few days later, after Iversen had gone ashore at Elsinore, he was also saluted with cannons as he came back on ship. They also saluted the king's formidable renaissance castle of Kronborg upon leaving Elsinore. Here, again, the ship's articles were most likely read aloud, as was customary (though Braad omits it).[34] While standing on the deck listening, Kronborg was a symbol of the power vested in the little book in the hand of the reader. The symbolism was not subtle. Then, a few days later, on 12 October 1682, the people were divided into 25 messes. The division was posted on the wall by the cabin door.[35] Now the unsteady rhythm of ceremonious departure was displaced by the steady churn of watches, the ship's bell ringing every four hours constituting the time-space of work at sea.[36]

What are we to make of all of this ceremony and the aural world it sought to constitute at the beginning of the voyage and then later, in appropriated forms, after the mutiny? Some scholars have argued that ceremony created a form of hegemony through performances that naturalized difference and order.[37] In stark contrast, others, such as James C. Scott, have argued that such rituals allowed for an image of community which denied 'the possibility of autonomous social action by subordinates'.[38] Such 'self-hypnosis' made ceremony effective in stiffening the spines of authorities, but not in inducing consent as such.[39]

Both these views are reductive. While ritual obviously did not create hegemony, it was not for nothing either. If so, imitation would not have followed so closely on the heels of events like the mutiny on the *Havmanden*. Further, we might argue, that as a form of self-hypnosis meant to induce authorities with the surety that their power was untouchable, they were highly ambivalent. Elites did not conceive of their subjects as incapable of action. Nor did these rituals omit the possibility that things might happen which were not supposed to. This is demonstrated by the oath and its paradoxical inclusion of those evading the ceremony itself. Thus, as 'self-hypnosis' it would have been ineffectual at best and anxiety-inducing at worst. The articles read aloud on such occasions bluntly stated that, 'if any other gathering than those necessary is made, the ship's council is to immediately be summoned and, without mercy and to the disgust and example of others, punish whomever has caused such a gathering as a person wanting to begin a mutiny'.[40] Thus, the possibility of resistance was far from omitted. Instead, we should read such ceremonious assertions as attempts at creating ways of listening to the many speeches bound to be uttered on the decks: the rituals of law clearly acknowledged that there were speeches that lived outside the ceremonious space of the public, but rendered such speeches as if they constituted only an atomized disorder whose only resolution could be reached by legal means. In this way, we might argue, ceremony was meant to create and train a way of listening in which speeches were identifiable as belonging to the public or the hidden, by subalterns themselves, but also by their petty officers whom authorities sometimes envisioned as their spies among the people.[41] In turn, illicit speech such as subversive storytelling or rumour comes to exist only outside proper community.[42]

This explains why the mutineers needed to reconstitute the ship with a ritual order of oaths, prayers and, eventually, spectacular violence. They knew more than anyone that ships were full of illicit utterances. They needed to enforce how such utterances were heard. This, in turn, created a state of anxiety in which Braad now found himself on the wrong side, terrified of being overheard.

A ship of terror

The task of recreating such order was difficult. The *Havmanden* kept being too full of words and stories. This is hinted at throughout. For instance, when commenting on Peder Frandsen's promotion to boatswain in February, Braad states: 'about whom it was rumoured among the other sailors that he, during the rebellion, had taken a boom and broken open the cabin door, where the dead Captain was, and also that in the morning he had been drinking brandy with the others below deck.'[43] Thus, by relating rumour, Braad provides useful hints about what had transpired below deck. Some such stories appear as outright bragging. Gulliksen himself had even 'boasted [about] being ringleader of the said revolt' as Braad remarked when the Company bookkeeper asked him who had been authors of the mutiny.[44] It is unclear why Gulliksen had felt the need to exert himself, but others had their reasons: Jan Sanders, for instance, had played a key role in the mutiny, devising the signal of stomping on the deck in order to prompt Mikkel Thomassen to lead the other convicts up on the deck. Sanders had also stolen the cutlasses.[45] However, the entrepreneurial English sailor did not receive an official role right away. Perhaps the other mutineers did not like this by all accounts quarrelsome sailor who would later get in a conflict with another of the mutineers, Roluf Lorenzen.[46] Or perhaps they had simply forgotten about him in the chaos. However, two days after the mutiny, while the sailors worked their best in 'rain and hail' to make headway towards Ireland, Sanders decided to rectify the matter and 'pretended to the chief rebels to have been of good service in the rebellion, as one of them, for which reason he also should have a new position'. They seem to have debated the matter 'and as they sensed and they knew his speech to be true, he became lieutenant'.[47] He took over the duties of the Irish convict Mikkel Thomassen, who instead became merchant. This all made a lot of sense; after all, they were headed to Ireland.[48]

Sanders' storytelling performance had worked. However, there was one catch to the shuffle. The real head merchant, van Bronckhorst, was still alive. He had been spared during the mutiny, though not out of any good will. He had been part of Blom's tight clique, but at the time of the uprising, he lay ill in his cabin. The mutineers appear to have considered him terminal. He was tended to by his 'negro boy', Michel Lacquei, likely an enslaved African acquired during van Bronckhorst's previous engagements in Africa.[49] Thus, when on 22 January the ringleaders appointed a new merchant, they did not reckon van Bronckhorst into the equation. However, he refused to die and their patience ran out. In the evening of 28 January, Thomassen, Blom's killer, decided to shoot van Bronckhorst as well and went into his cabin. However, his gun jammed. Then another convict, Jørgen Pohinske, to whom Gulliksen had promised brandy for helping in the deed, threw van Bronckhorst unto the floor where he stripped and searched him for valuables, finding nothing, before he and Niels Jørgensen carried the

Dutchman onto the deck and hurled him into the waves.[50] Braad used the event to illustrate Gulliksen's poor management. Gulliksen 'stood in the cabin and saw this misery, but [van Bronckhorst] received no pardon from him. And by God I was anxious about such a miserable death. As I saw it, I thought to myself that this would also entail me'.[51]

While the sick merchant died without much resistance, another man killed used his dying breaths to curse the new masters. We know him already. His name was Christopher Dichmand. He was a convict from the Stockhouse and he had taken part in the mutiny; one of the motley coalition, he emerges in the sources because he had been among those wanting to kill Braad.[52] When he was murdered on 7 February 1683, it was, however, for entirely different reasons. At noon, he was shot three or four times then thrown overboard, 'where, in the water, he acted in a bad way with bloody curses that he wished upon the chief rebels'. The reason was because of his reputation as a master thief, which incriminated him when he along with other convicts were found 'drunk from stolen brandy'.[53] The new masters knew how theft signified the existence of units of resistance. They themselves had participated in the same practices, just weeks prior. Possibly, Dichmand had helped provision the party on that occasion as well.

He was not the first convict to have stirred up trouble after the mutiny. Neither was he the first to die for it. In the early hours of 25 January, the ship's cooper had listened carefully to talk emanating from the lower deck. His ears picked up something prompting him to alert the new masters that: 'there were some convicts who had let it be known to the other convicts that if they were inclined as they, they would at daybreak see whether they or the chief rebels were to be masters of ship and goods.' Braad sensed that this was because they considered themselves 'as important as they [the new masters] in taking over the ship, but enjoy no part in it'. Thus, the egalitarianism enabling the mutiny was being felt as challenged by the new order. Further, they feared being 'abandoned on some desolate island'.[54] Whether Braad overheard such speeches is unclear, but he does quote fragments, as if he did. Gulliksen, knowing by experience the force of such discourse, reacted promptly to the news of his informant, locking up the gunroom and putting 'nine or ten mariners' in charge of guarding it, while 'in the cabin and the forecastle the chief rebels themselves were distributed with some of the mariners whom they knew to be loyal, and they were well supplied with grenades and other necessary guns'. Thus prepared, they interrupted the discussions taking place deep within the lower deck. However, they were more careful than Iversen had been five days prior. They called all convicts onto the deck 'and asked them who it was that wanted to start a new rebellion'. They were revealed to be four convicts, 'namely [Adolph] Gorgas, Anders Kuster, Simon Litschen and Joseph Jansen, who were immediately shot to death and thrown overboard'. This act of terror had the desired effect. According to Braad, the punishment was 'so terrible to the other convicts that they quivered from fear'.[55]

In his interrogation, Braad claimed to have felt terrorized by the spectacle himself. Asked why nobody had attempted to take back the ship from the new masters, he excused himself by saying that he was trying to keep a low profile, 'fearing any minute to lose his life, and dared not entrust anybody else'. His silence had been enforced, or so he claimed, by the spectacle of violence, 'as he had the example before him, of how Gorgas and his accomplishes, the rebels' own mates, were executed simply on the basis of the cooper's report of having heard them say a few words that might be against them'. Braad added that 'he as a single person could do nothing'.[56] Thus, we sense how shipboard order, predicated on ways of listening, worked to atomize its social world. Yet despite such anxieties Braad still relates a lot of details that can be interpreted only as rumours he picked up. Thus, while he felt the imperative not to speak out, his journal and the fragments it relates is teeming with rumour, demonstrating the dynamics of veiled shipboard discourse.

He also shows rumour to have circulated among the new leaders themselves. On 2 February, Braad was approached by the new merchant who asked 'where I kept the silver spoons that he had sensed that I had brought with me from Copenhagen for this voyage'. Braad 'said, as was the truth, that by God I had not a single silver spoon, but asked him heartily not to take heed of the speech of liars who in some way or another might want to see me dead'. A little later, Thomassen was there again, asking about 'the two casks with money supposed to be somewhere in the ship'. Braad replied 'that no other money had been brought for the voyage than the 100 [Rix-dollars] in cash found in the dead Captain Blom's chest. But I got the reply that if I did not reveal it [the money] things would go badly for me'. Braad then asked who had told him this and was answered that it was the cooper who 'swears sincerely that it is true'. Braad argued that he managed to persuade the convict-merchant that he was right by arguing how 'by speaking ill of others, they want only to be in the good favour of you [Thomassen] and the other officers, and therefore have no conscience that they might unjustly take my life'.[57]

This house, governed by fictions and even more disorderly than its predecessor, also contained other noises. The curious ear might have been able to pick up sounds that demonstrated that the new hierarchy, while powerful, contained a new way to move upwards in the shipboard community's hierarchy: sex. As the rebels took over the cabins, some of them had: 'each their whore with whom they lay and whored. These whores then ruled very strictly everywhere on ship, in a way that not a single person among the people, even if they had cause, dared speak to their faces out of fear that they would take the matter to the rebels.'[58] The fear that Braad describes was, in many ways, equivalent to the fear that marked life below deck prior to the mutiny as well; a fear of speaking out about injustices because of the way such speaking would be interpreted. While Braad gives no details, it is implied that the women in question were convicts from the prison workhouse. Indeed, some of them were, but there were in fact others. First, some of them were actually the wives of convicts. The two Irishmen, Mikkel Thomassen and Tønnes Willumsen both had their wives on board, and three and two children respectively. Second, one romantic relationship defied all categories. Sailor Roluf Lorenzen, who willingly left the ship at Flores in the Azores in the middle of February after having fought Jan Sanders, had seemingly fallen in love with Iversen's niece, who left the ship with him. One is reminded of descriptions of Stockholm syndrome. Other couples stuck together as well. When large parts of the ship's inhabitants were left at Flores, at least three additional women as well as Frandsen's sister were brought along for the voyage towards fabled Irish riches. According to Braad, their names were Birte, Annelil and Marlene.[59] They all seem to have been convicts. Annelil was described as Hans Biermand's 'whore'. One of the others was Jan Sanders' convict girlfriend. The relations of the last one is uncertain.[60]

It is worth noting that the two mariners who played the most active part (according to Braad's report) in the mutiny soon after had sexual relations with the convict women. This raises the question if these relationships had in fact pre-dated the mutiny itself. The instructions to Blom had warned of such relations, and how they might provoke God's anger.[61] If so, the sexual relationships could even have fostered solidarities between the different groups who banded together in the mutiny. No doubt the sexual politics of the ship were complicated. Braad, now on the lower deck, only heard its echoes.

Betrayals

The *Havmanden* had again become a ship on which discourse was silenced. On 8 February 1683, the day after Dichmand's murder, it transformed once more. Now it became an imitation of the slave ship that it had originally been destined to be during the second leg of its intended four-legged itinerary. At this point they were near Flores, the small westernmost island of the Azores. Winds had frustrated the attempt to head straight for Ireland and at some point, a new plan had been hatched in the cabin. Now the new masters made a move: allied with the mariners, they 'had the convicts with a party of the free folk driven beneath deck'. They then sealed the hatches. At mealtimes, the food 'was handed to them through a hole, at which there were guards, as [was the case] at the hatches'. If the convicts needed to relieve themselves, 'no more than three or four of them were allowed to come up'.[62] In this regime of separation and control, it is difficult not to hear resonances of the workings of Atlantic slave ships. Of course, Gulliksen and Frandsen had previously known the *Havmanden* as exactly that – a slave ship – although a very unsuccessful one.

At this point Braad, who was among those dispatched below decks, seems to have fully sympathized with the convicts. In his journal, he has them express: 'how much and how heartfelt it pained them that they had in this way let themselves be seduced by the chief rebels, having complied to their evil request in the rebellion, and getting no thanks for it.' In subtle ways, he makes the convicts the passive victims of somebody else's crime – a familiar plot of seductive tongues having misled the blind. It seems much more likely that what he had heard was actually bitter cursing and angry outbursts.[63] They were right to feel betrayed. Two days later, the mutineers had reached their intended destination. The sloop was then sent ashore with two of the rebels and a passenger, Matthias Skræder, who spoke Portuguese. They wanted the local governor at Fajagrande on the island of Flores to come on board. This happened the next day. The governor was presented with a gift of butter and other goods. He must have sensed the clamouring from the lower deck and wondered at it, but we have no way of knowing what story Gulliksen presented him with. The rebels wanted him to accept their decoy request of sending the people ashore while the ship was to be repaired. The governor did not see through the ploy and when he ventured back on land he was accompanied by Gulliksen and Frandsen. They returned later that same day and immediately went about their plan. Assisted by the mariners, they opened one of the hatches and brought some of the convicts up on the deck. Here, they were searched for the gold chain that Iversen's wife had lost during the mutiny and which had become a fabled object of desire. Then they were forced into the boat. Gulliksen 'commanded some [people] to stand ready with guns in case the convicts tried to resist'.[64] This must have included some mariners. The sailors were also key to the next part of the plan. The prisoners were taken to shore in the longboat with the sloop following right behind it 'with loaded guns, so that the convicts who were carried ashore could not take possession of the boat, or injure the mariners who handled the boat'. When they returned, it was night time. Early the next day, the scene was repeated, but this time they also sent a large contingent of the free passengers and indentured servants in the boat. One of the rebels, Roluf Lorenzen, willingly left the ship at this point, accompanied by Iversen's niece and with the 100 Rix-dollars given to Blom for emergencies. The two were the only ones to make a profit from the voyage.[65]

The two Company assistants, Niels Lassen and Laurits Tøgersen, were among the people who were sent ashore on 12 February. Braad, however, stayed on board. In his interrogation he claimed that he did not really know the reason, but that he thanked God that he did not suffer this fate as Flores was an island 'where you must toil as a slave, to get your food'. He again speculated that he stayed 'because he held prayers and had preached both morning and evening on board'. He also reasoned that it was God's plan that he should stay to give account of what had transpired, again using his own journal as evidence.[66]

Those who remained formed a murky community made up of friendships, sexual relationships, family relations and people who the rebels felt they could trust or somehow needed. On board were most of the original crew; the three doctors (one of whom was deadly ill); the remainder of the new masters, their families and lovers; and then there was a motley remainder. The latter included van Bronckhorst's African servant; the royal page, Friberg; a lieutenant who was sick and later died; Braad; Iversen's wife and son; Iversen's sister, her husband and two of their children (*sans* daughter); the Portuguese-speaking Mathias Skræder (who later left them at St Michael); and three of the indentured servants, all boys, who seem to have acted as servants in the cabin. Braad also explicitly mentions Jørgen Hoch, who had been a convict in *Trunken* as well as two other convicts. One is merely referred to as Henrik N (he died en route and was buried at Risö in Sweden). The other was Christopher N – the man who was injured during the mutiny when Blom fired his gun and whose wounds might have been the reason for his death on 1 April. He was buried on Risö as well. However, Braad forgot to mention Anthony Lovmand or Sigvardt Thorren, two other convicts from *Trunken*. These men might have been Gulliksen's and Jørgensen's friends from their time in *Trunken*. Hoch would later help Gulliksen write to the Admiralty. All four were, however, acquitted in the trial. Braad also fails to mention Hans Hansen, another steward, whose role is wholly unclear, but who had been the man to read the list of the new masters. He was, however, also acquitted in the trial.[67]

The fates of the people left on Flores are difficult to assess. The Company official asked Braad why they had not returned to Flores later 'to take the company servants back, as they had not been part of the revolt?'[68] This reveals their attitude to the convicts and passengers. They were counted as lost. In their state of disarray, the Company could only worry about the few people who were to receive a salary. These were the only people towards whom the Company held any sort of liability. Lassen and Tøgersen eventually returned to Copenhagen, but none of the convicts or other passengers appear to have done so. Going there to fetch a motley of convicts and indentured servants was simply out of the question.

It was perfectly clear to the Portuguese authorities that these were convicts. In a letter concerning the conduct of the two assistants (brought home by them and sadly the only archival trace of what happened on Flores), the local authorities appear perfectly aware that these men and women were criminals, referring to them as '*degredados*' – 'convicts'. They were also aware that many of them had participated 'in the death of the governor, captain, merchants and officers of the ship'. It appears that the two assistants had tried to bring the convicts to court 'which they didn't manage to do because they were in the Portuguese kingdom, where the courts wouldn't admit the offenses because it is against the kingdom's hospitality'. Thus, 'the town court refused to interfere in the matter because it involved foreigners'. A rumour was reported that 'some of these men wanted to kill the lads [meaning the Company servants] so they couldn't report the incident to the King'.[69] Nothing of the kind materialized, however. Thus, everything indicates that the convicts and indentured servants were not imprisoned by the Portuguese authorities.

What had they been surrendered to? Searching through the partially extant parish registers of Flores, there are no signs of Danes, but that does not mean that they were not there. First of all, they might not have converted to Catholicism; and second, very few foreigners appear in said records at all. However, we must at least consider the possibility that they did not stay on the island. The Azores were at this time no longer a place for penal exile as they had been previously. In fact, by the 1650s the tide had turned, meaning that the region now exported convicts to Brazil instead of importing them from Portugal.[70] Of course, another possibility is that the convicts found their way off the island by entering into the service of ships stopping to trade and take on water, but given that they were perceived to be *degredados*, that might also be unlikely. *Degredados* were not allowed to leave the provinces in which they had arrived, although given that they were foreigners, an exception to this rule might have been made.[71] If they did leave in this way, they must have left in small groups as it is unlikely that any captain would have been willing to take on that many people of dubious reputation. Further, the women and children would likely have been left behind.

Therefore, I reckon it most likely that at least some, if not most, stayed on Flores. Was Braad right in saying that this was an island on which one had to work as a slave to survive? Probably not. In fact, even as *degredados* in the Portuguese empire they were in many ways much better off than as 'slaves' in the Danish. The Portuguese ran a system that by comparison was much more humane. *Degredados* 'were not slaves and, at least in theory, were paid for their labor'. The only restrictions on them were that they were not allowed to return to Europe, and that they could not become city officials. Otherwise their status was that of commoners; a marked contrast to the state of perpetual infamy and non-subjectivity afforded transported Danes.[72] We might add that chances of survival in the Azores were much better than on St Thomas, where only few convicts survived beyond their first year. Thus, while their fate is uncertain, the abandoned almost certainly had brighter prospects than those open to them in a Danish colony.

The end

On board the ship, the silences of the abandoned were soon drowned out by other signifiers of human misery and uncertain motives. The new leaders had not headed back towards Ireland as Braad seems to believe was their plan. By 22 February they were at St Michael, a larger island in the Azores. They needed water, but Gulliksen had other plans as well: he wanted to go back to Copenhagen. Braad heard of this stratagem from Iversen's sister who still lived in the cabins and with whom Gulliksen, strangely, seemed to have some sort of rapport. Braad and Iversen's sister formed a friendship which then became the base unit for the transmission of information across the boundaries of the ship, as she 'told him [Braad] what occurred in the cabin'.[73] She had related how 'that same day [. . .] the rebellious Captain had comforted her and the Governor's wife that his intent now was to get rid of the other rebels in this country and then to take the ship to Copenhagen, though he forbad them to tell anyone'. Apparently Frandsen and Jørgensen were privy to the plan as well.[74] The task was difficult. Their fellow rebels were an unruly crew: the day before, Gulliksen had heard how Jan Sanders was hoarding guns and 'had roguish acts planned'. This made Gulliksen round up all the remaining weapons and store them in his own cabin. Then on 23 February, Gulliksen attempted to lure the others on shore under pretence of taking on water. They were, however, unwilling to do so 'because the rebels did not dare to go ashore all at once'.[75] Then the plot was altered. At dinnertime, a group of armed men consisting of Niels Jørgensen, the soldier Gyderich Hansen, Jørgen Hoch and Braad himself went first to the mess and apprehended Mikkel Thomassen and Tønnes Willumsen who were put in fetters below the foredeck. From there, they went into the cabin where Gulliksen had meanwhile been distracting Jan Sanders and Frans Vads and apprehended them. The two were shackled in the open on the quarterdeck and 'nobody were allowed to go near them'. Evidently, Gulliksen feared Sanders and his continual plotting.[76]

The situation had become tense. There was a reason that the arrest was carried out by a small clique: Gulliksen had feared that the mariners would in fact help the now imprisoned men. It is unclear exactly when, but it had demanded 'the utmost persistence [...] to make the mariners satisfied' with the new plan of returning. Thus, those who had been loyal to Blom in the mutiny were now the biggest hurdle to returning the ship to Denmark. The problem was that they had reckoned that even if they did make it back to Copenhagen, it would count as 'a lost voyage and, therefore, they would get no pay'. This caused some commotion, but at last they were assured on the promise of 'good things when they brought back the ship and goods in good condition, in order to make them inclined [to the plan]'.[77] However, the mariners had been right to be suspicious. Eventually, the Admiralty court ordered that they lose their wages, and serve six months at one-third of their previous pay for the original voyage.[78]

The rest of the people who were gathered by Gulliksen on the deck the next day also accepted the idea. They then set sail directly for Copenhagen and again raised Danish flags.[79] This signifies the final fracture of the coalition that had initiated the mutiny. The three sets of friends who had banded together (Gulliksen–Frandsen–Jørgensen; Thomassen–Willumsen–Sanders–Vads) now plotted against each other, to the extent that Gulliksen started torturing his prisoners. He seems to have wanted them to reveal the whereabouts of the riches that had disappeared from the cabins during the mutiny, most of which belonged to Iversen's wife. Perhaps Gulliksen was planning to gain her support in the eventual confrontation with the law that he was preparing for. For the task, he had Jørgensen apply thumbscrews. Vads soon confessed that he had taken a gold chain and five rings when he had found Iversen's wife in the cabin. However, he had been so drunk that he had no idea where they had gone. Thomassen was next. He denied knowing anything about the valuables. However, as if to defer attention, he revealed that Sanders had devised an elaborate plot to poison everyone except his own clique after the mutiny. If the opportunity presented itself, he would buy poison and then put it 'into the porridge kettle so that all of the people would in this way be poisoned, except for a few that he would warn not to take any porridge at mess'. The point of the plot was so that 'he and his accomplices could be masters of the ship and the goods'. It was also revealed that he had at one point plotted to kill everyone using the gunpowder as poison. This was a game of creating a scapegoat, and Gulliksen played along; a few days later he staged a strange scene on the deck, where he had the remaining shipmates gathered. In their presence, he asked Sanders if he had in fact been the one to devise the plan for the original mutiny. Gulliksen's intention here is likely to have been to convince everyone who had not been present below deck that night (the people on whose testimony his fate depended) that Sanders and the defected Roluf Lorenzen were the men to blame for the mutiny. Sanders, however, was intent not to go down alone. He publicly accused Hans Biermand of being just as key to the plan, and Biermand was apprehended and shackled. This, however, compromised Gulliksen's plan. Biermand did not deny Sanders' charge, but he muddied the waters when he swore how: 'in the morning before the rebellion, the Captain [Gulliksen] was also below deck and drank brandy and had full knowledge of everything, [and] how it was to proceed. He even bit off a piece of his finger nail and swore that he would be one of us.' This must have vexed Gulliksen, as what had been intended as a way of deferring blame unto others now placed him squarely in the centre of the mutinous coalition. However, the blaming continued, and later that day Claus von Kiel was apprehended for intent to murder several of the loyal sailors during the mutiny.[80]

In the course of these events, a friendship broke down. Mikkel Thomassen had been tortured in order to discover whether he had any of the missing valuables. He had vigorously denied it. However, his friend Tønnes Willumsen, was less hardy. He confessed that Mikkel Thomassen *did* have a wallet of money belonging to Iversen's wife. Then Thomassen was tortured again: 'but swore insistently that he had no more than a single Rix-dollar which was his own money, and when for the third time the screw was to be applied, he freely put forth his fingers.' However, his bravado faltered when he was told that his friend had ratted him out. He promptly handed over the money. Later, he surrendered another seven silver spoons. During the interrogations, it was revealed that Biermand had six silver spoons too. The valuables were then given back to Iversen's wife.[81] No doubt, Gulliksen had hoped this would buy him some goodwill. The gold chain, however, was never found.

Claus von Kiel was the only one of these prisoners to be later released. For the rest, the prospects must have seemed incredibly grim. They had been betrayed and made into scapegoats. They knew the fate they were headed towards. To Biermand, who had been made out by his comrades as being chief among them all, this was all too much. In the afternoon of 23 March when the ship was just north of Skagen, he decided to put an end to it. One of his hands was manacled, but somehow he got hold of a knife with the other and he tried to kill himself. Suicide was seen as a crime in its own right in early modern Europe. Further, it was a form of death that did not afford the atonement that penitence offered even the hardest criminal before execution. Biermand seemingly did not care for reconciliation with God, or perhaps he did not want to act out the deference towards authorities which was its price at an execution. Or maybe he simply feared the hangman more than the Devil. In any case, his attempt at suicide failed. His convict-lover Annelil, who appears to have stood by him to the end, somehow managed to disarm him. He then had his other hand manacled as well.[82] He was right in his assumption of how things would play out, however. On 3 July, the spectacular ritual of punishment portrayed him as the main perpetrator. While alive, one of his hands was cut off and nailed to the pole where the rest of his broken, but still living body was placed on the wheel.[83] According to one source, he was defiant to the last, asking for a drop of beer during the torture.[84]

By 25 March the ship was at Carlsund on the Swedish west coast, where five days later the vessel would be wrecked in a storm. Gulliksen was preparing for an encounter with the law. He wanted to test the ice, sending a few letters home. He had made attestations of what had been testified by his prisoners – although not of what Biermand had stubbornly claimed. He also had a statement made about his 'carriage and how he was, so to speak, innocent of all that had transpired'. Braad did not sign it: 'as I sensed that much of what it specified was untrue'. However, the mariners, 'thinking, perhaps, that even though they signed it would not be taken as evidence, when, God willing, they were to arrive in Copenhagen, because then everyone would speak freely about what was now covered in silence'.[85] From the final conviction, we know that it was the prisoner Jørgen Hoch who helped Gulliksen fashion these attestations. The writings themselves are unfortunately lost. We do, however, have one carefully fashioned letter (not in Gulliksen's own hand), which hints at their contents and the self-presentation they performed. On 25 March, Gulliksen wrote to the Admiralty:

> High and noble masters in the Royal Admiralty. On 24 March at night, I have arrived with the ship the *Havmanden* at Carlsund two miles from Marstrand, due to the strength of the currents. I cannot omit to let my honoured patrons know that we, [...] after Capt. Pahl [the Captain of the pilot ship] left us by the

Naze have suffered great misery in the North Sea for 9 or 10 weeks; not only with hunger and great thirst, but also with continual storms and bad weather, which I will relate in detail when we, God help us, arrive in Copenhagen. On 20 January, this year a great rebellion has happened in the Channel one and a half miles from Start Point, in which Governor Jørgen Iversen, Captain Blom, Master Christopher [Hysing] and many others have been thrown overboard. Its true masters have been four persons that are now in irons around feet and hands. On 9 February, we arrived at one of the Flemish islands called Flores, in which place all the free and the land people [meaning everyone not a mariner], except for a few who are still on board, were set ashore. The reason that these people were disembarked is that the rebels might thereby get a greater profit in selling the ship and goods. But God be praised their roguish plan has not been realized. In the course of the event, I was chosen to be the Captain, against my will, but to the fortune of many, God be praised, because next to God I, to say so myself, have saved not only ship and goods, but also many lives. This is in brief to inform the noble masters. I will always recommend myself to the noble masters' good and mild favour, as one who, through his acts, shall, for as long as God grants me my life, show himself a loyal and obedient servant to my Lord and King until death. Written on the *Havmanden* at Carlsund. 25 March 1683. Jokum Gulliksen.[86]

Here we find an instance of self-fashioning through storytelling before the law; what Natalie Zemon Davis famously called 'fiction in the archives'.[87] Gulliksen styled his letter directly to the authorities he knew would decide his fate in the trial he expected ahead. Interestingly, his protestations that he had heroically saved the ship were tied to a self-styling as an obedient servant to 'patrons'. In a way, he was speaking from a position that, as a convict, was not his to assume: he portrayed himself as a member of a community and as a subject. It was all to no avail, however; a futile attempt 'to appropriate the dominant vocabulary'.[88] Perhaps the authorities saw through it, or perhaps his fate was sealed by the fact that a few days later his ability to bargain had been severely compromised as the ship ran aground in a storm.

On April 9, the barca-longa the *Makrellen* (*The Mackerel*) had arrived at Marstrand at the request of the Company and command of the king. By then, Braad had long since gone to Copenhagen. He had probably already denied Gulliksen's version of the story. Meanwhile Gulliksen had stayed at Marstrand, apparently attempting to oversee the salvaging. He was still occupying his role as a subject and a servant of sovereignty. Peter Besemacker, the captain of *Makrellen*, assessed the wrecked ship and noted how 'the goods can be salvaged'. He was tasked only with the job of bringing the people home. Over the course of the next few days, Besemacker received most of the people from the *Havmanden*, including Gulliksen – still free at this point – and his prisoners. One sailor had deserted. He had been with Braad and Gulliksen when they had gone to send letters to Copenhagen the day before the storm. The storm had kept them back in Marstrand while the wreck happened.[89]

Gulliksen's scapegoats had been placed in Marstrand's dungeon by the local Swedish authorities. The prisoners had slandered Gulliksen by telling stories about how he had raped a woman – that one official deduced to have been 'the captain's wife' – only shortly after she had given birth.[90] However, the prisoners knew that such stories were not enough to avoid the executioner, and so they made one last bid for freedom. The night before embarkation, the watch 'sensed' that something was off: 'in the night the prisoners had broken out [of their shackles] and wanted to escape.' No other details are given. Besemacker notes only the outcome: 'then they [presumably the guards] had them locked up again.' Sound had given them away.[91] Three months later, their dismembered bodies were to be found right next to Gulliksen's.

Part Two

A Social History of Dissonance

4

Jan Hagel's Stories

The events on the *Havmanden* were singularly dramatic in the context of Danish maritime history, but the conflicts they reveal were not unique to this ship. Early modern Danes and Norwegians understood this. To them, ships were microcosms; small-scale societies in which power struggles played out over and over again. Maritime workers were regarded with fear and disdain by elites. The inhabitants of the maritime quarter of Nyboder in Copenhagen enjoyed a general reputation of drunkenness and riotous disorder. Sailors were among the lowest of the low in urban society. One relatively sympathetic eighteenth-century naval officer commented that they were society's 'true slave class'.[1] By 'slave', he could have been referencing either the workers of the Atlantic plantation complex or the convicts performing hard labour in the city itself, or both. At times, maritime workers themselves used this analogy as well.[2]

Thus, it is not surprising that contemporaries read the events on the *Havmanden*, in which those at the fringes of society grabbed power, as a political event. When retelling the story of the mutiny, they crafted political fables. For instance, in his 1729 history of Denmark-Norway, scholar and moralist Ludvig Holberg told the story as a 'rebellion' in which Biermand had 'seduced' his fellow sailors with the idea of becoming 'masters of the ship'. Such seduction was a common trope in early modern descriptions of the social dynamics of both politics and crime. In this way, the 'fall' of key players began with a persuasive tongue introducing disorderly, scandalous politics and a desire for power.[3]

Holberg's fellow scholar Erik Pontoppidan recounted the mutiny in his religious history of Denmark, *Annales Ecclesiæ Danicæ Diplomatici* (1741–1752). The most interesting part of his telling is the logic he attributed to the ship after the mutiny. The mutineers 'made an agreement among themselves' which was to be enforced by brutal punishments. However, Pontoppidan ensured his readers that such an improvised order was untenable, as 'every one of their regiment was desirous [of power] and held himself as worthy as anyone else'. Thus, the threatening egalitarian order established caused their 'government' to be 'overthrown two or three times'. So as to make sure his readers understood the analogy, Pontoppidan ended his retelling by asserting how the ship had been 'a true picture in miniature of how things proceed in so-called free republics'.[4] This was a cautionary tale of what happens when any man might falsely imagine himself able to hold power.

To members of the elite like Holberg and Pontoppidan, the mutiny resonated as a tale of the dangers of anarchic politics enacted by the easily corruptible common people that sailors embodied. In the reports on the *Havmanden's* voyage, they heard echoes of a larger drama: that of the chaos which presides where power becomes a game in which anyone takes part. Post-mutiny, the ship had operated not as the absolute monarchy it should have mirrored but as a dangerously unstable political community operating according to the politics taking place on the decks. Of course, such a self-governed community was, according to the logic imposed by Pontoppidan, almost impossible; the mutinous order did not create a free republic, but rather a 'so-called free republic'. Ultimately, an order established without an a priori (religious) mandate was no order at all. This was the moral to be taken from such events by the readers. It translated to a simple imperative: stay in your place.

Modern Danish maritime historians, on the other hand, have had difficulties infusing ships and docks with any type of political meaning. In turn, they have largely avoided the question of social conflict. Many have simply been too preoccupied with the tonnage of vessels, the number of cannons or the wills of kings to see the dynamics of the decks. However, a handful have at times recognized the hardships of life at sea and understood that social life on the decks was dominated by brutality and disparities in power. Unfortunately, these scholars have failed to ask how lower-class subjects responded meaningfully to such social conditions.[5] Thus, whereas seventeenth- and eighteenth-century commentators conceived of events like the mutiny as loaded with politics, *modern* historians have somewhat drained the lower deck of social meaning. In this way, events like the mutiny have become anomalous, and are seen as taking place outside of the history that can meaningfully be analyzed and recounted.

Yet if we pay careful attention to the rich (if patchy) sources that shed light on the lives of maritime workers at sea and in port, we can begin to reverse this approach and discern a maritime culture of conflict in early modern Denmark-Norway. Thus, it becomes possible to place the mutiny on the *Havmanden* in a larger context of maritime working-class traditions and struggles. Exploring the partial and incomplete sources of the Admiralty Courts in Copenhagen around 1700 as well as the logs and travel journals of ships, we begin to sense that conflict was indeed a regular feature in the lives of maritime workers. I use the term 'maritime workers' to signify the groups that laboured at the lowest rungs of the maritime community: sailors, common gunners, dockhands, craftsmen and artisans, at times even petty officers as well as occasionally groups such as soldiers and convicts (though I deal with the latter separately in the next chapter). From such sources, patterns emerge that highlight how these groups opposed the power structures they were subjected to, sometimes individually, but often collectively.

However, to fully appreciate the meaning of such actions we must also turn to a different type of sources: the writings of maritime workers themselves. Three uniquely rich texts written by members of the maritime working class in early modern Denmark-Norway exist, all of which are replete with stories of resistance. These texts provide a way to get at the meaning inherent to the patterns of crime and conflict evident in the court records, exactly because they echo the stories told among workers themselves – stories that offered them models of action. Thus, all three texts share a link to longstanding traditions of storytelling which itself can be interpreted as subversive. In this way, they help us re-think how maritime actors such as those on the *Havmanden* made sense of their conditions and understood their chances of countering them.

A culture of conflict

The crew of the *Havmanden* were a decidedly international lot. As we have seen, many of the officers were Dutch. The sailors included Dutch, English, Irish, Norwegians, Germans and Danes. Many, like Biermand (but also Blom), had come to Copenhagen as a result of recruitment campaigns in Amsterdam and Northern Germany during the Scanian War in what was a highly international market for maritime labour. While the crew on the *Havmanden* was unusually international, the Danish seafaring community in Copenhagen was, in general, polyglot. Both the navy and the merchant fleet struggled to get enough manpower to staff their ships throughout the seventeenth century. The navy was partly staffed with Danish, Norwegian and foreign recruits, partly with conscripts. In the seventeenth century, conscription was organized on a rather ad hoc basis, while in the early eighteenth century it became systematized in the so-called 'enrolment system', in which all sailors and fishermen in Denmark and Norway could forcibly be called up for naval service, often serving a year at a time. The foreigners recruited had usually 'capitulated', meaning that they had signed contracts to serve a set number of years. Until the contract expired, they could leave only with the express permission of officers or through desertion. The former was unlikely; seafaring men were a valuable resource to the early modern state. While naval recruiters often sought sailors from abroad, Danish and Norwegian sailors were forbidden to move the other way. Naturally, though, such sailors were attracted to the international labour market and its regional centre in Amsterdam, where wages would often be higher. Thus, various seventeenth-century kings forbade the emigration of maritime workers, considering it a form of desertion, as the merchant fleet was considered the reserve of the navy.[6] Thus, we see that the Danish market for maritime labour was inextricably tied (both through the agency of the labour force, and the agents dependent on it) to a much larger regional labour market.[7] With such a dynamic also came the circulation of knowledge and traditions, highlighting the need for maritime historians to think in terms not limited by 'methodological nationalism'.[8]

There are other good reasons to think comparatively when exploring maritime social history, besides the circulation of its actors. Life on the decks was similar across all European empires. The differences between types of seafaring, such as the length and end goal of voyages, were much greater determinants of maritime social life than the flag on the mast. For example, smaller vessels and shorter voyages usually produced social relations that were less alienating and allowed for more stable social and familial relations ashore on the part of the sailor. In contrast, life on large ships engaged in long-distance voyaging, either naval or merchant,[9] meant being part of starkly hierarchical, largely homo-social micro-societies for years on end. Thus, there is a reason why the theme of conflict seems to express itself most clearly in long-distance voyages like that of the *Havmanden*. Scholars have likened such ships to factories as their intensely stratified social relations and the commodification of labour organized in a complex, sometimes alienating division of labour foreshadowed industrialism in many ways.[10] Every four hours, the ship's bell signified the unrelenting churn of shifts of work. Sometimes the work would be physically demanding, even dangerous, but often it would simply be monotonous and alienating.[11] Sailors and officers lived apart, with sailors being afforded no real personal space.[12] The two groups also ate different food, the status symbolism of which is discernible in Iversen's writings. The rations afforded common hands were often meagre and of a low quality and death rates would sky-rocket as soon as ships neared African or American coasts, or when the inevitable rot set in on the provisions.[13]

Sailors across empires were subject to ship's articles that placed immense power in the hands of officers. Discipline was harsh and punishments draconian.

Even minor transgressions were often punished physically. Ships were worlds in which 'everyday violence played an important role as an incentive for work and discipline', as historian Matthias van Rossum recently put it in a discussion of working conditions in the Dutch VOC.[14] Ships also afforded their own special forms of punishment such as keelhauling. Other punishments on board ship were highly symbolic. For instance, in some places, including Denmark, murderers were to be tied to the body of their victim and drowned. Anyone pulling a knife was to have said knife pinned through his hand into the mast.[15] The power of the captain has often been compared to that of absolute sovereigns.[16] Intimidation was a part of their power.[17] As discussed in the previous chapter, ship's articles were often read aloud, so sailors were constantly reminded of the potential punishments for misbehaviour, and encouraged to listen for signs of the social order unravelling. Such readings also asserted that the captain was a substitute for the king himself. Underlining class differences, sailors and officers were punished differently as well, with officers usually being exempt from physical punishments.[18] Petty officers often stood in an awkward place inbetween these groups, as indicated by their frequent complicity in shipboard unrest, while they were often also themselves targets of the actions of common hands.

In the events on the *Havmanden* we have already sensed how sailors had an array of strategies to make their lives in such environments endurable. Religion offered solace, though the highly international character of crews often meant that religious dogmatism was subdued at sea as it otherwise held the potential to stir unwanted conflicts.[19] Comfort was also afforded by the drink that could be pilfered from the stores. Drunkenness and petty theft was a constant feature in life on ships bound for the Danish colonies, as it was on the ships of the larger empires. From time to time, things would escalate beyond forms of everyday resistance. Across empires, mutiny was perhaps the most extreme response of workers to such conditions and authorities constantly had their ears out for grumbling sailors. In a recent collection of essays on mutiny, the authors argued for a broad definition of mutiny, 'that includes all forms of collective resistance to the constituted authority of the ship, from muttering and murmuring all the way to bloody resistance'.[20] Employing such a definition makes sense. Murmuring sailors on board Danish ships, and elsewhere, were often interpreted as being on the verge of rebellion, especially in times of distress such as during storms or when rations were cut. For instance, at the point of joining up with several other ships in Norway after a long and difficult return from an East India voyage in 1711, the sailors of a Danish ship managed to send a complaint about their treatment to the officers of one of the other vessels. This prompted the captain to bring a sizeable contingent of soldiers on board because of fears of rebellion.[21] A Danish naval officer writing an instructional manual for seafarers in the 1740s warned that rebellions 'seem to happen sooner in a ship than almost any other place'. This was because there were so many potential catalysts, he argued. The problem, he surmised, was that the power of captains and officers was given to them from outside, by a sovereign who to grumbling sailors would be 'many hundred miles away'. Besides, the world was large, so there were many places for a mutineer to hide. The biggest problem, however, was the despotic way that many officers handled their vicarious power. If not for the fact that large numbers often found it difficult to agree to anything, mutinies would happen much more often, he reasonably concluded. The most important remedy was for commanders and officers to be attentive to the people's 'whispers and talk' and to try and read their faces for signs of 'secrecy'.[22]

Outright shipboard insurrections were rare, but they did happen.[23] They were most common on slave ships, with about one in ten seeing attempts at mutiny on behalf of the enslaved.[24] Slave mutinies appear to have been as common on Danish ships as they were on those of other empires, and the first one recorded occurred on a Company ship in 1698, the first to be sent after the Company's long hiatus. Instances in which sailors themselves took direct control of the ship happened on Danish ships other than the *Havmanden* as well. Most seem to have occurred on ships engaged in colonial trade. For instance, in early March 1710 two Danish slave ships, the *Fredericus Quartus* and *Christianus Quintus*, were the scene of a double mutiny after having crossed the Atlantic (during which crossing the enslaved packed into the lower deck had themselves mutinied[25]). The ships had overshot their destination in the Antilles and had ended up near the Nicaraguan or Costa Rican coast. Supplies were running out quickly, and so the people on one of the ships devised a plan of setting the enslaved Africans ashore in order to make what little was left last them longer. As was the case in 1683, we sense how, in such situations of destitution, the decks of ships became spaces of interpretation and deliberation. The captain, however, refused the plan laid out by his people, causing matters to escalate. After further discussions in which the crew demanded wages so that they could survive wherever they might be able to go, they fully rejected the captain's command and plundered the cabins, sharing all the gold they could find equally among them. They then set the enslaved ashore and abandoned the ship, which they set on fire. They wanted to head for Portobelo in Panama in English sloops whose crews they appear to have been able to force to take them there. The crew on the other ship then followed their example, although its captain seems to have held no pretensions that he might stop them. The English sloops, however, were taken as prizes by a Spanish privateer. Both crews eventually made their way to Portobelo where they were examined. They had agreed upon a story about being forced to leave the ships because of a storm. However, they were then held prisoners for months on account of Spanish suspicions that they had planned to sell the enslaved Africans illegally in Spanish territory.[26]

While recurrent features abound in such events when studied comparatively across empires (as I have attempted to show throughout the first part of this book), the study of such large-scale collective actions also raises important questions. Perhaps most importantly, a comparative perspective shows that while maritime social histories were interconnected through the migrations of maritime workers themselves and the transfers of technologies (including disciplinary ones), they were not synchronous. We can take the English Atlantic as a sort of measuring stick: there, two great waves of struggle took place in the early modern period. The first was the so-called 'golden age of piracy' that came at the conclusion of the War of Spanish Succession (1713), which had seen the large-scale mobilization of sailors across the major European empires. It lasted until the middle of the 1720s. It was partly triggered by the mass of unemployed sailors who lost their jobs at the end of the war and sought a means of living outside the regular Atlantic economy. Meanwhile, Denmark and Sweden fought in the so-called 'Great Northern War' that ended only in 1720. Therefore, there were very few Danes among these pirate crews that so unsettled Atlantic trade. Another period of radicalism, and along with it waves of mutinies, hit the British (as well as the navies of several other European powers) in the last decades of the eighteenth century. Again, this was at a time when Denmark was neutral in international politics, and whereas other navies witnessed what Niklas Frykman has called 'shock-proletarization', the Danish did not.[27] Instead unrest and resistance seem most common in other periods in Danish maritime history, and also tends to take slightly less dramatic forms. One period stands out: that between 1680 and 1730 – and perhaps the first and last decades of this period especially, both of which followed the conclusion of wars with Denmark's Swedish arch-rival. Both wars had seen large-scale mobilization of maritime workers and both left the Danish state coffers empty, causing naval pay to be withheld.[28]

Thus, the mutiny on the *Havmanden* happened at a time of general distress and heightened tensions in Denmark's maritime community. Many of the sailors and officers on the ship were naval men who had personally experienced the effects of this time. In general, the king allowed the personnel of his navy to enter into the service of the large trading companies based in Copenhagen, likely because it gave them valuable experience. The sailors themselves learned of such opportunities through word of mouth or from seeing the recruitment posters which in the spring and summer of 1682 had hung in various places around Copenhagen as well as in the maritime community of Elsinore. While such service came at a risk, well-known because of the stories and rumours in circulation, it at least promised much-needed pay.

Being without pay was a brutal blow to the members of a class that already ranked among urban society's poorest, and many sailors and their families took to begging. In the spring of 1682, officials in Copenhagen lamented that sailors would send their wives and children into the streets and when arrested in order to be taken to the local prison workhouse, they would put up a considerable fight.[29] These were desperate times.

The general distress in these periods have left a mark on the archives. While the records of the Danish Admiralty Courts are incomplete, especially in the first part of this period, they offer glimpses of a maritime culture defined by a great variety of conflicts. First and foremost, they reveal lives steeped in violence and alcohol. Fighting is a constant theme: some occurs on a personal level in the form of domestic abuse and fighting between sailors themselves, but much appears to be collective. Often groups of sailors and soldiers clashed in what at times look almost like turf wars in Copenhagen. Sometimes petty officers would be involved in such fighting as well, hinting at a sort of professional identity, as distinct from other professions.[30] Sometimes such violence, however, pitted gangs of sailors against the officers themselves; instances in which sailors would often excuse themselves with drunkenness, but where a recurrent subtext hints that such aggression also expressed grievances about perceived abuses.[31] Perhaps the largest incident occurred in July 1729, when one day after work on the docks a large group of more than sixty sailors attacked their superiors with stones, after having grumbled repeatedly during the day because of a dispute over their working hours. Their protests had made the officers call the guards in order to force the sailors to work. In court, the sailors complained that the quartermaster who was their main target had also abused them verbally during the day by calling them 'dog's cunts'.[32]

The court records also reveal telling patterns in the frequent cases of property crimes. Thus, we see how common sailors and petty officers would react to their poverty by resorting to theft. This resonates with AnnaSara Hammar's analysis of Swedish Admiralty records in which she has found that the general destitution of sailors influenced their patterns of crime with petty theft being a recurrent strategy in a life that was defined by the hunt for ready cash and the next meal.[33] In 1686, a memorial from the Danish naval authorities argued that it was a 'weekly, almost daily' event that their workers were caught stealing naval stores.[34] We rarely get a sense of the motivations behind such acts, but when we do they are striking. In 1690, a sailor who had sold his shirt argued that he did so, because in the past year, he had only been paid a month's wage.[35] Hammar also found that the general poverty among Swedish sailors created horizontal relations of solidarity. Therefore, we should not be surprised to find that, at times, and perhaps especially during hard times, theft could materialize in relatively large-scale collective projects. We find many such thieving operations in the Danish Admiralty Court records.[36] For instance, while working as dockhands, sailors would steal from the ships they unloaded. Metals appear to have been an especially attractive target, perhaps because they were abundant and because it was easy to find a buyer of such goods among the blacksmiths of Copenhagen. Other naval staples such as sail cloth were popular as well, and indeed the storehouses of the navy and the trading companies offered a host of potential goods for thieves. Other maritime workers simply formed gangs and robbed in the streets or became burglars.[37] Perhaps the most dramatic case occurred in 1722 when a small group of sailors murdered the skipper of the ship on which they had been hired, in order to steal his valuables.[38] It is very rare, however, to find common mariners stealing from each other.

Other types of crime found in Admiralty records also speak of a maritime social life defined by tensions. We find many cases of insubordination, especially against petty officers. Food was often a source of conflict. Sometimes such unrest was read by authorities as the beginnings of mutiny. For instance, bad conditions on board the hulk of *Trekroner* in 1721 ended with two men being sentenced to three years of hard labour for inciting rebellion.[39] Similarly, in 1726 a large group of sailors complained about bad food and an abusive captain. The author of the complaint was then placed under arrest for almost a year before finally being released when the authorities found that the criticism of the substandard meals had in fact been justified. They found that the long arrest was a sufficient punishment for the part of the complaint concerning the captain's abusive behaviour, of which they found no proof.[40] Another recurrent act was rioting in or around the maritime quarters of Copenhagen.[41] Such events sometimes involved pilfering from other neighbourhoods. In the 1690s, this caused the maritime community of Nyboder to employ its own guard, which itself became the target of such crowds.[42] Labour relations also caused grievances. For instance, in 1728 a group of several hundred naval sailors abandoned their work on the docks because they considered themselves to have the right to take the week off. They also coordinated what to say to authorities and it took weeks, and more than a hundred interrogations, for the Admiralty to get even a vague sense of how the illegal strike had been organized.[43] A similar conflict erupted the following year.[44]

Desertion was another common crime, both in the Admiralty Court records and in material from long voyages. There are many cases in which sailors deserted by deliberately missing the embarking ship.[45] During the Great Northern War, authorities tried to prevent such desertion by fining people who housed sailors who were signed on to embark.[46] In wartime, we find several cases in which mariners deserted in order to become Swedish privateers.[47] Similarly soldiers often enrolled in more than one regiment at once, taking pay from one employer before leaving in order to enrol and take pay from another, sometimes under a different name.[48] Such a form of 'desertion' was certainly a way for workers to bump up their pay, while other desertions appear motivated by the opportunity to get better overall pay with another employer. This was common in foreign and especially in colonial ports, where labour shortages would often drive up wages.[49] In home waters, Dutch merchantmen proved a great attraction.[50] Non-economic factors could motivate desertion as well, such as sea- and homesickness, dislike of the job or the social environment onboard ship or the abuse by superiors. Causes could be intertwined, as when in 1693 a sailor before the Admiralty Court explained that he had joined the only navy because of his excessive poverty, that he was unable to perform any useful work onboard ship and was thus ridiculed by his fellow sailors. He added that during the four months he had been in the navy, he had been paid for only one.[51] In other cases, desertion was a way to recoup lost agency, as when in 1691 an abusive captain had threatened to hand over a disobedient sailor to the army. This prompted the sailor to desert in order to be recruited by the army under his own steam, as he had a personal preference for a specific army regiment; facing the arbitrariness inherent in his captain's threat, the sailor took matters into his own hands.[52] Punishments for desertion varied greatly, and became much more severe during wartime. Faced with the problem of punishing large groups of deserters, the Admiralty Court sometimes resorted to the method of letting the transgressors play dice to decide who would be punished.[53] Collective desertion was also seen as an aggravating factor. While desertion was common in both the navy and the merchant fleet, the archives afford no apparent way to quantify desertion rates.

Thus, we might read the mutiny on the *Havmanden* as being only a singularly violent expression of a much wider culture of conflict and resistance intensified by the social conditions maritime workers experienced in these decades. The mutiny on the *Havmanden* was not even unique for seeing sailors and convicts join hands in collective action. We have already seen how the prison workhouse at times received the children and wives of sailors. In general, maritime workers belonged to the urban poor whose ranks filled the prisons. Of course, the stigma of dishonour could at times create differences among sailors and convicts, as some sailors took their honour very seriously. For instance, in October 1709 a sailor was brought before the Admiralty Court for having stabbed another sailor to death. The reason he gave was that the two had been at an inn drinking when the deceased had repeatedly mocked his adversary because he had previously been in irons at *Trunken* for a case of theft. Further, as 'an honest man' he had refused to drink from the same pitcher as the former convict, even though he actually still had his honour formally (otherwise he would not have been released, nor re-entered the navy). The former convict had defended himself saying that he had atoned for his crime, which provoked the deceased to a fight which eventually ended in the stabbing.[54] Thus, notions of honour and criminality could be a divider but not always: many maritime workers appear to have felt like the Norwegian purser's mate, Ole Amonsen Stavanger, who in the winter of 1715 was drunk on his guard watching over those awaiting trial at the Admiralty Court when he exclaimed that 'if we are not going to help our friends, then who are we going to help?' before assisting a prisoner to escape.[55]

Stavanger's case was far from unusual. Convicts often got assistance from accomplices or otherwise used their personal connections to the men at the docks when escaping. For instance, the convict Johannes Grosch fled his captors in 1722. He had been in the custody of Joen Ellingsen, a sailor who was to oversee his work, but had instead taken him drinking, at which point Grosch escaped.[56] There are several similar cases in the records, suggesting that the practice of sailors abandoning work to go drinking with the convicts was not altogether uncommon.[57] At other times, sailors actively assisted convicts or prisoners awaiting trial to escape.[58] Thus, some convicts ran with the aid of passports or other instruments given to them by sailors. I explore such cases at more length in the next chapter.

Convicts and maritime workers would steal together as well, just as sailors would act as handlers of goods stolen by convicts.[59] The most dramatic instance occurred in 1727 when a group of rowers and sailors ganged up to steal irons with a large group of convicts, the leaders of whom appear to have been former sailors themselves. This plot unfolded over several months, possibly years, and even involved the prison wardens. The convicts would steal the irons, bury them until the time was right to hand them over to the mariners who would then sell them and share the profit with the convicts. The convicts needed the money in order to buy alcohol, tobacco and other goods from the prison guards, who kept an illegal inn for the convicts. Perhaps most telling, while awaiting trial, one of the convicts involved managed to escape, aided by a file given to him by a ship's carpenter during his arrest.[60]

Maritime crime, whether as dramatic as on the *Havmanden*, or as subtle as the cases of small-scale theft, often had to be collective. Life on ship was a life lived in tight spaces and which therefore was by necessity social. Even ships not filled with convicts were almost impossibly crowded, affording little to no space in which to operate undetected. The dock work that naval sailors were obligated to perform when in port or the tasks carried out in naval workshops is a similar story. If we look at the inmates of *Trunken*, maritime workers were the cohort most likely to arrive in groups, which hints at the collective character of their actions.[61] However, when appearing in court they would often efface the social logic behind their acts in order to offer what authorities heard as acceptable explanations. Thus, the common tropes of drink, stupidity, being seduced by others and youth offered by sailors before court officials, were strategic; they showed how maritime workers knew what elites wanted to hear and understood the theatre of power in which they performed. They consciously effaced the importance of horizontal relations and solidarities when faced with authorities' intent on punishing any sort of organization or collusion.

Stories of transgressions / transgressive stories

The strategies employed by maritime workers in court when faced with persecution show how we should consider the court records to be fragmented. Not only are they incomplete in the literal sense, but the answers they contain are purposefully evasive – even if they do hint at a culture of conflict and resistance from below. Thankfully, there are other ways to explore this culture and to get at the meaning of the acts of maritime workers. Indeed, three unique texts written by members of the maritime lower classes in the period allow us to get a sense of the way maritime workers themselves made sense of the conditions they were subjected to and understood their options of taking action. Danish historians should thus feel privileged, although they have too often neglected these working-class voices.[62] The words of Jon Olafsson, Nils Trosner and Arni Magnusson can help us begin to fill in the strategic silences in the court records.

Both Jon Olafsson and Arni Magnusson were Icelanders. They travelled to Denmark in order to work as common gunners and soldiers in the Danish navy, but both also sailed on a host of merchant vessels. Both saw much of the world: Olafsson went on one of the first Danish expeditions to India, while Magnusson not only travelled east, but also saw Greenland first-hand. Both at times lived within Copenhagen's maritime community, and like many members of this community, both came into conflict with the law. They even experienced the coercion of Copenhagen's jails and prisons: Olafsson was arrested and locked up in the jail *Blåtårn* (which held some of the mutineers awaiting trial), while Magnusson spent several years in the Stockhouse for a case of fraud. Finally, long after the fact, both produced texts that blended autobiography with travel writing, describing exotic encounters in distant locations as well as their experiences on deck or in Copenhagen. Both these texts speak extensively on conflict in ways that utterly fail to comport with the conventions of the at the time already well-established genre of travel writing in which transgressions were usually related to serve as moral or even political lessons for a reader often assumed to be a future traveller.[63] All these similarities, both in terms of experiences and voice, become all the more striking because Olafsson and Magnusson lived a century and a half apart: Olafsson wrote of what he experienced on his adventures in the 1610s and 1620s, while his spiritual successor Magnusson sailed on Danish ships in the 1760s and 1770s.

The first of these surprisingly candid odysseys of conflict, violence and transgression, Jon Olafsson's, is the lengthiest. As with the other texts examined here, it remained unpublished in its time, but was translated from its original Icelandic into both Danish and English in the early twentieth century.[64] Its protagonist is constantly at the centre of quarrel and trouble. The text presents Olafsson as a daring, almost reckless, man. He often mirrors his own personality in that of his king, Christian IV, who has enjoyed notoriety for being brave and boisterous, but somewhat thoughtless. In Olafsson's estimation, he is a true and faultless authority; however, everyone beneath the king is not; among these people are figures whom Olafsson at one point conceives of as 'the go-between' and who 'often has much power'. They were the objects of Olafsson's scorn. Such a man, Olafsson warned, could 'cause trouble and harm if it be his desire, as is daily shown in practice'.[65] Thus, on several occasions Olafsson had confrontations with authorities whom he deemed thoroughly unjust. One high-ranking official was presented in a particularly bad light. One of his many faults is that he wanted the workers on the docks to work more than what was 'ancient usage and custom'. Olafsson's personal hatred, however, stemmed from the fact that at one point this officer wished to have Olafsson submitted to *Trunken*. He did not succeed. Olafsson then goes on to tell several pages on the completely unrelated downfall of this man – styling it as a form of divine retribution.[66] Indeed, many of the stories he tells show a sense of how at least God is on his side in his struggles against adversity.

An even clearer sense of *Schadenfreude* runs through Magnusson's text, which was also translated and published in the early twentieth century. On several occasions, Magnusson even shows how such retribution did not only come from up high, but also from below. For instance, in one voyage the people suffered greatly from 'thirst, meagre food and hard command'. The mate especially was not well liked, no doubt because he seems to have lived in a state of plenty, but also because 'he was the worst of all when it came to punishing the people, even for mere trifles'. Then one day, the sailors played a trick on him. While he was on a drink break, they placed a louse in his telescope. This prompted him to rejoice when moments later he thought he had spotted a rowboat coming towards them. As the captain came to the scene, he was befuddled: he saw no such thing through his own lens, but the mate insisted, although now he was also somewhat perplexed as suddenly 'the front rowers held the oars up into the sky'. An argument ensued and eventually the captain took the drunken mate's telescope in order to try it out, but by then the louse had fallen out.[67] The prank succeeded in every measure. Cultural historians have asserted the subversive qualities of the jokes told among early modern workers.[68] The drawn-out days on the deck of a voyaging ship provided the perfect opportunity for retelling such stories over and over again – a scene pictured by Magnusson as he explains how there were sometimes occasions when the wind made the work so negligible that the sailors instead lay on the deck 'sleeping or telling each other stories'.[69]

Olafsson does not shy away from making himself the centre of similar acts. One anecdote he relates came from his experiences during a winter when he worked as a guard at the Bremerholmen docks. One day 'it so happened that I and six of the best of my young comrades made up our minds to neglect our work and fail to appear at the muster at the Arsenal, and we clubbed together to have a feast'. They found an inn on the outskirts of the city, where they 'fancied that we should be able to hide undetected'. Olafsson presents no qualms about their actions. Instead, it seems to be the authorities that are excessive, and the party ends when one of the naval provost catches them. As he entered the room, Olafsson told his friends 'not to show any trace of shame'. Thus, when he approached them, 'I bade him welcome'. The provost took it all in good spirit, but when he brought them back to the docks, another provost was vengeful. He subjected them to be 'placed out on the ice, each with an iron bolt about his feet and twelve pails of water were poured over each of us'. This man, Olafsson told, was 'skilful at that kind of punishment'. He then recounts how the provost who had inflicted the punishment was the subject of their mockery because he had a habit of 'being very hostile to us and often reporting and exaggerating our transgressions, the which he could have left undone'. Puzzlingly, one of the terms they call him is 'Roast Lamb', possibly referencing the sexual act of 'spit roasting'.[70]

As was the case on the *Havmanden*, friendships are a foundation of resistance in Olafsson's writings. In one instance, such practices were prompted by the widespread tradition of having subordinates punish each other. When one of Olafsson's friends on his Indian voyage, a young man called Franz, stabbed a man on the ship, he was spared the symbolic punishment of having his hand pinned to the mast with the knife in question because 'all the crew made a general plea in his behalf'. Instead, he was sentenced to be lashed with a cable-end once by each of the people on board, except for the chief officers. In total, there were eighty people, each of whom had to give one lash each. The small clique that Olafsson was part of, however, had 'agreed among ourselves that when our turn came we would spare him'. Therefore, they put on a show, so when their time came to hit their friend, they only feigned doing so. They did this because they were 'attached to him in innocent friendship and comradeship', but unfortunately their attempt to foil the workings of the law failed as they were discovered, which caused them to be lashed by the provost instead.[71] It is perhaps not surprising that to an unsettled, somewhat cosmopolitan, bachelor like Olafsson, friendships were the most important relation in his social life. On the Indian voyage, his best friend was a man named Bernt Andersen, whom Olafsson compared to 'a good wife in his thoughtful care and in everything concerning my daily necessities'. Andersen 'could not bear to see or hear that I suffered in any way'. When Olafsson fell ill, his friend was so concerned that he could not eat. This friendship was also the base for illicit actions: the two secretly brought eight cheeses with them to India, which they sold to make a fine profit.[72] Like Frandsen and Gulliksen, they had formed a powerful bond in the face of adversity.

Magnusson's text places a similar emphasis on friendships, but in his own account Magnusson was a bit of a loner. He portrays himself as somewhat isolated, feeling as a foreigner among his Danish colleagues. There is a sense of resentment, even bitterness, running through the narrative he crafted. It did not help that he felt he had been tricked into the service and he cursed the enrolment system. He expressly sympathized with German soldiers tricked into being recruited for the Danish army.[73] The fact that he, at one point, spent several years in the Stockhouse prison after what he found to be a false conviction in a case of forgery, also seems to aid his feelings of regret.[74] However, despite his outsider position, he must have enjoyed the company of fellow maritime workers enough to remember the stories he picked up on the lower deck of the ships he travelled. The stories he relates speak badly of the power relations on board. For instance, he crafted a somewhat angry anecdote about a ship's surgeon who passed away on the ship in a voyage to India. Usually the death of a surgeon would have been a terrible event jeopardizing the safety of the crew, but not this time. Instead, the sailors were delighted, because 'whenever the sailors were ill, [he] used to say that they merely suffered from laziness. Their disease would go away if they were severely beaten'. They experienced a sense of relief 'by throwing him overboard'.[75] Magnusson also hints how such antagonisms might result in direct violence, as it did on the *Havmanden*. For instance, he had himself voyaged on a ship whose purser was 'amused to hear sailors scream'. However, the story takes a darker turn: one night, the captain rushed to see what was going on as he heard the people begging for the purser to stop his tormenting and punishments. However, before the captain arrived at the scene he heard 'a great noise which came from the sailors yelling "oh, God save us! Our purser has fallen overboard!"' Arriving on the deck, the captain inquired 'under what circumstances this had happened, but the sailors feigned to be so sad that none could provide the particulars'. Then, when he left them, 'they all started to laugh and sing songs of ridicule'. They were happy to see him gone. The captain seems to have suspected that the purser had been murdered, as the story implies, but nothing came of it.[76]

Collective insubordination is also a feature in Olafsson's retelling, especially in his story of his voyage to India in the 1620s. In one passage, he tells of two soldiers at the Danish fort on the Coromandel Coast who got drunk and committed an unspecified act of insubordination. They were imprisoned, but kept provoking their superiors by threatening them and by expressing their intention of running away and breaking their oath. They were then sentenced to the brutal punishment of squassation or *strappado*, during which the rest of the fort's men, Olafsson among them, begged for their friends to be spared. Pardon was not given, so they 'aimed our muskets on them with burning matches, whereat they were much humbled'. The tense situation was only resolved when a couple of local merchants interrupted the scene and as they also asked for mercy for the two prisoners, they were pardoned.[77] In general, Olafsson disliked the colonial service. Outside the fort they heard nothing but the 'threatening talk of the heathens' and inside 'the strict and harsh superintendence of our officers and their continual reprimands, of which I need not speak further'.[78]

The type of mutinous deliberations that took place on the *Havmanden* also took place on the ships that Olafsson sailed on – although they manifested in less dramatic action. In the return leg of the India voyage, the crew was suffering from starvation. A governor returning from the colony, however, had two live stags on board which he stubbornly refused to slaughter, probably because he considered them to be a valuable souvenir. The people below deck were of a different mind and deliberated at night, laying plans in order to foil their superiors. Thus, one night, they killed the animals. Trying to ensure that the meat would end on *their* plates and not on those of the cabin-dwellers, they killed them in such a way that it appeared they had suffocated. Animals that died of unknown causes were surrounded by intense magical beliefs and taboo. Considered to be supernaturally unclean, they brought a fear of pollution, and only the dishonoured social caste of nightmen were supposed to handle their carcasses; going by this principle, the sailors hoped that their superiors in the cabin would think it beneath them to eat the dead animals. In this way, they were trying to play their superiors. Unfortunately, in the morning when the dead stags were discovered, the men in the cabin ate them anyway, although they at least shared the food with the crew.[79]

Both of these Icelandic storytellers often delve into what we can surmise to be retelling of things they had not experienced themselves. Such stories hint at the everyday practices of storytelling in maritime communities and how some such narratives were noted and remembered. The last text to be discussed here, the diary of Norwegian common sailor Nils Trosner, is more clearly indebted to such an oral tradition. Trosner took part in the Great Northern War (1709–1720) and recounts his experiences on Danish warships. However, he did not see all that much action. Instead he provides us with summaries of the rumours and stories circulating within the ships on which he laboured. Many of the entries in his text begin with the phrase, 'it was said . . .'. In this way, the stories he tells are of the sort that Magnusson tells us filled the idle hours of seafaring – a rare glimpse at lower-deck everyday storytelling. Evidently, such stories were concerned with a great many different subjects. Naturally, there is a constant preoccupation with rumours about the war and the battles playing out elsewhere. Interestingly such informal news was sometimes wrong. They were also mixed up with a host of different omens which were interpreted to reveal the immediate future and the outcome of the fighting.[80] A very tangible concern was with the plague that broke out in the summer of 1711 and took a heavy toll on Copenhagen's population – many of the sailors' families and friends among them. In light of such relations, the constant preoccupation with rumours about deaths is perfectly logical. In terms of both of these subjects, rumour reads as a response to uncertainties and the anxieties experienced on the decks. Thus, Trosner offers us what is perhaps the most direct access anywhere to the usually lost discourses of early modern sailors and their world of 'useful' stories, as well as the informal circulation and interpretation of news. Yet of the three, his text has enjoyed the least attention from scholars – possibly because it, as a sort of communal testimony, offers its reader a much weaker sense of the personality of its author than, for instance, the tales of reckless bravado offered by Olafsson.

However, like the Icelandic autobiographies, themes of retribution and justice, often supernatural, are ever-present in the text. For instance, Trosner relates an evocative ghost story that revolves around the theme of vengeance. It was one which he had picked up during the daily conversations with the other mariners onboard ship. It told of a ship's master who was considered 'ungodly' because of his arbitrary abuse of a common sailor whom he made 'bonkefeyer [a derogatory term for the one who handles waste on ships] and made a wooden sword [possibly a Harlequin reference] and tied it to him, and always beat him much'.[81] These acts of ridicule, difficult for us to parse, ended only when the sailor killed himself by throwing himself into the waves: 'as he jumped, he said: "You who is to blame for my death, will get misfortune."' The night thereafter, 'the ship's sentry guard saw the same dead man enter . . . the ship, in his previous way'. The story turns as: 'that same night he was by the master in his cabin and broke his neck so that his head sat all wrong on him'.[82] Like the tales told by Olafsson and Magnusson, the story is clear in its message: abusive authorities will get what they deserve.

This is only one among a host of yarns rotating around the theme of a poetic justice manifesting itself in Trosner's diary. A telling one casts such conflicts in a more general light as it relates a clash between rich and poor in a struggle over the rights to the commons. A river next to the town of Halmstad in Sweden was the source of the grievance. It had provided the poor well with eel and salmon before spite drove the rich to enforce their claim on it. This caused the fish to disappear, seemingly a divine act of sorts. Only by donating 'much money to the poor' did the rich see them come back, and even so, in smaller numbers.[83] This was levelling fantasy as it resonated on the decks of early modern ships.

The subversive mockery that we sense in the other narratives is here as well. For instance, Trosner tells a tale of a scholarly man who could read the future from the stars. He had a daughter but when she was born, he saw that she would die at the hand of the executioner. Having seen her fate in the stars, he himself decided to drive her to the executioner.[84] Elsewhere, Trosner related how the wartime navy pressed people into service – a recurrent topic throughout the text which at another point describes how even newly-wed men exiting Copenhagen's churches were dragged off.[85] In the passage in question, he then changes subject almost mid-story to recount a yarn about trickery which involves ten sailors stationed on the island of Stevns, where Trosner himself was at one point lodged too. Desirous to leave what is, by the context, cast as a form of forced labour, these ten men put on white shirts at night in order to appear as ghosts and scare the guards. They succeeded in running away. His sympathy shows in the story's moral: instead of being apprehended and punished, the runaways found happiness by running to Copenhagen and eventually all getting married.[86] Other stories speak in similar ways on the conditions for maritime workers, but read as much less funny. Several deal with the real-life impact of abusive officers. One such story tells of a sailor who was incarcerated for having killed his child when, one day, it had cried out for food. He had been in the navy for years and, resonating with the conflicts over pay outlined above, he was owed 'a heap of money, but the masters kept his pay for so long that he, his wife and child had almost starved to death'.[87] In this way, the circumstances of the story make it read as a critique on behalf of the impoverished naval workers bereft of pay.

While Olafsson and Magnusson appear bullish, Trosner himself is somewhat absent as a protagonist in his writings. He does not tell of instances in which he himself transgressed, and in this way he represents the many sailors who did not appear in the Admiralty Court – those who did not come into direct conflict with authorities. Perhaps more importantly, he shows how such staying put did not mean that the common hands believed the abuses they regularly suffered to be just. This shows in how the stories which Trosner relates on some occasions read as echoes of deliberations about potential acts of resistance, having the character of repertoires of action. One anecdote from December 1711 is particularly interesting in this regard. At this time, Trosner heard stories being told by mariners about discontent on another of the navy's ships. Trosner tells us how: 'on [the naval ship] *Høyenhall* 60 men stood at the mast [meaning they were punished] this summer, because they had written a complaint about a lieutenant called Spincke whom they had. All of these had put their names in the letter, as in a compass.' This complaint appears entirely justified, as the ship was defined by abusive officers. For instance, Trosner tells us how the captain of the ship at one point accidentally killed a sailor.[88] The practice of written complaints being signed in circles is well known to maritime historians. It was a practice that was widespread in other maritime empires. It can be interpreted as a form of formalized solidarity designed to render the atomizing work of exemplary punishments impossible. For instance, Rediker has discussed the social logic of these so-called 'round robins' which enabled crews to complain formally, demonstrating their numbers, yet at the same time concealing the specific origins of the collective protests.[89] In this way, there was none who had signed the complaint first and could thereby be singled out as ringleaders to be punished. However, I have not come across examples of such round robins in the Danish maritime archives. That only makes the anecdote the more important, as it demonstrates how Danish-Norwegian sailors knew of such traditions and what their use was. The plot thickens further due to the fact that the logs and journals of the ship that Trosner recounts to have been the scene of this conflict still exist, but contain no trace of the incidents. This reveals the stories to be the stuff of yarning: sailors discussing how to approach situations in which the outcome could be fatal. This is storytelling as the transmission of knowledge of potential actions and their dangers.

All three texts confound conventions of how to emplot crime and conflict in early modern writing. The defining features of social life on board ships and in ports is the stark and potentially unjust hierarchy and the informal relations of friendships that enabled sailors to subvert power relations. All three texts show a strikingly similar outlook. If such similarities across 150 years were to be explained by literary convention, we would have expected to find their tales of transgressions as cautionary moral tales. However, in the cases where the three texts imply that readers should take caution; the implicit lesson is radical. Collectively, they warn of the bad intentions of officers and the need to keep them out of earshot. Thus, if the similarities between these three texts is to be explained by common genre conventions, these conventions are not the ones found in literary traditions, but those of the very oral traditions on the lower decks. As remarked by historian of folklore David Hopkin in his study of nineteenth-century France, sailors and soldiers 'had their own concepts of what constituted proper military behaviour, which were inculcated through storytelling and other unofficial practices, concepts that could include desertion, marauding and conflict with superiors.'[90] What we hear in these memoirs and diaries are echoes of precisely such storytelling, communicating a widely shared lower-deck culture of resistance.

In this way, these texts are similar because they share a link to a world of stories transmitted over work or drink when at a remove from officers. In turn, we can argue that the outlook structuring all three texts also structured and legitimized the transgressive actions filling the court records in the period. While we should not make them speak for all sailors, they at least partly make up for the occluding narratives that maritime workers offered up in court in hopes of evading punishment. And of course, such storytelling traditions go a long way towards helping us understand the transformation of the lower deck of the *Havmanden*. Maritime workers were skilled storytellers and their words transmitted knowledge.

5

Birds in Cages

Captain Blom had been warned. In their instructions for him, the Company directors had brought attention to the disorder that the convicts could wreak upon his voyage. They feared their flight especially. If, in case of emergency, Blom was forced to seek harbour, the directors demanded him to take extra precautions so that the convicts would not be able to steal the boats or attempt to swim to shore. In previous voyages, convicts had escaped during stops in Bergen, forcing authorities to take on Norwegian convicts from Bergen's prisons in their stead.[1] Iversen had experienced this first hand. Preparing for the voyage of the *Havmanden*, the directors feared that such plans could take shape either in secret or materialize in outright violence – fears that seem to have heightened because of the sheer number of convicts on board. Therefore, Blom or a trusted officer was to patrol the ship hourly at night. In a sense, foreshadowing events three months later, the directors conceived of the convicts on the lower deck as a 'multitude of indomitable people who by means of authority and respect needs to be forced to obedience'.[2]

These remarks suggest a link between the mutiny and the most common form of resistance that convicts everywhere in the scattered Danish-Norwegian empire practised. As an attempt to run away with the ship itself, the mutiny can be conceived as a momentous attempt at mass flight. The mutiny expressed a will to escape mirrored in myriad plots formulated in the many different penal institutions created as the militarized state of the seventeenth century mobilized larger and larger crowds of convicts to labour. Like the mutiny itself, such practices were predicated on storytelling. However, such storytelling is decidedly of the dark-matter type bereft of archival representation. Thus, whereas the previous chapter dealt with stories that on some occasions made it to paper, the traditions of knowledge accumulation and storytelling that escape hinged on are much more elusive.

Escape followed carceral schemes everywhere in the Danish-Norwegian empire. As argued by Rediker and Linebaugh in their study on class struggle in the early modern Atlantic, the early modern prison 'organized large numbers of people for purposes of exploitation, but it simultaneously was unable to prevent prisoners from organizing against it'.[3] Thus, 'the theme of incarceration brought with it a counter-theme of excarceration'.[4] Yet despite such a status as an emblem of resistance, surprisingly little research have been conducted on the actual experiences and practices of escape from early modern penal institutions. This neglect becomes all the more remarkable considering the intensity with which scholars have studied other groups on the move such as deserters, the itinerant poor or maroons.

Studying escape practices allows us to appreciate how the men and women on the lower deck were part of a culture of flight that expressed itself on both sides of the Atlantic. This chapter, then, will first study escape from the institutions from which the convicts on the *Havmanden* came, principally the dockyard prison, then turn to practices of running in the colony for which they had been headed. In both places escape was predicated upon knowledge, often formed through trial and error, but also disseminated in the long idle hours of incarceration and transportation. We get a sense of such storytelling primarily from looking carefully at *how* convicts escaped, occupying ourselves with the specificities of escape and the 'rival geography' that such flights expressed.[5]

Centripetal and centrifugal flows

The convicts who escaped with the *Havmanden* had come from three institutions in the empire's centre of Copenhagen. In this way, the flow that brought convicts to St Thomas in the 1670s and 80s had been grafted onto an already existing set of flows which circulated convicts both centripetally and centrifugally within the Danish-Norwegian empire. This had been happening since the early seventeenth century, when the militarized Danish-Norwegian state had taken increased control of the machinery of punishment, which involved instituting new forms of penal labour that were tied to the military ambitions of the Danish rulers. This move created a quantitatively small but nonetheless enduring system of circulation of convicts within the Scandinavian empire, which in various forms persisted until the middle of the nineteenth century.

The result of this reconfiguration of punishment was a bifurcated system, split between two different types of institution that also represented two different and highly gendered ways of connecting punishment and labour. On the one hand, female felons, juvenile delinquents and vagrants were incarcerated in prison workhouses (from 1605 in Copenhagen, later elsewhere in the realm as well). In creating this system, the Danish authorities took heavy cues from the Dutch who had invented what was to become the model for this type of institution in the late sixteenth century.[6] On the other hand, male felons were sentenced to hard labour in military or naval institutions, either in the naval dockyard prison of *Trunken* (1620–1741) or in various military or naval fortresses throughout Denmark-Norway. The convicts on the *Havmanden* came from both strands: one in about five were women from Copenhagen's prison workhouse, while most of the rest came from *Trunken*.

Both strands aimed at mobilizing the labour force, although in quite different ways: while the prison workhouses trained their inmates in the hope of transforming the poor into a productive workforce to be of use in workshops or manufactures, the institutions of hard labour simply aimed to exploit the physical toil of malfeasants. Both forms were attempting to fashion Copenhagen into an economic and military stronghold. The proto-industrial complex of the prison workhouse provided cloth for the state's military. The establishment of the naval dockyard prison was similarly motivated as the initial push for bringing larger groups of convict workers to Copenhagen around 1600 appears to have been the need for workers in constructing military infrastructure at a time of armament. They also served as galley rowers, although this practice was given up much earlier in Denmark than, for instance, in France or Spain. The naval dockyard prison was established around 1620 as an institutionalization of these earlier practices. Chained convicts performed an array of labours, usually the meanest and hardest, such as dredging or hauling building materials. They were also dragooned into public initiatives of different types, often side by side with sailors and soldiers, and in general we might argue that all three groups were part of the same labour market driven by the needs of the state.[7]

While these institutions were new, convicted criminals had laboured in the service of the state for centuries. Thus, the figure of the convict as a forced labourer was not the product of the seventeenth century. Medieval law had contained clauses that allowed courts to sentence thieves to enslavement in the 'King's yard' – a peculiar state of enslavement from which the convicted could not be sold, thus foreshadowing the status of the convict labourer who, echoing such precedents, was widely referred to as a 'thrall'. In this way, the figure of the convict labourer in the service of the state had precedents in earlier forms of unfreedom.[8] As argued in Chapter 1, this conception changed somewhat at the same time that Denmark entered into the transatlantic slave trade, from which point onwards the term 'slave' came into fashion.

Both Copenhagen's prison workhouse and the naval/military institutions received convicts from the entire realm, including Norway and Iceland. This metropolitan flow was in operation from the beginning of these institutions, and as noted above, even preceded them in some cases. Convicts were usually shipped individually or in very small groups from the port nearest to the court where they had been sentenced. Others were also transported over land. For most convicts, this entailed a separation from kin. Of course, the cost of transportation also meant that local courts far from the capital were more likely to use other penalties, principally corporal punishments. Thus, looking at the inmate registers of Copenhagen's early modern prisons, we can deduce that the further away the destination, the fewer the convicts.

During the time it was operational, from 1620 to 1741, the prison of *Trunken* on Copenhagen's docks (Bremerholmen) was perhaps the most important of these institutions in that it also functioned as a hub in that part of the system in which male convicts circulated and laboured. Besides the West India and Guinea Company, the navy itself used these convicts in other locations as well, for instance in its efforts to build and maintain the fortress of Christiansø in the Baltic. Another destination was the fortress of Kronborg at Elsinore. Speaking of the convicts under his command, the commander there argued that convicts were an 'indispensable' labour force as they carried out jobs that the soldiers could not take on. He added that it would be a costly affair if he was forced to pay wages for labourers to do them. However, they were also a source of friction; of the ten convicts he had at his disposal, three had fled and of the remaining seven, four had attempted to do so. One of them was a 'daring bird', who had attempted escape many times.[9]

In sharp contrast with the prison workhouse and the army prison, known as the Stockhouse – from whence smaller contingents of convicts also arrived on the *Havmanden* – the naval dockyard prison has left a plethora of sources scattered throughout the navy's archive. They provide a rare opportunity to examine the workings of an early modern penal institution and its inmate population (averaging seventy-nine people at any given time in the period examined here) in some detail. Partly, this opportunity arises because the system that circulated convicts also circulated knowledge. Whether arriving by boat from afar or on foot from a local court in or near Copenhagen, each convict was accompanied by paper. In this way, copies of the court documents that detailed the transgressions of the convicts landed on the writing desk of the naval clerk. He would read through them and enter the convict into his books, often along with his own short summations of the crime, before placing the documents in his archive. Eventually, he or a successor would return to the entry and note how the incarceration had ended: whether by death, release, transportation elsewhere or escape. Such books exist in an unbroken series from 1690 to 1741, when this institution was closed and the convicts transferred to a similar institution administered by the army. They allow us to examine patterns of escape quantitatively. Nothing really changed in the lifetime of this institution, so what we learn from this period likely holds true for the preceding decades as well. The clerk's entry books note the number of 1,490 men,[10] but this does not include all of those inside, as the institution at times appears also to have held sailors awaiting trial (Gulliksen appears to have been detained there upon his arrest), vagrants who had been arrested but not yet sentenced, and prisoners of war. Those groups were not recorded in the books. Of the 1,490 convicted men listed, at least 290 escaped. I say 'at least' because various (although unfortunately less complete) court martial records show that those apprehended the same day were not registered by the clerk, so the actual number of escapes was higher. Of those who got out, 223 managed to stay on the loose, while the rest were caught.

Interestingly, the inmates' propensity for escape varied greatly. Thus, specific groups were over-represented among the 290 escapees. We can delineate two clear variables that influenced whether a convict was likely to run:

1. the length of the sentence. 93.4 percent of those who attempted to break out carried life sentences. We can conclude, therefore, that this dramatic form of resistance was chosen primarily by those who knew that they were very likely to be confined to hard labour for the rest of their lives.
2. whether the convict had 'retained his honour'. This ties into the first variable, as those with life sentences who still had their honour still had the chance of being pardoned by the king, many of them crafting petitions to improve their chances. That this was a variable in the convicts' propensity to attempt escape is demonstrated by how, out of all who carried life sentences, two-thirds were dishonoured, yet out of those with life sentences who ran, the total percentage of dishonoured was 82.4 percent.

Further, we might propose a third, albeit less clear-cut, variable: a background in the army. 33.9 percent of the convicts serving life sentences who were former soldiers escaped, while the percentage among their civilian peers was 26.3 percent. This can be interpreted in a number of ways, the most likely being that former military personnel had knowledge of the tactics and skills that would have been useful during a prison break. In fact, many of them were former deserters. The crimes of having taking part in a desertion plot (meaning collective desertion) or serial desertions could warrant a life sentence. Stealing in the process (for instance, stealing your military garb or gun) could also factor in.

Thus, thieves and deserters with life sentences and dishonouring scars across their foreheads or backs were among the most common escapees. They, the thieves especially, were also the most likely to be selected for transportation.[11] By extension, the convicts received by the Company were truly among the most 'indomitable'.

Patterns that speak to the motivations of prison breakers can also be teased from these sources. They resonate with the motivations of the mutineers, especially their experiences of hunger and the rumours of death and violence in the colony. The numbers allow us to calculate death and escape rates. Across this fifty-year period the mortality rate averaged 8.74 percent. This number is somewhat inflated because of the year 1711, when the majority of the inmate population died from an outbreak of the bubonic plague. In general, death rates were much higher on the inside than outside. In turn, this goes some way towards explaining why convicts fared so badly on the ships bringing them to St Thomas in the 1670s. Thus, we are not surprised to learn that self-preservation appears a clear motivation in escape. Many of the years which saw the most 'runners' were also years in which death rates were well above average. They include the years 1700, 1709, 1711, 1716, 1727 – years in which food prices were generally high, and in which the convicts are likely to have experienced diminished rations. The three years from 1697 to 1700 were times of scarcity because of failed harvests,[12] but the harvest also failed in 1709, again driving up food prices and meaning that convicts were already vulnerable when the plague hit in 1711. 1716 was yet another year of grain shortages in Copenhagen,[13] indicating that convicts probably ran because of hunger, which then prompted death rates to spike in the following year. The spike of 1727 was similarly motivated by hunger due to a failed harvest.

As can be seen, then, convicts' experiences in Danish prisons worsened in times of general crisis. Other factors could affect their situation badly too. The *Trunken* prison cook was repeatedly accused of tinkering with the rations, apparently in order to skim a profit off of what he denied the convicts.[14] In 1726, desperation drove the deserter Jacob Kolberg to stab two other inmates, both of whom died. According to his own testimony, he simply hoped that he would be taken elsewhere and fed before his inevitable execution, as his hunger had become unbearable. Kolberg also explained that his fear of being flogged for having sold his clothes in order to buy food and drink had factored into his suicidal act as well.[15] The incident had been preceded by a conflict over food in which the prison wardens had withheld food as a punishment, apparently because the convicts had demanded a fairer share. Shortened rations were also a common way to punish escapees. The general low quality of the food was a recurring problem as well. In 1727, the convicts complained about the quality of the peas which led the cook to explain that sometimes the vegetables were of such a low quality that they simply could not be prepared in a satisfactory manner.[16]

Another push factor was the violence that was an integral part of this institution. Everyday punishments were not recorded, but in some cases we get glimpses. For instance, a runner in 1691 explained that he had been tormented by the prison warden. During one of the beatings, the warden had reportedly stated how he thought no differently about killing a convict than about drinking a glass of beer.[17] At least one warden in the period was murdered in revenge for his violence.[18]

Authorities were blunt about the fact that convicts suffered a terrible fate. In several trials, it was argued that convicts acted out of 'desperation and despair' in the face of 'prison and thraldom'.[19] Yet we should not see running as a blind reaction. Instead, we must tease out its social dynamics and the strategies involved.

How to escape early modern prison

Escaping early modern prison meant traversing several distinct *thresholds of confinement*. *Trunken* stood in the centre of the Bremerholmen dockyard complex and consisted of a large brick building with no windows. It was overseen by prison wardens who lived, with their families, in a house adjacent to the prison. Bremerholmen itself was also a sequestered space. It was the daily workplace of many of the navy's men and contained workshops and different worksites. While the sea closed off paths to freedom on one side, channels, walls and gates did so on the other – thresholds that were also to regulate the movements of the sailors with whom the convicts shared this workspace. Bremerholmen lay at the heart of Copenhagen, itself walled off and gated, in part to contain the soldiers in the city's garrisons. Finally, the sea around the island of Zealand constituted a natural, but also political, threshold which many of those who ran would attempt to violate as well. Thus, escape not only meant to escape the prison itself.

Because of the nature of such thresholds, preparations were key to a successful escape and only few escapes were truly spontaneous. This was especially true of those escapes that were collective. Just about one in two escapees (45.6 per cent) made it out with others. The largest groups that succeeded numbered five convicts. Attempts at running by larger groups did occur, but all failed before exiting the docks. For the same reason, they do not figure into the numbers presented above. Whether the groups were small or large, the very fact of having company was important. As remarked in a study of deserters, having 'a running-mate encouraged desertion because soldiers benefited from the companionship, and shared resources and advice offered by accomplices in an enterprise of considerable risk'.[20] The same can be said of prison breakers. Some even stuck together through several attempts, as was the case for two former soldiers, Christian Nieman and Hans Henrik Beck, who arrived in *Trunken* only five days apart in April 1709. Perhaps because both were new to the institution (as Gulliksen and Jørgensen had been), they formed a friendship before making two unsuccessful escapes together that autumn. They finally succeeded in what was their third attempt together two years later.[21] It was far from unusual that inmates who arrived around the same time bonded and subsequently ran together.

In the court martials of unsuccessful runners, we see faint, but constant imprints of the storytelling that premeditated their practices and formed an important step in the planning phase, especially as the convicts planned where to go and what to do upon escape. We must understand such planning as a transformative moment that also bound people together. Further, to those without local knowledge, the words of their fellow inmates were an invaluable source. Interestingly, an inmate's origin – either his place of birth or where he lived prior to his conviction – appears to have had no noteworthy influence on his propensity to run. Thus, knowledge of the surrounding area and beyond must have been widely dissimulated across different groups on the inside, as a lack of local knowledge would otherwise have been a deterrent for many. Unfortunately, there are no memoirs or diaries written by inmates in the period. However, at one point around 1620, Jon Olafsson was actually incarcerated for a month in a jail in Copenhagen and he even knew men who entered and escaped *Trunken*. He met men from all over the realm, many of whom are bound to have ended up in *Trunken*. His narrative shows how the incarcerated told stories to while away the time. While awaiting trial for having abandoned his duties as a guard, he bonded with another prisoner, Jørgen, a servant from Jutland, who 'had fallen into displeasure with his lord'. He was a great storyteller and entertained Olafsson with tales of 'remarkable happenings in Jutland amongst noble and humble men and women'. He was eventually sentenced to spend three years in *Trunken*. In this way, prisoners filled their time of incarceration with meaning. Another friend Olafsson made on the inside told him of his dreams, and Olafsson listened carefully. Dreams were thought to make predictions, so when Olafsson was going to trial, he asked the man what he had dreamt in order to interpret what awaited him. The man had dreamt that he and Olafsson had been free and feasted together; a happy omen which according to Olafsson came true when both were eventually released. Thus the bonds formed under confinement could live on beyond prison walls, as they also did on the *Havmanden*. Finally, Olafsson's narrative hints at how escape itself could become the subject of yarns, as he recounts how a third friend of his ingeniously managed to escape through the *Trunken* lavatories.[22] This was before a rebuilding of the prison in 1640 that was explicitly prompted by the great number of escapes.[23] He also related how he had heard of men having escaped the jail of *Blåtårn*, 'but only with the help of the devil'.[24]

An account by the convict Christian Larsen Kjær, who saw a host of different penal institutions from the inside in the early nineteenth century, confirms this soundscape of storytelling. He details how he bonded with many different 'brothers in misfortune' on the inside. The locus of such bonding was plans to escape, which was a constant theme in the discussions among the convicts. He even argues that they at times resorted to speaking German or even French among themselves so as to frustrate their guards' attempts at eavesdropping.[25] Kjær styled himself as a major escape artist, bragging how he tried his luck a total of nine times. Such self-fashioning testifies to how prison escape was imbued with a certain romanticism in the popular imagination. The fact that prison escape also features heavily in the writings of other nineteenth-century convicts who wrote their memoirs highlights this.[26] Unfortunately, a lack of accounts makes it difficult to determine if escape already had a romantic air to it before then, although Olafsson's account does hint this. So does the account about the privateer John Norcross, who was put in chains in the fortress of Copenhagen in 1726. An account written in Danish but based on Norcross' own account was published in Copenhagen in 1756. His story of adventure turns on the theme of escape many times, first during Norcross' life as a privateer in which capture was a constant threat, and later from the prison itself.[27] The book was popular enough to warrant another edition in 1786. Whether such accounts also flourished in oral storytelling is impossible to know, but it would not be surprising as prison breakers elsewhere in Europe certainly captured the popular imagination as well.[28]

There is, however, another even more important layer to Kjær's bragging about escapes in his memoir. Some of his stories about attempts actually turn out to relate escape attempts that he had not personally been involved in, but which he nevertheless relates as his own experiences. Some of those attempts had even happened about a decade before he personally arrived at the prison.[29] Thus, his narrative implicitly shows us how stories of escapes kept circulating on the inside of penal institutions as well as outside.

In Hamish Maxwell-Stewart's brilliant discussion of life in a nineteenth-century Tasmanian convict station, *Closing Hell's Gates,* he argued how 'the prisoners believed every little rumour that filtered back to circulate among their ranks'.[30] They needed the stories, because of the unfamiliar territory in which the convict station was placed. Escape hinged on knowledge, and as a collective they slowly built such knowledge, as escapees tested out routes then told their fellow inmates about them when caught. Thus, storytelling enabled emulation. Even the boat crews sent to catch the convicts in the hostile environment they attempted to traverse told stories which the convicts mined for useful knowledge. Like the convicts escaping life in *Trunken,* such escapes were planned and hinged on the circulation of knowledge. However, whereas the main obstacle facing runners who escaped into the rugged Tasmanian nature was how to eat, the main obstacle of those in Copenhagen's dense, urban environment was how to cross thresholds undetected.[31]

The many facets that needed preparation and were thus the subject of the discussions of the incarcerated reveal themselves as we consider how convicts violated the thresholds around them, and I will discuss these below. However, we should first mention one possible aid that also hinged on storytelling: magic. Convicts inside *Trunken* at times sought supernatural aid. In 1721, a convict and former soldier, Hans Georg Furchthammer, was executed for having written a letter to the Devil, hoping for money and satanic assistance in breaking out.[32] We will later see a similar plot among the convicts who escaped into St Thomas' forest.[33] As historian Tyge Krogh has shown, the act of writing to the Devil became a recurrent theme in trials against soldiers around 1700.[34] Several of the convicts in *Trunken* in the period were there because of such acts, and so it is unsurprising that it became a tool for convicts on the run as well. They knew of other such tricks as well. For instance, the soldier Johan Otto Berchelman was sentenced to *Trunken* after having been sent to prison for theft. From inside the jail, he convinced a woman to fetch him a Communion wafer as well as other ingredients necessary for him to make him and his accomplices invisible.[35] Invisibility magic was key to another case as well. In 1706, two convicts and a fisherman coerced into serving as a soldier at the fortress island of *Munkholmen* at Trondheim planned to make a joint escape attempt and head for Russia in a small boat. During the trial, it was reported that one of the convicts, Gudmund Møller, had planned how they were to take an old piece of neck cloth, tear it apart and throw it backwards over their heads during the escape in order that 'no one would then be able to catch them again'. Upon discovery, the two convicts were sent to *Trunken*.[36]

Storytelling was absolutely key to large-scale attempts at collective exit. Such cases highlight the need for preparation and collaboration. In the late 1720s and 1730s several such exits were attempted, involving an overlapping group of inmates. While these schemes involved a great degree of planning and concerted effort, they repeatedly failed because of informers. Structurally, they were very much akin to acts of mutiny: their plans were compromised by the spatial layout of *Trunken*, in which all the convicts lived and slept in large dormitories, just as they did on the lower decks of ships during Atlantic crossings. Like the lower deck, this dark, sequestered space had all too many ears. Thus, by necessity such attempts had to be agreed upon by all, or those who were not in agreement had to be paid off or intimidated into staying silent.

One night in early January 1730, a large group of convicts worked towards a collective exit by making a hole in the wall near the roof. (One of them was a former bricklayer, so he may well have come up with the plan.) They hoped to leave Copenhagen and get a boat near the village of Køge, to the south of the city. Managing to break down the wall, several of them climbed out, but were then forced to stay put because of a guard outside who stayed on his post the entire night. As morning came, they climbed back in and covered up the hole with clay. They evidently hoped to run the next night, but during the day the prison wardens made a search of *Trunken*, finding the exit.[37] Such searches were carried out weekly by the wardens who looked for instruments of escape or other illegalities. Several of those involved in this attempt were central to events when, in September of 1730, a large group of sixteen to eighteen convicts dug a pathway underneath the exit of *Trunken* using equipment stolen from a ship during their daily work at the docks. However, because the September nights were clear and bright they waited for the weather to turn 'dark and rainy', so that they could all make it out onto the docks without being spotted. Like the previous attempt, they hoped to find a boat and eventually make their way to Sweden. However, at some point their exit was also discovered by the wardens.[38]

An attempt made over the summer of 1732 was perhaps the most spectacular. It appears to have involved more or less all of the convicts in one of the prison's dorms. They planned to go underneath the building itself and managed to dig a tunnel that was forty feet long before they were discovered in the late summer.

They had been digging since Whitsun. The two former soldiers singled out as ringleaders had been key to the second attempt of 1730 as well. The most noteworthy thing about the plot, however, was their plans upon exiting the docks, which clearly hint at acts of storytelling in the long nights of preparation. Their sentence, which unfortunately is more or less all that is left of the plot stated that: 'exiting the city and reaching the fishing villages they wanted to take a vessel with force and, once at sea, to take the first vessel they came upon and then sail on.' This, the court summarized, was equal to a plan of 'murder', although we may call it piracy. The ringleaders were sentenced to death, and the rest to play dice to decide who would follow them, but the king stepped in and they were spared capital punishment, being required instead to live off bread and water for a year.[39] This might have prompted their next attempt. In October that same year, sailors heard the convicts murmur during their daily labour on the docks, saying that they wanted to make an act that would 'echo across the entire world'. Unfortunately, there is no archival trace of what this plan consisted of and if it differed from their previous fantasies of roving, as the convicts refused to disclose their plans when they were apprehended a few days later. The escape itself had consisted in a new attempt to break through the walls, apparently in the same place near the roof that they had attempted in 1730. However, this time they had failed in getting the hole big enough to get out before morning and had instead tried covering it up with old clothes. They had hoped that their very numbers would scare off the guards.[40]

A recurrent theme across these cases is the convicts' fears of informers. This is natural as such large-scale attempts were impossible to keep secret. They were right to be wary. The convict Mikkel Hummel, who gave away the first piratical plot of 1732, was released, apparently for his safety. As an encouragement for others to inform this worked, as the second plot that year was also revealed by a whistleblower. Of course, informing carried its own risks. After the escape attempts in early January 1730, two men suspected by the other convicts of having been 'traitors' were badly beaten up. Similarly, in March 1728, a convict was suspected by his fellows of having given them away during a breakout attempt. They threatened to hang or kill him, which prompted him to make a desperate attempt at distancing himself from his pursuers by loudly threatening to kill them in the presence of others, hoping that this would get him isolated in the small dungeon known as the 'black hole'.[41]

The difficulties of such a form of prison break mirror the difficulties of acts such as mutiny. However, escape became much easier if the convicts could exploit the fact that during the day, they were not inside *Trunken* itself. In such cases, successful escape did not depend upon the forming or agreement of large coalition. Smaller groups were much more viable as units of escape and many prisoners managed to make it out with some of those they worked with. Discussing escape among a smaller work crew meant running a smaller risk that someone might inform, in part because there were simply fewer ears to pick up what was exchanged, but also because working together forged bonds among them. Many escapes began while the men were working on the docks, thereby bypassing the difficulties of exiting a building. In this way, the character of the labour enabled escape. Yet having circumvented one threshold, the convicts still faced several others, not least having to evade the eyes of guards and wardens and finding a way out of the walled-off site. There were two ways to get off the docks: by land or by sea. The former was the most common. One method was to wander off during working hour and find a hiding place somewhere on the premises until night fell, then exit by climbing the walls in the darkness. But there were variations on this theme: for instance, bad weather could provide natural cover or opportunities by which to make a move, such as the hailstorm which in the summer of 1728 allowed two convicts to run as their guards sought cover.[42] Others managed to trick the guards. For instance, on Boxing Day 1691, Ole Baltersen saw his opportunity to sneak into the empty ropewalk where he managed to get out of his chains. He then crawled out of the window on the other side, at which point he encountered a guard whom he tricked by asking whether 'he had seen the escaped convict?'[43] Others exploited the drunkenness of guards overseeing their work.[44] Exiting the docks by sea was the other method. One possibility was to steal a boat, as did the deserters Cornelius Prunck and Rasmus Rasmussen in November 1707.[45] Very few appear to have swum across to Christianshavn on the other side, probably because of the weight of their chains. However, sometimes you could exit over sea by foot. Because of the cold winters of the early modern period, the waters often froze, opening up new avenues. This, however, could also prove fatal as the convict Jens Jensen learned, when on 16 December 1696 he tried his luck in escaping over the ice, but fell through and drowned.[46]

Of course, it was sometimes possible to bypass this threshold as well. Often convicts were taken outside of Bremerholmen to work. Sometimes groups of more than a dozen convicts would be under the supervision of a single warden or a few guards and because of the nature of their work, convicts would be dispersed across a given worksite. This gave frequent opportunities for escape, especially if the worksite had pathways unknown to the wardens. This was the case when four convicts ran while working in a large crew digging moats at the castle of Amalienborg in 1727. They were under the supervision of the warden and a small group of sailors, but still managed to escape through a hole in a fence by which they sat while eating their lunch.[47] The walk to and from worksites outside of Bremerholmen also provided an opportunity for many to escape.[48] Apparently, so as to hinder opportunities of escape while walking through the city, a 1732 resolution demanded that all convicts who were to labour outside of the docks were to be chained together in pairs while going to and from such sites.[49]

At some point during successful escape attempts, the convict had to lose his irons once he was out of prison as the next step – moving about and exiting Copenhagen – was predicated on camouflage. The irons were usually only a thin band around the waist connected via a chain to a smaller band below the knee. They were relatively light and functioned mostly as a visible marker of the convict's unfree state, because heavier irons would render the convict unproductive. However, they were effective in rendering convicts on the run easily identifiable, even if a few actually managed to exit the city gates by covering over their irons with clothes.[50] Because of their thinness, the irons could be removed by beating them with a rock for a while if the convict could find a safe place to do so. This was how convicts Johan Handers and Jens Pedersen Slagter managed to get rid of their chains when they ran from a worksite in August 1729. However, they were apprehended when trying to exit Copenhagen's gates because they had no passports. Slagter was also found to be in the possession of a skeleton key given to him before he arrived in *Trunken* by a horseman on Funen who had got it from a former inmate. Slagter 'planned to use them when he got out' in order to get the resources to go back to Lübeck, where his wife lived.[51]

Losing one's irons could be done quickly if they had been prepared in advance. Some filed them so thin as to be able to break them with their hands, while others loosened the rivets that kept the irons together or inserted fake wooden ones,[52] as was the case for several convicts brought before the court in October 1729. One of them excused himself by saying that he had broken the irons because he had been sick and swollen, while another plainly admitted that he had done so to facilitate his escape.[53] Such preparations allowed convicts to take advantage of any sudden opportunities. This was the case of deserter Jørgen Isenberg, who ran from the prison in August 1727. He had crafted a fake rivet, using a file that he claimed to have received from another convict who was then at large, and whom Isenberg expediently claimed had taken the instrument itself with him.[54]

Having exited the docks and lost their irons was not enough for convicts to attain their freedom. Almost all sought to leave Copenhagen as well, and for good reason. In modern terms, it was still a relatively small city and everyone knew of the 'slaves' on the docks. Several attempts failed because of civilians alerting the authorities, and in such cases the informers were paid a form of bounty from the convicts' fines. However, the biggest threats were the search teams headed by the prison wardens that accompanied each escape. As the wardens often fell under suspicion when convicts escaped, they appear to have made a great effort in catching those on the run. Exiting Copenhagen was thus pretty much essential for escapees.

In order to do so safely, one needed to be able to blend in with the crowd, but also to be able to mask one's identity. The gates were guarded and the guards were obliged to check the documents of those entering and exiting. Though some convicts did manage to exit the gates without being asked for their papers, most did not want to try their luck. Passports could be obtained through many different means, but sometimes forgery was the easiest. Questioned before the Admiralty Court on why he had assisted five of his fellow convicts in escaping prison in this way, convict Abraham Bølge explained that he had only followed Solomon's proverb: 'rescue those who are being led to death.' Of course, Bølge's wayward religious sentiment had a hollow ring to the men interrogating him; he was a former soldier who had deserted in the summer of 1721, making his way to Sweden. Blind drunk, he sat under a bright night sky when he made a small cut in the middle finger of his left hand. With the blood as his ink, he wrote a letter to the Devil in which he promised his 'body and soul' if the Devil would deliver him 500 Rix-dollars and ten years to spend them before his damnation. When he was later apprehended, the letter was found among his belongings. With his back still bloody from the executioner's whip, he was shackled and put to hard labour. A year and a half later, in the summer of 1723, he was revealed by another inmate (who was afterwards beaten up by a gang of inmates) to have forged passports using a stolen seal given to him by a man who had long since escaped. Three fake passports in Bølge's hand were presented as damning evidence. Defiant, he proclaimed to the Admiralty officials that a convict was 'like the bird in the cage: seeking the open sky'. His offence merited that he should have his right hand cut off, but out of mercy (and so as to not render him unproductive) only his thumb was severed. Bølge spent almost two decades in chains, before managing to escape it on 21 January 1740.[55]

Another forgery plot was discovered in late February of 1729 when a group of convicts centred around a German, former sailor Johan Schwartz, committed an act of theft inside the prison. Because Schwartz was a Roman Catholic, he did not attend sermons on Sundays, and instead he used the occasion to break into the attic where some confiscated goods (from the case of large-scale theft discussed in the previous chapter) were being held. He gave some of them, mostly clothes, to other convicts and some to the wife of a convict during one of her visits. Convict wives were not supposed to be allowed on the premises, but several cases show that this happened frequently anyway. The woman in question then sold the clothes around town. Word spread, so the group 'deliberated amongst themselves' and decided that two of them should escape in order to 'take on the blame'. One was Jørgen Isenberg, already introduced above. The other was a German soldier, Arnold Wilhem Osenberg, who seems to have been high in the internal hierarchy among the convicts as, on another occasion, he was found guilty of holding court over a thief caught among the convicts themselves. Osenberg had run before, an attempt that ended when he let himself be recruited by a regiment in Slagelse on Western Zealand, on which occasion an officer described him as 'quite tall, with long brown hair'.[56] Osenberg and Isenberg both had ample clothes, so they thought they would stand a decent chance in the winter cold. They were then assisted by Henrik Seeman, a thief who had also broken out of his jail during the trial. Seeman fashioned two passports, forging the signature of the Admiral and marking them with a fake seal crafted out of a small piece of lead by a now dead convict and former goldsmith. A few days later, while working away from the docks, the two managed to hide in a hideout fashioned on the worksite by a third convict. As Osenberg detailed during his interrogation, the hideout was not meant to be used for escape 'until the summer'. Having gotten away, they took off their prison garments and walked across the ice to Christianshavn. The next step was to find the woman who had acted as the group's 'fence'. However, they could not find her house, and soon they were apprehended by a guard alerted by two women who had spotted the convicts searching the street where their helper was supposed to live.[57] Both of these forgery cases reveal glimpses of social dynamics on the inside and we can almost, but not quite, hear their deliberations.

Exiting the gates, the convicts needed to get far enough that rumour would not circulate back to Copenhagen. On 18 May 1718, two convicts ran from the prison warden overseeing their work at the docks. The warden was arrested on suspicion of collusion, but when the convicts were spotted near Copenhagen, he was released in order to join the hunt for them. An innkeeper could identify the two based on account of a description of their clothes, as they had been drinking in his establishment. He gave further hints as to where they had gone. Eventually, the warden found out that the two had stayed with the father of one of the convicts who was a farmer in Nørre Jernløse, a small village in central Zealand, quite some distance from Copenhagen. The warden then went there to find the missing convicts. Confronting the father, matters escalated as the warden wanted him arrested, but was then chased away by the men of the village. The only achievement resulting from his efforts was an attestation from the bailiff of Nørre Jernløse that he had done all he could, but this was enough to win him back his trust with his superiors.[58] Both convicts were later apprehended elsewhere. One of them, Niels Larsen, a deserter who had previously been in *Trunken* before being forcibly recruited into the army because of the manpower shortages of the Great Northern War, managed to stay at large for six years (during which time he let himself be recruited to the army once again). He deserted once more, taking up work as an agricultural labourer before he was caught poaching in 1724.[59]

For those escapees finding themselves on the run in Zealand, a problem quickly arose: how could they sustain themselves without their cover being blown? Many fell back into a life of crime, and were often caught again as a result. Begging was another common strategy, but this too posed a risk because statutes against vagrancy meant that only people who were authorized to beg were allowed to do so. Thus, it could draw unwanted attention. Getting a job was more tenable. Larsen was far from alone in becoming an agricultural labourer. Another example is the case of Anders Jensen Amager, a thief who ran with two other men from the docks in February 1737. During their escape, they lost track of each other and Amager ended up in the town of Ringsted, where he got a job on a farm. He told a cover story of being from Copenhagen, but having no friends. At one point, fearing he would be conscripted, he moved on to another town, Husum, where he found several other jobs. His last gig, however, entailed him repeatedly driving a cart to and from Copenhagen, prompting him to leave for fear of being recognized. Instead, he wanted to go to his native island of Amager where his sister lived, but he was caught stealing en route.[60]

For many, and for former soldiers especially, the military labour market provided another option while on the run. I have already noted several examples of convicts being revealed as they let themselves be recruited at garrisons around Zealand. The military labour market was driven by fierce demand. Often recruitment hinged on coercion, as the ever-growing European armies' insatiable demand for personnel had no 'respect to the actual supply on the labour market'.[61] Vagrants and petty criminals were common targets for recruiters. Similarly aggressive recruitment is known to have been common in German cities, where many of the mercenary soldiers who ended up in *Trunken* had come from. In a similar vein, the archive of *Trunken* reveals examples of offenders being impressed into the army at the behest of officers. However, even what we might consider 'regular' recruitment hinged on predatory strategies that often involved large amounts of alcohol. In turn, this demand also explains the opportunities the military labour market provided not only for prison breakers, but also for deserters. For instance, foreign deserters could let themselves be recruited into the Danish army, thus substituting one master for another, and putting a little money in their pocket along the way. This was the case with Swedish deserters who fled from Sweden to Copenhagen, where they were often recruited directly into the Danish army or navy. The same was evident in the German cities where there existed a highly international labour market for military recruits. In such places, deserters could always find someone willing to take them on.[62]

In this way, the practices of many prison breakers mimicked that of bounty jumping among deserters. Unsurprisingly, we find many cases in which former deserters (often Germans) let themselves be recruited upon breaking prison. For instance, Johan Henrich Henschen, who was among the four who ran while digging moats at Amalienborg mentioned above, found himself roaming Zealand. The prisoners' escape had been planned, and Henschen had taken precautions by buying a shirt from a woman on the street while working so that he could quickly change his appearance. During the escape, he wore it under his regular clothes, which he shed as soon as they got out of sight. First they went north, staying in a forest near a village south of Elsinore. Their plan was to find a boat to go to Sweden, but in their attempt to steal one they were spotted by a pack of dogs whose barking alerted the farmers in the village. The villagers chased them and Henschen lost contact with the others. Over the following week, he walked across Zealand to the city of Slagelse, where he pretended to be a shoemaker journeyman and joined the Cuirassier regiment stationed there before being identified. He later made several other escape attempts.[63] Thus, the military labour market offered an opportunity, but also posed a considerable risk of discovery. This might explain the differences in success rates across different groups of runners among the convicts: the success rate of former deserters was only 63.8 percent, far lower than that of any of the other groups discussed, while prison breakers with a civilian background had a success rate as high as 83.3 percent. The tendency of ex-military prison breakers to seek employment in the military partly explains this discrepancy, but it was probably also influenced by the fact that many ex-military convicts were foreigners and lacked a personal network that might facilitate hiding.

A recurrent theme in the cases of convicts who roamed around Zealand is their fear of discovery. Being on the run was to live in a state of anxiety and often entailed roaming from one place to another. During his first escape Osenberg had first let himself be recruited at Tryggevælde, but left after seven weeks because he sensed that somebody in the regiment knew who he was. He deserted and let himself be recruited somewhere else instead.[64] Much greater anonymity was offered if the prison breaker was able to leave the island of Zealand or even the country altogether. However, doing so was not easy, as demonstrated by the case of Henschen. In part the difficulty was due to the fact that this route was also an intrinsic part of the rival geography of desertion. After the treaty of Roskilde in 1658 when Denmark lost Scania, Sweden was temptingly close. It offered not only freedom, but also a competing military labour market. All you needed was to cross the slender body of water known as the Sound (*Øresund*). This made authorities take pre-emptive measures, which subsequently came to frustrate prison breakers. For example, ships were regularly posted in the Sound for the express purpose of keeping lookout for deserters. It was also illegal for anyone to ferry passengers without them showing a passport or documents from an employer, and fishermen along the coast were demanded by law to chain up their vessels at night and to remove the oars.[65]

Despite such measures, many still succeeded in crossing the narrow strait. There were many ways of doing so. As noted above, because of the general cold climate of the period, the sea froze at points during some winters. In such instances patrols were posted on the ice, but it was impossible to keep people from crossing. This pathway helps explain a seasonal pattern among prison breakers. Thus, most (about 38 percent) ran during summer, likely because the prospects of sleeping outside were much less grim; December, on the other hand, has the fewest numbers of escapees. That said, the number then spikes in January, making it the third most popular month for escapes. Escape bids then remain relatively frequent in February. In fact, we know that the January that saw most escapes, January 1726, was a particularly cold one.[66] A similar seasonal pattern existed among deserters.[67] Those who were not lucky enough to get assistance from the environment could sometimes get a helping hand in other ways. For instance, in January 1729, four fishermen arrived in *Trunken* for having transported deserters to Sweden. During their trial, it was revealed that one of them had ferried more than forty men in this way, while it was reported that another had helped ferry runaway convicts along the same route.[68] During their incarceration, the four men met two other fishermen, a set of brothers from a village just north of Copenhagen, sentenced for the same transgression in April 1730. Just a few months later, the brothers managed to escape when a sailor overseeing their labour decided to take them drinking – a practice discussed in the previous chapter. In the tavern, they met with their wives and took off, never to be heard of again. The sailor, however, was incarcerated in their stead.[69]

Foreign shores offered freedom. For those who were caught, it was another story. Beatings and floggings were common punishments, as were fines to be paid off by prolonged periods of nothing but bread and water. Short stints in the 'black hole' were another measure. Many were put in heavier irons and some chained together in pairs. Interestingly, we only see one instance in which a runner was sentenced to death and did not receive pardon – a case in which the convict had also assaulted the warden. This is curious as a 1673 statute against those who broke out of the king's prisons actually called for death sentences for prison breakers.[70] Thus, while executions were often called for in court, they rarely occurred in practice.[71] Finally, many runners were selected for transportation elsewhere. In the 1720s and 30s particular troublemakers were among those sent to the naval fortress at the island of Christiansø in the Baltic, perhaps because the island was thought inescapable. However, despite its isolation, convicts also tried running from there, stealing boats or arranging to be picked up and moved elsewhere. One such plot was uncovered in 1734 and involved all of the about one dozen convicts on the island. They had discussed their plans during their daily work, which consisted of breaking rocks. The plot even involved the prison warden, himself a former convict. Somehow, they arranged for a boat to arrive from the larger island of Bornholm to pick them up. The plan was that they should kill the guards and hide out among the rocks. The exit was prepared, but for some reason the plan never materialized. A similar plan was hatched the next year, and involved killing the guards and stealing vessels.[72]

Other convicts who became part of centripetal flows plotted their escapes as well: even more remotely, the group of the twenty-four convicts sent to labour in a colonial outpost in Greenland in 1728 as a one-off experiment in convict transportation to this arctic location made plans to run away and join Dutch fishing vessels.[73] Most importantly, in the context of this book, many of those who actually made it to St Thomas tried their luck as well. They were faced with the difficult task of violating the spatial confines of the island itself – a challenge they shared with other groups of subalterns.

Escaping colonial bondage

Practices of running were widespread among enslaved and indentured workers in the Caribbean. In smaller colonies like St Thomas, viable escapes relied on finding maritime routes to other islands. The practices of maritime marronage of the enslaved Africans in the Danish West Indies have been discussed at length in a groundbreaking essay by Neville Hall. These traditions developed as the island became increasingly deforested over the first decades of the colony. The primary destination was Puerto Rico to the west.[74] Searching through the archives, I have found what might be the men who inaugurated this tradition. This was a group of three enslaved who sought to go to Puerto Rico 'to get fish and other things to eat' in October 1673. They might have known of this destination because one of them was not of African, but rather of local descent. He was called Jan Indian and had been the author of the plot. Punishments were different for the enslaved, so Jan Indian became the first of many to have a leg cut off for seeking his freedom.[75]

Maritime escape hinged on vessels. They could be stolen or built. Rafts were the preferred means of escape for the enslaved. Various governors repeatedly sought to limit their labourers' access to vessels. It was forbidden to own a canoe or vessel if one was not able to pay the potential damages. It was also forbidden to cut down trees that might be turned into rafts.[76] This did not successfully hinder such attempts. For instance, a group of enslaved Africans ran away from a plantation during a summer night in 1680. They had secretly gathered materials for a raft, which they unfortunately had to abandon when their owner went running after them. With no way of getting off the island, they were caught and revealed to have co-conspirators on other plantations.[77] As discussed in Chapter 1, Iversen harboured intense fears about such maroons – anxieties based on rumours from English colonies.

While we never find enslaved Africans and coerced European labourers running together, their practices show a close kinship. Convicts, indentured servants, sailors and soldiers tested the same routes that Hall describes for the enslaved in the eighteenth century. They did so from the beginning. As early as June 1672, only a few months after the arrival of the first ship, two convicts who had been taken on in Norway as well as two Danish indentured servants ran away in a Company boat. Their plan is unclear, but they brought stolen muskets, an axe and a pot with them.[78] They went to St Croix to the south. According to testimonies, the idea of running had been proposed by a convict by the name of Henrik Henriksen, who had come from *Trunken*.[79] The two indentured servants were later apprehended under unknown circumstances, having been gone for two and a half and four months respectively. They became subject to the first trials in the colony.[80] In order to deter others from following their example, the code that Iversen had in the interim proclaimed dictated the punishment of added time in servitude. This time was calculated on the basis of the time absent. Other measures were meant to deter running as well. Masters were also allowed to put any servant who ran away in irons 'until he gives up his evil habit'. This law hints how indentured servants were only a misstep away from becoming indistinguishable from the convicts. Any escapee, whatever rank, was explicitly defined as an 'outlaw'.[81] Runaway convicts appear to have been in an even more precarious situation; for instance, planters were given the freedom to 'break the arms and legs' of convicts found on plantations.[82] The fine for housing escapees was the steep sum of 1,000 pounds of sugar and all ships that left the harbour were to be searched for stowaway workers.[83] Continuing through the 1670s, such anxious escalation of measures read as a sign of the vulnerability of the colony, whose authorities desperately needed labourers, but saw them die in throngs. However, no matter what he did, Iversen's letters, discussed in the first chapter, demonstrate vividly that it did not stop attempts at running on the parts of servants and convicts – the latter as indomitable on St Thomas as they were in Copenhagen.[84]

As was the case in *Trunken*, the nature of the labour enabled escape. While convicts slept in a locked-up house, not completely unlike *Trunken*, they laboured outside during the day. The tasks they were put to allowed them to scout the island. Some jobs, such as fishing, even allowed them to scout neighbouring islands, many of which were abandoned. Yet inspiration and knowledge might also have come from outside. The enslaved labourers imported by planters from other islands in the region brought Caribbean traditions and knowledges with them. Foreign sailors were another source of knowledge, as were runners from other colonies. From its beginning as a Danish colony, St Thomas was a destination for such people. Iversen appears to have used these runners as leverage in order to foster good relations with his neighbours by apprehending them. So, for instance, when in 1674 five sailors and two enslaved men arrived without a passport in a vessel, they were interrogated and found to have been in the service of a master from Barbados, having run due to maltreatment. The vessel and the enslaved Africans were then returned to the English at Nevis, while Iversen sentenced the rest of the escapees to penal labour at the fort.[85] However, in the period from 1680 to 1684, when St Thomas became an open port, it became a magnet for runaways from elsewhere, many of whom joined pirate crews (discussed at length in the next chapter). This might very well have enabled the circulation of knowledge about routes and destinations.

A piece of evidence from a case concerning a small-scale mutiny at the fortress of Christiansværn (on Danish St Croix) in June 1751 provides an illustration of how knowledge of destinations was passed along in the form of everyday storytelling among colonial workers. The mutiny – resulting in about a score of soldiers laying down their arms in a refusal to work – had been triggered by events transpiring months earlier when a soldier had been drinking with a sergeant in an inn. There the soldier had spoken of how life on nearby Puerto Rico was so much better than the conditions experienced by the soldiers in the Danish colony. The soldier had first-hand knowledge of this due to his former employment as a sailor. This piece of information seems to have sparked the imagination of the sergeant, who then tried to bring others into the plot. According to his own testimony, he had done so in order to test to the soldiers' loyalty, but his superiors were not convinced and he was jailed briefly. Upon release, he faced further problems due to rumours that he had been informing on the soldiers in his testimony, and the situation was aggravated still further by whispers that he had been heard threatening to avenge himself on them. It was this that prompted them to mutiny, in what essentially looks like a protest against him for having broken their trust. The case ended in one of the mutineers being banished and two others being flogged.[86]

Soldiers tried to escape in the early decades of the colony as well. For instance, a group of eight soldiers ran away in a Company vessel in August 1684. One of these eight was later returned to St Thomas, where he was pardoned. This plot is very likely to have been a source of inspiration for the most dramatic instance of convict escape from the colony which transpired in the late summer and autumn of 1686. Involved in that plot were two soldiers who had worked side by side with the pardoned soldier of the 1684 plot. However, the idea of running seems to have come initially from a group of convicts transported from *Trunken* to the colony. They had arrived as a group of about thirty felons in the spring of 1686 on the ship *Fortuna* – the first larger vessel to reach the colony after the *Havmanden* mutiny. This was in fact the last major contingent of convicts sent by the Company to the colony. Incidentally, the case against these escapees after they had tried to escape was the cause of deep concern for the governor, resulting in a paper trail that allows us to trace it in more detail than any other escape attempt by convicts in the Danish empire. Thus, it seems fitting to end this chapter's exploration of the processes of escape and their similarities with the mutiny by seeing how the men and women who actually arrived in the colony struggled to escape it.

The plan seems to have been conceived during a trip in the Company canoe harvesting salt. On 30 July 1686, the Dutch skipper at St Thomas had been ordered to take a group of male convicts to harvest salt from the natural salt ponds on a small uninhabited island located to the east of the abandoned St John. On 3 August they returned.[87] During their stay on the small island, a man named Jens Pedersen, a cattle thief from Falster, had approached the others, detailing a plot which involved getting one of them to steal a spike from the Company storehouse. This step was needed because Pedersen's wife, Mette Nielsdatter (who had been sent to St Thomas along with her convict husband), was locked up in the fort jail for having stolen some cotton, and Pedersen clearly wanted to break her out first.[88]

In the days following their return, Pedersen approached several other convicts as well. A fellow criminal, Peder Vognmand, who seems to have been Pedersen's friend, aided him as he tried to persuade others to join him. The two later covered for each other in the interrogations, despite being tortured with thumbscrews.[89] Vognmand's background is ultimately untraceable in the archive, as Vognmand was not his real name, but there is a good chance that he was the man whom the convict muster dubs 'Peder Nelausen', in which case he was also a thief, and had in fact escaped from *Trunken* on a previous occasion.[90] The two appear to have formed the original core of the collective which they now sought to expand. Some of those they approached seem to have turned the plan down, but a handful agreed to it. The two soldiers mentioned above, Søren Islænder and Niels Krog, also became part of the plan at this stage. Reportedly, Islænder had complained that they 'were young people, but were like convicts here', poignantly expressing the hardships of colonial servitude and the solidarities it could foster. Islænder and Krog were the ones to come up with the plan of stealing guns from the fort to aid them after the escape. The arms were located in a room where the constable slept, but the soldiers assured the others 'that you can take him in his hammock and carry him out, and he would still be sound asleep'.[91] The soldiers were key to another aspect as well. Approached by Pedersen, one of the convicts had some reservations about the plan because the gang lacked provisions to sustain them on the run. Pedersen reassured him that they would break into the storehouse next to the fort while the two soldiers were on guard duty. This was carried out on the night of 12 August. They wanted to steal a sloop one of the following nights in order to disappear into the complex Caribbean geography that they had studied during their trips fishing and harvesting salt.[92]

By then, however, the plan had already been compromised. Pedersen had been placed in the jail at the fort with his wife. It had been 'rumoured that he and a group of the other convicts were committed to running away'.[93] Thus, like the men in *Trunken* or those of the second mutiny on the *Havmanden*, the convicts were frustrated by informers as they had sought to expand their group. On the thirteenth, the colony's governor, Christopher Heins, gathered his council and had the convicts brought before them. It was an extensive case, involving many interrogations, which forced the council to reconvene three days later. Due to the statements given by their fellow convicts, Pedersen and Vognmand were found to be the ringleaders of the plot. As punishment for their planning, both were to be flogged and branded by the executioner before being shackled together and sent to work among the enslaved Africans on the Company plantation. A long drought had dried up the countryside, but rain in early August made the governor eager to put people to work, first and foremost in producing foodstuff. Thus, starvation might have been the immediate reason for their running, but also for the particular sentence they received.[94] The rest of the convicts involved were sentenced to be 'sold, to get the company the most and best profit, to some other nation, so that one can get rid of such roguish and loose people'.[95]

The two soldiers involved in the plans were not in court on 16 August. The previous night, they had managed to break free of their bolts with a large knife and to exit the dungeon in which they had been kept.[96] The guards probably turned a blind eye when the two climbed wall of the fort before heading into the colony's primeval forests, which at this point still offered temporary cover for runaways. In contrast to the previous plan to move east, they hoped to build their own raft and use it to go west to Puerto Rico – the route used most often by the enslaved workers. However, the two soldiers had no tools to cut down the trees needed. A few nights later, they broke into the house of the Company cooper but found nothing of use. During this period, they kept going by stealing foodstuffs from plantations. At one point, they were spotted, but got away.[97] Pushed to extremes, they flirted with a more dramatic plan. Later, in court, Islænder revealed: 'that some days after they had run away, Niels Krog had said to him that he should give himself over to the evil man and walk into the bushes, curse and swear, then the Devil would appear and help them [go] away from this country'. Krog did not deny making this suggestion but put the blame on his companion, whom he said had proposed it at a time when they 'saw no other way out'. In the woods, he had exclaimed how: 'by God I wish I had ink and paper. Then I would write a contract and leave it, and after that the evil Spirit will come. He is such a crook that when you need him he will not be there, but when you don't want him there, he will come all the faster.'[98] Not receiving any such supernatural aid, Islænder was apprehended on 27 August while Krog stayed free for another ten days before being brought to the fort. They were then sentenced to be bolted together and to join the convicts Pedersen and Vognmand at the Company plantation, where they worked in chains for three years.[99]

However, by this point, the governor had become uneasy. Heins had arrived in the colony with Blom's first voyage in the spring of 1681 and had served as the Company's lieutenant for five years, before being chosen to serve as governor by a naval commissioner, a man called Mikkel Mikkelsen, who had arrived in St Thomas in the spring of 1686, along with the convicts discussed here. Mikkelsen (who had also been the judge in the case against the mutineers of the *Havmanden*) had been sent to regain control of the island, whose spinning out of control is discussed at length in the next chapter. He had achieved some order among the unruly planters and servants before leaving the colony in Heins' care in June. Heins was the first truly 'Company' man to serve in the role since Iversen. His inexperience, however, explains why he appears unsure of his mandate in the case of the runaways. In early October, he sent a letter to the directors in Copenhagen, in which he described the whole process. The punishments of Pedersen and Vognmand had been 'well-deserved', while the punishments of Krog and Islænder were more problematic, in spite of the fact that they had actually deserted and had even contemplated Satanic magic, whereas the convicts had only planned to run. Heins described how the two had broken out of their bolts and had jumped over the fort wall, and he argued that because of the severity of this, they had to be punished. Yet Heins wished that the directors would reduce their sentences because of their youth and because 'both are supposedly of good people'. Thus, the inexperienced governor wanted them to be pardoned, but had not dared to do so himself.[100]

His anxieties, however, should not be attributed to him alone. Instead they can be interpreted as the product of stories told by these subalterns themselves. The day after Krog and Islænder had been sentenced to work on the plantation, the governor had sent his clerk to investigate who the two soldiers were, how they 'had gotten here' and especially if they were 'free or unfree'?[101] Likely, these questions had arisen the day before when the governor had heard the two soldiers tell fragments of their life stories in court. Islænder had explained to the council that he was twenty-five years old and had been born in Rotterdam, while Krog had told how 'his father was an official in the Meddelsom district court' in Jutland, adding that he was only eighteen years old.[102] This tale of youth and a background among honest people seems to have prompted the need for clarification – no such questions were asked of the convicts, whose scarred faces and backs revealed traces of the thief's marks that told everything Heins needed to know. Krog and Islænder seemed to merit more careful attention. The next day, Krog told the clerk that he had been a soldier and was innocent, but that: 'his master Colonel von Plessen had placed him on Bremerholmen [shorthand for the naval dockyard, but also for its prison], and because he would no longer serve him, he had given 20 Rix-dollars for his provisions going here with the ship Fortuna. Mr. Gyldensparre [one of the Company directors] had supposedly met him and promised him that he would be brought back home with the ship and be given free provisions at the fort.' Islænder also presented a tale of coercion. He told a story of indenture sliding into something more akin to bondage: 'he had been promised a spot on the plantation of the heirs of the former governor [Iversen] or to be employed in another good service, but upon arrival the commissioner [Mikkelsen] had forced them to become soldiers and given them each a musket on their backs.'[103] This tale of coercive labour relations resonates with the initial report given in the first interrogations in which it was said that Islænder had joined in the original desertion plot because he found conditions as a Company soldier equivalent to being a convict.

Krog and Islænder were crafting stories about the injustices faced by lower-class subjects. They were doing so in a context of uncertainty about their status. Both presented narratives of subterfuge and coercion in the Atlantic labour market, yet while articulating the deeply oppressive nature of colonial recruitment, the two were also, in a sense, manipulating the truth. To Krog in particular, this whole situation presented an opportunity of which he seems to have been keenly aware. Searching through the Admiralty archives, I have found a sentence of Krog's that reveals him to have been lying. While he had indeed been a soldier, he had actually stabbed another man and had been sentenced to death in a court martial as a result. As this happened while the Company was preparing Mikkelsen's dispatch to St Thomas, the sentence had then been commuted to transportation by the king.[104] No branding or other dishonouring form of physical injury had been part of the sentence. Thus, when confronted with the telling question whether he was free or not, Krog had seen and seized his chance to escape his past through storytelling. Thus, his tale about being tricked into Atlantic bondage played off the truths of labour relations in the Atlantic in order to escape a different tale.

Krog was exploiting a deficiency in the colonial knowledge circulation regarding convicts. Elites in the Admiralty knew their convict labourers from the documents in the clerk's archive, but the Company did not receive copies of these sentences when convicts were transferred into their hands. In theory, they received paperwork only for those who carried life sentences, and therefore no more knowledge was needed; they were to work in the colony until they died. Further, the convict musters detailing felons' names were often incomplete.[105] Had Krog figured on such a list, it would have been enough to give his background away. However, he did not, as he had arrived only after the paperwork had been completed. This was common; for instance, Gulliksen did not feature in the convict muster for the *Havmanden*, as he had also been sentenced only after the muster had been completed, while the ship waited for embarkation. Like Gulliksen, Krog had arrived just days before embarkation and therefore his name was nowhere to be found in the documents later received by the governor. At some point, it appears to have been decided by the leader of the voyage taking him across the Atlantic (commissioner Mikkelsen, who by October was back in Copenhagen) that Krog was to be deployed as a soldier. Thus, because of a lack of visual markers of dishonour as well as a lack of documentation, Krog effectively changed status. It was this change that was confirmed by the clerk's revealing question about his freedom. The loophole allowed him to tell another story and present another identity to the inquisitive authorities.

While the words of the other convicts seem to have carried no weight, Krog was heard and his speech recorded at length precisely because he fashioned himself not as a convict non-subject bereft of social standing, but rather as a free man whose subject-status was threatened by the coercion and dishonour that made convicts ideal colonial labourers. It was a lie tailored to the situation. Asked why they had broken out of the fort jail, he gave a detailed story, explaining how: 'the other soldier Søren Islænder had cried and complained strongly, saying that he took it much to heart that he who was of honest parents and had done nothing evil, was to be held captive and imprisoned.' Further, Islænder had said that: 'it was certain that one of them would be hanged, and the other flogged under the gallows. Therefore, they both resolved to do their utmost to break out and thereby escape and run away.'[106] This short narrative appears strategic in every facet. The soldiers must have known full well that they had not been in danger of execution, as they knew people who had run before but nonetheless been pardoned. So the remark that they feared the death penalty serves both to show their respect for the power of the authorities but also, in a subtler way, to underline Krog's portrayal of youthful ignorance. The real threat that faced them was a loss of honour. The story invokes this stigma powerfully by underlining that the two were of 'honest parents'. Had Heins known that Krog was a convict, such a narrative would not given him pause for thought.[107]

Of course, having provoked anxiety was not enough for Krog. He had hoped to talk his way out of irons altogether. While his performance eventually did save him and Islænder from punishment (as I will discuss briefly), it did not give them the pardon they must have been eyeing up. Instead, on 25 September, the two soldiers joined up with the two convicts on the Company plantation, chained together. However, they would soon attain a degree of freedom. It had only taken Pedersen and Vognmand a handful of days to break their irons in a way 'so that at night they can be free, and again in the day take them back on'.[108] We have already seen such manipulations among the convicts in *Trunken*. On St Thomas, it allowed them to venture into town at night in order to steal food and other things.[109] Thus, they made several raids on Company stores, hiding their plunder under a destroyed canoe in an old shed on the plantation. Pedersen's wife Mette Nielsdatter had been released after the trial in August so she contributed to these nightly expeditions by acting as their spy.[110] It was she who spotted the old canoe that lay abandoned by the Company sergeant's house. On 5 November, the five broke into the smithy and stole various tools.[111] The next night, they carried out their escape. Under the cover of darkness, Islænder left the plantation, lugging their stolen provisions to a small bay to the south west. Meanwhile, Vognmand, Pedersen and Krog met up with Nielsdatter near the fort and stole the canoe, then picked up Islænder and escaped into the night.[112]

Unfortunately, the party was apprehended only a few days later, when the skipper was ordered to take a mixed group of workers fishing.[113] The canoe gave them away. It was spotted on a small island between St Thomas and St John. The escapees had tried to head for St John, but had not progressed that far, possibly because the canoe was simply unable to hold them all safely at sea. The weather may also have been rough. Later in court, it was claimed that they wanted to go to St John and then onwards to some Caribbean port in order to make their return to Europe. This rather innocuous story might have been offered to gloss over other intentions. When the skipper discovered the search party, they hid in the bushes on the island. It took two trips to apprehend them all, and even then Pedersen managed to escape, apparently by swimming back to St Thomas. Eventually even he was apprehended.[114] On 16 November they were all back before Heins' council. Prompted to explain the reasoning behind their actions, Islænder answered 'because he had suffered so much pain from prison, work and hunger'. He was given only a little cassava 'which he could not possibly live on'. Vognmand echoed his story: 'because they had endured much evil from prison and hunger.' Krog joined in: 'because of hard prison and hunger which he like the others had suffered.' Lastly, Jens Pedersen 'answered like the rest of them from hunger and the coercion of prison'.[115] It appears that they had rehearsed and coordinated their answers, perhaps so as to avoid the kind of contradictions Krog and Islænder had been caught in, regarding their Faustian plan earlier that autumn. Yet even though they appear strategic these words powerfully articulate the conditions of convicts everywhere in the Danish empire and what pushed them to flee.[116]

As had been the case in the first trial in August, Jens Pedersen was convicted of being the ringleader. The council decided to follow the letter of the law and to execute him, along with Vognmand. Again, the lives of Krog and Islænder were spared. They were sentenced to flogging by the gallows and then to be banished from the colony. However, Heins then spared them these punishments as well 'because of others' intercession' so that 'their honour was saved'.[117] This concern can only be interpreted as a reaction to Krog's masterful camouflage and storytelling performance. In stark contrast, Mette Nielsdatter was not spared the flogging and was even sentenced to be branded as well. As the wife of a dishonoured convict, her status as a subject was already compromised. This extensive ritual of spectacular punishment, dishonour and death was to be carried out on 19 November. The night before, however, the executioner, a black enslaved man, ran away. In need of someone to perform the ultimate sanction, Heins then gave Vognmand a startling choice: accept a conditional pardon to become the executioner and kill your friend, or die. The next day, Vognmand placed the noose around the neck of his friend Pedersen and hung him from the gallows outside the fort.

In many ways, demonstrated perhaps by this case in particular, but also by the multitude of cases in the Admiralty archives regarding *Trunken*'s inmates, failure is the condition of examining convicts' escapes. Yet there is one last fragment to this story – an act of flight that we know only a little about. It turns out that Vognmand had a final victory in his brutal quest for freedom. He served as hangman without notice until 6 August 1687 when a journal kept at the fort notes: 'Tonight the executioner Peder Vognmand, Svend Madsen who looks after the horses and Albrecht Olsen who was on the bark have run away from the harbour in a boat belonging to the noble company. They went together and took the jib with them as a sail.'[118] Thus, like the 223 men who escaped *Trunken* without getting caught and the handful of other convicts who successfully escaped St Thomas, Vognmand finally became unknowable.

* * *

Against the backdrop of all of these acts, some of them quite dramatic, the seizing of the *Havmanden* stands not as an isolated anomaly of convict resistance (just as the sailors' involvement in collective resistance was no anomaly either) but rather as the most spectacular moment in a long series of struggles for freedom that challenged confines everywhere in the Danish-Norwegian empire. Making off with an entire ship was a plan that involved an act of piracy, as did several of the other plots discussed here. It succeeded in the short term, but ultimately failed, crystallizing a greater history of convict resistance fought over and over again as the early modern state attempted to exploit the labour of the convicted – and usually succeeded. Whenever we find convicts labouring, we find them testing their chains – often collectively.

Such practices rested on solidarities formed in the face of brutal exploitation, but also on context-dependent knowledge gathered through trial and error or plucked from the stories that were disseminated inside prisons, below deck or on plantations. They seem to have drawn on the experiences of other groups such as deserters and maroons. Exploring the fragmented archival records, we encounter echoes of stories about routes to freedom. And everywhere we see the dynamics of trust and distrust as these small communities formed and struggled to avoid untimely revelations. Like the decks of ships, prisons and colonies rarely afforded convicts a space in which to speak freely. Instead, they struggled against informers. Thus, the story of the *Havmanden's* mutiny is not only connected to this history of prison break by the fact that the mutiny was aimed at making an escape, and by the involvement of the most 'indomitable', but also by sharing its dynamics of veiled discourse and inquisitive ears. Such acts reveal the conditions of subaltern storytelling in the early modern Atlantic world.

6

Dissonant Empire

The *Havmanden* had been eagerly awaited in the Caribbean, although not so much by the small community of Danes, Dutch, Irish, English and Frenchmen on St Thomas. They likely expected the ship to bring an end to the lucrative trade with smugglers and pirates which had begun flourishing after Iversen left the island. In some ways, this had helped keep the colony afloat in the absence of consistent connections with Copenhagen. However, in the neighbouring English colonies, news of Iversen's return had offered the prospect of a welcome change to local elites. Thus William Stapleton, governor of the English Leeward Islands, was sorry when, in August 1683, he reported from Nevis to London that 'he that is sent out by the King of Denmark is thoht to bee taken by the Algerins or Sally men for he has beene expected 8 moneths'.[1] While the deduction that Iversen had been taken by corsairs was wrong, the result was the same: the region's worst pirate haunt was still a huge problem.

St Thomas had become one of only a few safe havens for pirates in the first years of the 1680s, after Iversen had left it. This was a crucial point in the history of buccaneering. In the earlier stages of Caribbean colonization, piracy had been eminently useful to the French, the Dutch and especially the English as they carved out spaces for themselves in the scattered Caribbean archipelago over which the Spanish claimed dominion. Piracy and imperialism had become entwined. Pirate ships had served as a primitive maritime bulwark against the Spanish, and pirate riches pillaged from ships as well as cities on the Spanish mainland had helped kick-start the plantation economy of Jamaica.[2] But piracy had also proven difficult to control, especially in peacetime when robbery at sea could not claim the full legitimacy of privateering. Thus, as the seventeenth century went on, the authorities of the colonial empires began to look less favourably upon piratical behaviour. At the same time, pirates grew increasingly autonomous as they developed egalitarian traditions and increasingly turned against ships of their own nation.[3] Thus, after the Treaty of Madrid in 1670, in which Spain recognized the English possessions in the Caribbean, the English began to suppress piracy, outfitting ships and handing out commissions for people to hunt them down, turning some former pirates against their own peers.[4] In the same period, the English sugar economy fully transformed previously peripheral territories such as the Leeward Islands and Jamaica into bustling, but inherently oppressive plantation economies, built on coerced labour. Not only did maritime predators endanger the trade from such plantation colonies, but it also lured indentured servants and other workers away from their brutal labour.[5] Such allure circulated through storytelling. As a result, Caribbean authorities came to see pirates not as a useful resource in their quest for new territories, but as an 'enemy to mankind' and a threat to the economic growth of empire.[6] A long slow war on piracy in the Caribbean began, one that would conclude only decades later, when pirates' corpses dangled as spectacles of terror at the entrance of every respectable British port.

Because of this turn of events (which at this point was only in its early stages), pirates were in need of refuges. Port Royal no longer offered a safe place to spend one's loot, so crews instead sought out old haunts such as Saint-Domingue where, until 1684, the French authorities gave out commissions allowing pirates to operate, in theory, as privateers, much to the chagrin of the British. Other well-known safe harbours could be found in the Bahamas and in the logwood communities in the bays of Honduras and Campeche.[7] Yet some also found new and welcoming hideouts. St Thomas was among these places and as of early 1682 its natural harbour became a valuable place to provision and careen, and was used by several pirate crews preying all over the Atlantic world. This function is well known to those versed in the scholarly literature on seventeenth-century Caribbean piracy, in which St Thomas has often enjoyed mention as one of the region's most important pirate haunts.[8] St Thomas' arms were open to pirates for a relatively short spell, yet it was an important one for the history of Denmark's Atlantic empire in that it marked the decisive beginning of the colony's opening up to the maritime Caribbean of inter-imperial trade and trans-imperial actors, a move that was never reversed successfully. While St Thomas' inhabitants had led relatively secluded lives during Iversen's reign, they now became firmly integrated in the micro-region's maritime networks and its sliding scale of trade and smuggling as Nicholas Esmit made St Thomas a free harbour.[9] This development, and its implication of an existence inbetween empires, was to define the history of the Danish West Indies for the next two centuries and its emergence owed much to the vacuum created by the mutiny of the *Havmanden*, which for years left the Company paralyzed and unable to intervene in the events transpiring on the other side of the Atlantic where local interests instead reigned supreme. Thus, we might argue that the mutiny was a breaking point, in which the tensions of empire finally brought the Danish colonial project to snap out of joint.

While this is itself an important story, it also allows for something more: to explore the workings of the speech communities of these pirate ships themselves. The men who used the colony in the absence of Company intervention were driven by stories in a way that resonates with the case of the *Havmanden* itself. Thus, just like the mutiny that cut off St Thomas owed much to subaltern storytelling, so did the phenomenon that was to fill the vacuum.

Parallel mutinies

The first known pirate crew to have come to St Thomas was a small group of men who in late January 1682 arrived in a former Spanish vessel, the *Santissima Trinidad*, renamed simply the *Trinity*. Governor Nicholas Esmit described the arrival of the pirates in a letter to the Company, the original of which Iversen later had among his papers on the *Havmanden*, probably as a form of documentation. According to Esmit, thirty inhabitants had helped salvage what goods were left in the ship and he himself had bought a batch of prize Spanish cocoa from them. He had abstained from confiscating anything because he did not want any conflict with the 'pirate class'.[10] In part, his relations with these pirates were only a logical extension of his opening of the harbour to smugglers and interlopers, something hinted at in the letters sent home by the merchant Jonsen in the preceding spring, in which he alerted the Company that their interests were being side-lined – a fact they also found empirical proof of in the meagre cargo loaded on the hip that arrived in Copenhagen in the late summer of 1681.[11] Thus, St Thomas and the small city of Charlotte Amalie – founded against the will of the Company by Esmit in order to house and entertain foreign traders and seafarers – had become increasingly entangled in the maritime Caribbean. The *Havmanden* had been sent to clean up the mess.

The pirate crew that arrived at St Thomas on the *Trinity* in January 1682 had stories to tell. They had been on a three-year cruise that had begun as several pirate crews joined forces in the Caribbean. In 1680, about 300 of them reached the Pacific after crossing the isthmus of Panama on foot. They seem to have attempted to emulate the feat of Sir Henry Morgan who had famously taken the city of Panama in 1671, bringing home massive spoils. Their attempt failed, but as part of their efforts they managed to steal the *Trinity*. In this spectacular vessel, they sought to explore other opportunities of emulating legends in the South Sea, known to them only through stories. In August, while staying off of the coast of Ecuador on the small Isla de la Plata, which they called 'Drake's Isle', they feasted on goats and played dice while recounting legends.[12] Their imaginations were aided by the stories of a local prisoner who told them how the very place in which they now were had a century ago been the scene of Sir Francis Drake's division of the spoils after his taking of a Manila-bound galleon.[13] In their journals, some of the pirates echo the stories told that night, relating how Drake had stolen so much silver that it was distributed 'unto each man of his company by whole bowles full'. It was even said that the crew had been forced to throw silver over-board so as to keep the ship from sinking.[14] Dreams of easy riches were a key part of the allure of piracy, but it was alluring precisely because of the contrast to the coercive labour regimes so prevalent in the Caribbean at that time. Another pirate author, who sailed with some of the men involved in the 1679–82 cruise, told a story of a pirate crew abandoning command, as 'being under no Government, [they] said, That they came for Gold and Silver, and not to be made Pedlars to carry packs at their Backs'. Piracy offered a way of escaping a world that was out to exploit you. Thus, while piracy is often associated with legends, in order to understand its driving force, we must also note that it lived *because* of legends. 'Such vast expectations had we framed now unto our selves, in the vain Idæa's of our minds', as one of the men involved in the cruise phrased it. Having told stories of riches in August 1680, they then set out to emulate Drake's feats.

Their efforts resulted in the most thoroughly documented pirate cruise of any in the period. At least seven of the crew members kept journals on the deck of the *Trinity*. Of these, six were published before the end of the century.[15] Their stories of exotic places and daring pursuits against the Spanish titillated readers in London, where books like these were also valued for the practical information they offered the seafaring community.[16] However, such narratives had to either efface or distance their authors from the scandal at the heart of the pirate community: the anarchic, political community of speakers and storytellers 'under no Government' on the decks. For instance, one of the narrators, Basil Ringrose, was prized by his editor as a man of observation and distinction 'at the same time making Quadrants at Sea, that others sate idle and murmuring upon the Decks'.[17] Only one of the seven authors identified himself with the men on the deck; this anonymous journal was the only one not to get published.

The pirates took the *Trinity* up and down the east coast of South America, attempting to re-enact the legends of Drake whose image they had conjured repeatedly to themselves during the early stages of the venture. Compared to the visions they must have had of abundant silver, the voyage was not successful. They had failed to take Panama City, and everywhere they went along the coasts of Chile and Peru the Spanish had been prepared for their coming which had been rumoured in advance.[18] Meanwhile, the men on the deck murmured. Around New Year of 1680–81, the crew took on water and provisions at the island they called Juan Fernandez (now known as Isla Mas A Tierra, or Robinson Crusoe Island). This was when they mutinied. It was not the first time that they did so; after the failed attempt at Panama, there had been a conflict surrounding then leader John Coxon, who had been accused of cowardice. The anonymous journal adds that Coxon had taken 500 gold pieces 'which hee wronged the party of by keeping of itt to himself, hee being sworn as well as any other man not to wrong any man'.[19] In this complicated set of equivalences we sense the workings of this pirate speech community in which 'any man' spoke, and in which no one was seen as being worth more than anyone else. We also hear resonances of the process we have seen at work on the *Havmanden*. The pirates had sworn the same oath because they were equals – an oath that came to work in ways that were radically different from those sworn at the beginning of normal merchant voyages across the Atlantic empires, but which might not have been so different from the one sworn in the mutiny on the *Havmanden*. Like the men on the *Havmanden* had planned to, pirates shared their spoils equally. Having booted out Coxon, a new captain, Bartholomew Sharp, was elected, but he too failed to gain his men's esteem. The animosity towards him may well have been fuelled further by his luck at playing dice, by which he amassed a small fortune. Their grumbling gained in amplitude throughout the autumn as they continually failed to obtain fresh provisions. One of the journal-writers explained how he lay awake at night, unable to sleep from thirst.[20] Then at Christmas they sought refuge on Juan Fernandez, itself a place of legends and pirate lore. The island offered ample stores for pirates. In this situation of sudden plenty, their anarchic speech community erupted again on 5 January 1681.

A journal-writer – an officer among them – described the event in distancing terms that strongly hint how these anarchic communities conflicted greatly with contemporary views of order and truth. The political speech spoken by mutinous sailors could not be real discourse because it was spoken by subjects who did not know the world of politics they sought to appropriate. Instead, it was to be understood as a kind of dangerous play in which the parties acted out fantasies. He remarked: 'A party of the disaffected to Captain Sharp got ashoar and subscribed a Paper to make John Watling Commander, pretending liberty to a free election as they termed it, and that Watling had it by vote.'[21] Here, we find lower-class subjects able to accomplish something that was ruled out by authoritarian logic. Thus, their appearance as political actors takes the form of a misappropriation of language as they are 'pretending' that their voices could speak a 'political' language. The allergic framing 'as they termed it' closes off what seems to be a dangerous appropriation of political forms (reminding us here of Pontoppidan's 'so-called free republics'), signalled by the terms 'liberty' and the dangerously anarchic 'free election' that was modus operandi among pirate crews.[22] The implicit statement is clear: piracy operated through fiction, scandalous stories made real, by making impossible claims. Later in the same passage, the journal-writer likened it to the political stigma par excellence: 'civil War'. Another eye-witness argued that the people turned out Sharp, 'pretending they could do it, as being a free election. And so they might do, for they were the greatest number by far; and power may pretend to any thing.'[23] Other South Sea voyagers would complain of similar crimes against a backdrop of reserved political language and phrases such as 'justice'.[24] Such appropriations were also often accompanied by the uneasy refrain 'as they termed it'.[25] In their writings, travellers warned future commanders of the dangers that men on these types of long idle voyages would become 'possessed with any imagination'.[26] Sharp himself framed it more succinctly – but according to the same logic – when he said that 'From Consultation they proceeded to Execution, took my Ship from me, clapt me up Prisoner'.[27] The danger as conceptualized in all these echoes is the same: that of a people acting on a fiction that is their own, appropriating language. Such liberties, the ability to fashion a social reality 'as if' one had the power to do so and, thereby, in effect gaining that power, formed the other key component in the allure of piracy. Pirate ships were famously anarchic, in the sense of being without a sure foundation outside of their own politics. Just as pirates shared their spoils, they shared their opinions about the running of the ship. They elected their captains and chose the rules that governed them. Such improvisation, again finding its modus in storytelling on the decks, stood in marked contrast to the rest of the Atlantic world, ruled by small and decidedly exclusionary elites.[28]

Over the next year, the improvised community in question kept roaming the South American coast. They ended up re-electing the captain they had ousted in January, when their new chief died in a failed attempt to take Arica on the Chilean coast. Sharp saw the number of men under his command diminish as subsequent mutinies split them. In his groundbreaking study of pirates, Robert C. Ritchie described how crews like these: 'wandered the seas, dividing and coalescing like amoebas. They lived in small self-contained democracies that usually operated by majority vote, with the minority asked (or forced) to leave in order to keep the remaining crew in happy consensus.[29] Such 'dividing and coalescing' defined the speech circulating within the shipboard community as well.

During the winter of 1681–82, the remainder of the crew (numbering less than half of the original contingent) sailed the ship south of the American continent. They fought the entire way.[30] By late January they were in the Caribbean.[31] The crew then split for the final time, leaving the ship to the small group among them who had gambled away their meagre prize money on the decks, the anonymous author among them.[32] The ship was leaky and during a storm they sought harbour at St Thomas. While the crew was ashore, the cable snapped and the ship ran aground at Charlotte Amalie.[33]

The power of storytelling that had fuelled Sharp's crew to seek out distant territories resonated in the inn at St Thomas. Even if Sharp's men had enjoyed ill success, most were still driven to pursue legends (though one of them settled down and became a planter on the island).[34] As was the case with many other Atlantic pirate crews in the period, their stories also moved other crews to emulation.[35] One of these was that of the merchant vessel the *Summer Island*, captained by George Bond. He had originally been destined to Bermuda from London. From Bermuda, he had gone on a trading voyage to Africa and thence to the Caribbean. Having sold his cargo of enslaved Africans at Curaçao, he headed for St Thomas to careen the ship whose bottom had become overgrown with weeds and barnacles. Here he and his crew met the remainder of Sharp's unruly crew: 'Richard Moreton, John Trunkett and other South Sea travellers.' They appear to have listened to their 'persuasions' and subsequently agreed to go 'upon a pirating account'.[36] Having outfitted their vessel from the remains of the Trinity, they went to Newfoundland where they successfully plundered a few fishing vessels. From there they sought Cape Verde, where they met with another pirate crew captained by John Eaton. Eaton's crew was headed for the South Sea and Bond and his men agreed to go with them.[37] This made sense; after all, tales of pirating in the South Sea had been the initial allure. However, on their way they failed at keeping pace and instead they went for Surinam on the coast of which they took a Dutch ship.[38] This was when their improvised community split. A group of them left Bond in the Dutch ship, reportedly 'to be rid of his hard service'.[39] They then took the ship to St Thomas, where the governor bought their stolen goods and entertained the crew merrily.[40] Lists of the members of the crew given later at a deposition reveal that they were a motley gathering consisting mostly of runaways, principally from English colonies or ships.[41]

Bond and his remaining men also returned to the Danish colony. At St Thomas, they were welcomed by a new face: Adolph Esmit, brother of Nicholas. Adolph had successfully unseated his brother in the autumn of 1682, with the aid of the planters.[42] He had then proceeded upon the same course as his brother, aiding pirates at the island, going so far as to help settle a dispute over the payment of one of the crews, by paying them out of his own pocket.[43]

The most notorious of the crews using St Thomas was the one led by the Frenchman Jean Hamlyn. He captained the ship the *Trompeuse*, which had originally been a French royal frigate before being surprised by pirates in the Bay of Honduras.[44] The ship was reported to be a 'stout handsome frigate' outfitted with about thirty guns.[45] Hamlyn had cruised the Caribbean before being chased out of his first hiding place on Île-à-Vache. He then sought St Thomas, where he was welcomed by Adolph Esmit in early 1683. There he careened and also found a navigator who knew the African coast; it is possible that this could have been another of Sharp's men. Crossing the Atlantic, Hamlyn and his crew enjoyed a solid run along the Gold Coast reportedly taking a total of seventeen prizes.[46] Many crew members from stolen English vessels joined the crew. Eventually, in the usual fashion, the crew split. Hamlyn headed up one group and returned to St Thomas, where he appears to have made an arrangement with Adolph Esmit, who bought around twenty enslaved men and women taken by Hamlyn as plunder and who, shortly before arrival attempted to take the ship, resulting in three deaths.[47]

Local conflict

At this point, Esmit had come to the attention of his English neighbours. William Stapleton, governor of the English Leeward Islands at Nevis,[48] was especially aggressive towards him. Stapleton worried about the Danish governors' claims to other islands besides St Thomas. The Virgin Islands were important to local merchants, in part because these had 'noe other place to gett timber', but also because of their natural harbours. The fact that Adolph Esmit apparently considered his own authority in the region greater than Stapleton's did nothing to mend their ill will. Esmit was even reported to have bragged that the Danish king was 'more sovereign' than the English monarch because the Danish king could single-handedly decide to go to war, while his English counterpart 'was obliged to pull off his hat to his Parliament'.[49]

The biggest threats posed by the vicinity of the Danish colony were social and economic. Stapleton lamented how English merchants suffered from the actions of the 'Dutch and Danes' because they harboured 'fugitive servants white and black' as well as 'seamen and other personnes indebted who runaway to them and will never restore them alleadgeing the freedome of their ports to protect all'.[50] For instance, Stapleton had been frustrated in his attempt to restore seven runaways to their owners in 1682, as Esmit had argued that Charlotte Amalie was a 'free port'.[51] With these freedoms the Danes, as well as the Dutch, 'steal trade and in sloopes carrie the growth of the country'.[52] These were not freedoms granted by the Company, but by Esmit himself. They were grounded in local interests, not in mercantilist logic. In this way, piracy was part of a larger problem in which a nearby free port short-circuited the way people and goods were supposed to move. It was, however, the most urgent part of this problem. Stapleton called St Thomas the worst pirate's nest 'this side of the tropics'.[53] It was a 'receptable of theeves and sea robbers'.[54] Pirates could find no place so welcoming as the authorities on St Thomas 'harbours them, mans and victuals them'.[55] Hamlyn was the worst of all: an 'Arch Pyratt, Murderer and Ravisher of women', as Stapleton dubbed him on account of his reported brutality towards prisoners whom he was said to have tortured.[56] While Stapleton's accusations against Esmit at times seem hyperbolic, a flurry of depositions testified to Esmit's assistance of Bond's and Hamlyn's crews. In his letters, Stapleton did everything he could to spur diplomatic sanction of the Danes, though little actually came of it.

However, Stapleton did more than that. In late July 1683, he sent a small warship to St Thomas under a captain by the name of Charles Carlyle. He was to search out the pirates who were expected to arrive at their haunt soon because of the immanent hurricane season. Carlyle was also to apprehend local Amerindian crews from places such as Hairoun (St Vincent).[57] He found Hamlyn's frigate in the harbour of St Thomas. As he approached, a loaded gun was fired from the ship towards him. He kept a distance, waiting for his chance during the night, when in a pinnace he managed to surprise the men in the *Trompeuse* and overpower them after a brief gunfight. They turned out to be Esmit's Company soldiers guarding the ship while most of the crew was ashore. Carlyle then set the pirate frigate on fire. It blew up when the fire reached the gunpowder. The noise was terrible. A fiery log fell unto the wreck of Bartholomew Sharp's ship, which caught fire. Just as the stories told on the decks during Sharp's voyage had travelled and become appropriated, so had the ship itself. Now its remains 'burnt down to the water'.[58] Carlyle then waited outside of St Thomas for a few days, hoping to catch Bond, whom he expected to arrive there as well. However, eventually a storm forced him to abandon his search. Meanwhile, Hamlyn and his crew made new plans; the loss of the ship did not stop them. Aided by Esmit, Hamlyn purchased a sloop which was used to take a new ship, which was renamed the *Nouvelle Trompeuse*.[59] It was apprehended in Boston only in September 1684.[60]

In Copenhagen, the authorities were powerless to interfere. Due to the threat of an invasion from the increasingly hostile English and the attention they raised in London, the king fashioned Adolph Esmit with the title of governor, so as not to give Stapleton an excuse for further action, but he also instructed Esmit not to engage in anything that might compromise the colony's safety. This was only a temporary measure, but the financial disarray of the Company in the wake of the *Havmanden*'s voyage meant that a forceful intervention was some way off. Eventually, in late 1684, a new governor, Gabriel Milan, arrived on a small ship. He was assisted by soldiers from Stapleton in his takeover of the island.[61] However, his reign was chaotic and despotic. While he put an end to the piracy epidemic and in so doing smoothed out relations with his English neighbours, he did not attain any sort of order in the colony itself. Then, in 1686, yet another new man arrived to clean up the mess. This was Mikkel Mikkelsen, the naval prosecutor who had been responsible for the trial of the mutineers of the *Havmanden*. He lamented how 'unrest in the government' had caused the fledgling plantation economy to suffer greatly, and hoped that he would lay a 'foundation' for future prosperity.[62] Mikkelsen also brought the last significant contingent of convicts to the island, among them the runaways discussed in the previous chapter. However, in general, we might say that the Company's hopes of peopling the island with Danish subjects appear to have been abandoned.

We have continually encountered the Danish Atlantic empire in a state of dissonance; becoming fragmented and disjointed. The mutiny on the *Havmanden* seems to have accelerated this process, bringing it to a point of no return. However, we must also recognize that this dissonance was more a transformation than a dissolution of empire: this was an empire caught in dissonance slowly becoming an empire *made from* dissonances. The Danish Atlantic became a space in which hegemony was continually being remade and contested by multiple actors (smugglers, pirates, runaways etc.). These actors did not undo the empire, but sustained its bustle, and in turn brought it out of kilter with that mercantilist fever dream of Copenhagen.[63] This was empire 'poached' in the sense put forward in Michel de Certeau's famous study of everyday appropriations; or perhaps we might say, in a more befitting metaphor, that the empire was 'piratically seized'.[64] This is most evident in that turn towards the maritime economy of the intra- and transimperial Caribbean taken by St Thomas in the vacuum created when Iversen and his decidedly exclusionary vision of empire was hurled into the sea at Biermand's command. The activity that filled this space did, in a sense, enact its own peculiar form of empire-building and it created an economic dynamism previously absent. It also supplied the colony with enslaved African workers, some of whom arrived on board pirate ships.

Polyglot community

A flurry of governors ruled St Thomas over the next few years, which saw the colony become increasingly embedded in regional maritime networks as well as the inter-imperial slave trade. The most unlikely of these governors was Adolph Esmit who, after having been brought back to Copenhagen, returned for a brief stint as governor. He had promised that he knew the whereabouts of a rich Spanish shipwreck, and apparently the allure of his story had been irresistible to the cash-starved Company. At this point, the king seems to have abandoned hope that the floundering Company would regain a sure financial footing in the near future, and so in late 1685 he struck a thirty-year deal with Brandenburg. The first negotiations had taken place in 1684 in the wake of the chaos wrecked by the events on the *Havmanden*. Denmark and the Company retained sovereignty over St Thomas, but the Brandenburgers were allowed to use the island as a base for their rather extensive slave trading[65] – the beginning of the island's function as a key regional slave trading entrepôt.[66] Under the cover of neutrality, the Brandenburgers' German and Dutch merchants sold enslaved persons to merchants and planters from all over the region. They also traded with pirates and privateers when, in the 1690s, war turned the Caribbean into a privateer's dream.[67]

In 1690, a private merchant from Bergen in Norway took over the Company monopoly on trade.[68] Thus, for nearly a decade the Company sent no loads between Copenhagen and its Caribbean colony, but instead subsisted (barely) on the tax revenue and income derived from its own plantations. Not until 1697, after the Bergen merchant had failed in establishing a stable commercial link between colony and metropole, did the Company itself re-emerge as an active (albeit tiny) player in the Atlantic trade, as had always been the intention. At that point, the key to its new footing was, unsurprisingly, slave trading.

However, even after this re-emergence, the colony retained the polyglot character that had become so pronounced in the chaotic decades during which the island had been sustained principally by its embedding in the maritime

Caribbean. The Company's renewed attempts at closing off the trade to and from the island, which the directors had been forced to officially open in 1694, proved unsuccessful.[69] Local authorities knew the problems that a monopolistic policy posed to them, and actively worked against the wishes from the metropole.[70] The island retained its function as a node to inter-imperial trading, privateering and smuggling networks – a function aided by Danish neutrality in the major conflicts of the other Atlantic empires, such The Nine Years War (1688–97) and Queen Anne's War (1702–13). During said wars, the port attracted privateers, but also smugglers and traders who wished to bypass the navigation laws of the larger empires.

As argued by Linda Rupert, speaking of Curaçao which she explicitly argues formed a southern Caribbean parallel to St Thomas: 'Smugglers and their far-flung networks provided structure and coherence—often an entire quasi-infrastructure—in entire areas that were outside the effective control of imperial state apparatus.'[71] St Thomas became an important intersection in this web. In this capacity, the colony became increasingly tied to the Dutch Caribbean and its circulations of contraband, credit and information. In the scholarly literature on the region's economic history, the island is usually discussed in that respect, and sometimes conceptualized almost as a Dutch satellite, although never really with an understanding of how it came to be so.[72]

Thus, a colony established as a classic monopolistic project for the closed circulation of goods between colony and metropole came to live a life in which most of what happened was not in any meaningful way determined by metropolitan interests. To local traders and seafarers, St Thomas was like a magnet. When the famed Frenchman Jean-Baptiste Labat visited the island *c.* 1700 he described it as a rich, multinational entrepôt for both legal and illegal trade, and he found the local merchants stocked with what he deduced from rumour to be pirate goods. He found the trade there utterly disproportionate to the minuscule size of the island. Privateers could sell their loot and merchants could trade their contraband.[73] Similarly, the famous pirate, circumnavigator and writer William Dampier (who had sailed with Sharp) called the island a 'Sanctuary for Privateers'.[74] He had never been there himself, but had heard the rumours from the pirates he sailed among, some of whom had visited the island when it was ruled by the Esmits. St Thomas had become an interstitial space in the confused political geography of the maritime Caribbean; an interface for the dynamic exchanges that the increasingly exclusionary definitions of mercantile empires had in the latter half of the seventeenth century come to rule out.[75] This nodal function and the prosperity it had brought to the small colony stood in marked contrast to the relatively isolated and poor agricultural community that Iversen, backed by the Company, had attempted to lock into a mercantilist formulaic; yet the empire had persisted only because of this disarray. Left to its own devices, in large part because of the mutiny, such maritime connections had kept the island afloat.

The floundering of the West India and Guinea Company in the 1680s and 1690s was not determined by economic constraints on the part of merchants and capitalists in Copenhagen, as has sometimes been assumed by Danish historians.[76] In the years when the West Indian business nearly dissolved, the Danish East India Company gained momentum, ushering in what has been dubbed a 'great age' (from 1687 to 1704) by scholars.[77] There were also enough people in Copenhagen willing to invest in Atlantic, and especially African, trade. In the aftermath of the mutiny, the Company abandoned all hopes of regular visits to the Gold Coast castles and instead let private merchants, including the Company's own bookkeeper, fill the void. They sent several ships, one of which was taken by a pirate crew associated with those who stayed at St Thomas. However, this was not enough to secure Danish possessions in Africa. One of the two forts was lost in 1685 to the English 'as forfeiture for a heavy financial debt'.[78] Then in 1689, a charter was given to a private Copenhagen merchant to take over the Gold Coast business, relieving the dormant Company of the task. He made a whole-hearted attempt, but failed, in part because of his inability to negotiate political relations with the local Akvamu leaders, an issue that came to the fore in 1693 when the Akvamu captured the remaining fort and held it for a year, using it to sell enslaved Africans directly to European ships. The fort was only given over to the Danes in 1694, when they paid 3,000 Rix-dollars for it. In the aftermath of this event, another Danish slave ship was attacked by pirates, this time the legendary Henry Avery.[79] Even despite such failures, ships kept leaving Copenhagen for the Caribbean.

Thus, it was not a lack of risk-embracing capital in the metropole that kept the Company dormant. Had it not suffered repeatedly (and in large part by the hands of its own subalterns), it seems likely that such merchants would have invested in the Company, instead of seeking to take over its trading monopolies. Instead of structural limitations, it was the blow of the mutiny and subsequent shipwreck that decisively side-lined the already struggling Company and allowed for their Atlantic enterprise to become so profoundly embedded in the maritime Caribbean. While the transportation of convicts from Copenhagen had been key to the attempt at making the colony distinctly Danish, by strengthening the Company with inexpensive labour and peopling the island with Danish bodies, it proved to be the undoing of this fever dream as well. The actions of coerced workers, spurred on by stories told on the lower deck, created a situation in which other speakers and words came to dominate the colonial soundscape, some of whom enacted their own anarchic politics. In this way, the noise inherent to this moment of empire-building and early modern capitalism had denied the vain vision of simple exchanges and human exploitation that had motivated it.

Conclusion

Only in 1697 did the Company fully re-emerge. At that point, their model of empire had changed. They abandoned convict (and to a lesser extent indentured) labour and focused almost exclusively on slave trading – in stark contrast to the vision of twenty-five years earlier. However, throughout the first half of the eighteenth century, kings and various other authorities showed a continued interest in using the colonies for the purpose of punishment. The Danish West Indies were perceived as a potential destination for convicts that could solve the rising pressure on Copenhagen's increasingly crowded penal institutions. Yet every time enquiries were made, the Company argued against it. We can trace at least one such attempt for every new king in the period. The first show of interest came in 1701 when the king ordered the chief of police in Copenhagen to enquire whether the Company was able to ship a notorious criminal to St Thomas. In their reply, the Company directors argued that such miscreants would negatively effect trade if the act of going to the colonies became associated with punishment and crime. In this way, convict labour was still tied to questions about the reputation of colonization, although now in a different way. Further, they noted how 'the disaster that such malefactors caused the last time is still in fresh memory, which is the reason we must have honest people and not criminals to send there'.[1] The wound of the *Havmanden* had become part of the institutional memory of the West India and Guinea Company. Convicts were no longer seen as a potential source of labour, but only a source of unrest.

The convict in question appears to have been transported anyway, and so were several others. In this way, St Thomas gained the same status as the East Indian colony which the kings also used intermittently as a site of banishment. It was a very slow trickle, with only a few convicts being dispatched per decade, but by 1737 the king enquired if the colonies could again be used for housing convicts on a larger scale, as 'there are currently much greater numbers of such delinquents than what is needed for the work on Bremerholmen and in the Spinn House'.[2] This came at a time of general reform of the Danish penal system lasting until the 1760s – a period in which a host of new penal institutions were opened and closed in order to render the burgeoning number of convicts useful to an ever stronger state. The same push resulted in experiments in using the northernmost parts of Norway known as the Finnmark as a site for transported convict labour as well. However, once again the directors refused. In a letter responding to the king's request, they argued that they had taken 'past horrible examples' into consideration and found that convicts would be of utmost danger to the colony. Not only was it 'to be feared, both that during the voyage they might rebel or do other evil misdeeds as had happened earlier, and then later, instead of being of service to the colonists, might cause great harm, not only with their scandalous living, but also with seduction to desertion, insubordination as well as causing other disasters'.[3] The king seems to have listened, although the following year the Company agreed to take on twelve male inmates from the prison workhouse on the premise that they had not been incarcerated for any 'dishonest reason'. They were to serve not as convicts, but as indentured servants. This practice was repeated several times in the 1740s.[4] It indicates how the Company's unwillingness to take on convicts was ultimately not rooted in any lack in the demand for labour. The purchase of the island of St Croix in 1733, in fact, meant that they needed labourers. As a consequence, they had revived their use of indenture. The adverse reaction to the notion of convict labour rested on a specific distrust of these specific unfree labourers.

By 1746, a new king of Denmark, Frederik VI, was crowned. Soon he also enquired about this issue.[5] On this occasion, a more elaborate answer was presented.[6] In it the Company directors argued vehemently that transporting convicts would cause 'the corruption of the colonies and the ruin of the Company'.[7] The inspiration for the king's request seems to have been English, as the directors argued that while the English had been able to send convicts from London's Newgate prison, the Danish case was different. Their argument rested on several points. The English colonies were argued to be qualitatively different and stronger than the Danish. This was important because of how convicts would challenge the colonial enterprise as such. It was argued that there was a fundamental difference between 'African slaves and European [ones]'. While enslaved Africans were (in the directors' view) ideally suited for work in the plantations, and were able to grow foods in small gardens to feed themselves, convicts were 'quite unable to endure the heat that exists in those countries, as it drains them of all the power needed for hard labour which they can [therefore] not endure, and to which they are of no use'. Further it was 'impossible for them to get their own subsistence in the way of the negro, so that their food and clothes, in that country where everything is expensive, would cost the planters much more than the worth of the labour'. Therefore, no planter would be willing to take them on. Neither could the Company use them as soldiers, as they could not arm them, and further, it would make anyone else unwilling to serve in the colonies because of the dishonour of the convicts. Most disconcertingly, the mixing of these racially defined categories of enslaved would deteriorate 'the discipline among the slaves [meaning, the enslaved Africans]'. As the Company directors argued: 'It is necessary to keep the blacks in great awe and to make them have a great fear of whites or Christian people, which cannot be any different since these negroes are in many ways superior to the Christians'. This superiority would be realized when 'they see that whites or Christians are also enslaved, and are treated in the same way and with as much humiliation as negroes'. This would cause the fears of the enslaved to dissipate. Thus, the directors feared that the carefully engineered, but fragile, social world of their colonies would become dissonant. Another way this would happen was when the two groups of subalterns mingled. The convicts would be determined to regain their lost freedom 'and when they become mixed or come in the least contact with the blacks who themselves are inclined to rebellion, they will strive towards it all the more, even taking up the most desperate means and cause miserable revolts in those countries'. At this point, the directors referred explicitly to the large slave rebellion on St John in 1733–34, in which newly transported enslaved Africans had taken over the entire island, which was only reconquered with the aid of the French. Such risk of violence would merely be intensified 'when the negroes get whites as companions [Staldbrödre], who are here so well trained and know so well how to encourage them, yes, even as instigators to instruct them of their power and might to carry out their evil intentions'.[8]

All of this would, of course, also deter the attempts to recruit free colonists. Further, it would become difficult to recruit mariners. This was when the directors recounted the story of the *Havmanden*:

> [...] no sensible captain, master or mariners will dare to embark with such people if they are not in irons and the ship's crew many times superior to them in numbers, from fear that the same things should happen as in 1683. This would cause such a transportation to be too expensive, even if someone agreed to do it. This above-mentioned example, even though it happened more than 60 years ago, is still in our and in most seafarers' fresh memory and happened like this: It had been decided to send a group of convicts from Copenhagen to the West Indies. [They came] from both *Holmen*, the *Stockhouse* and the *Børnehuset*. They were embarked on a ship called the *Havmanden* which sailed from here in

November 1682, but in the voyage the convicts revolted, killed the governor travelling with them on the ship, as well as the captain Jan Blom and other Company servants. Strangely, the ship arrived at Marstrand in March 1683 where these convicts were arrested and then transported here. They were examined in the Admiralty Court and found guilty on 20 June of that year, and a large part of them were executed and placed on wheels. Even without such an example and if it was decided that the transportation of such delinquents to the colonies is safe, the colonies would still become stricken with fear, terror and anxiety because of the miserable acts which would be caused by this. Any inhabitant would feel unsafe and expect nothing but revolt, murder, arson and other terrible acts from such criminals and their unavoidable trade and conversation with the blacks.[9]

Here we encounter the story of the *Havmanden* told in an anxious mode, very different from the way it was cast by contemporary historians who told it from the vantage point of a reconstitution of proper power relations through law. Of course, the letter glosses over the uneasy fact that sailors were also key to the mutiny itself. Yet despite this epistolary sleight of hand, this was not a comforting story of order reasserting itself through justified violence. Rather, it was a story about the powerlessness of authorities and the complications of the antagonistic social world of empire. In this way, it is a story that renders the empire-building project much more truthfully – one in which we glimpse the very precariousness of empire itself.

Importantly, these anxieties on the part of Company elites are what have allowed for the retelling of the story presented in this book. They mar the provenance of the archive itself. In an anonymous note from 1746, likely to have been fashioned by the Company's bookkeeper, Per Mariager, we find an earlier draft of the arguments outlined above. It seemed to have been part of an internal correspondence. In it the *Havmanden* is again referenced in a way that chimes with the above-cited retelling and it was claimed how 'this lamentable example is still in memory'. Most interestingly, however, we learn that the author of the note had learned the details of the story from the narrative of Braad, the supercargo. Mariager explained how he had 'procured a copy of the journal kept in said voyage as well as the examination and the Admiralty Court sentence, of which I have made a copy which is here for the sake of enlightenment'.[10] These copies are the only surviving ones of Braad's journal, examination and the full sentence. Along with it, the bookkeeper gathered a number of documents now found in a single box, numbered 181, in the Company archive. Outside of this box, the actions of convicts are almost entirely invisible, but inside it, we encounter the empire unravelling because of their agency.[11] Thus, without the clerk's anxious archival practices trying to fend off what was seen as an impending disaster, this book would have been impossible – as the originals of these documents are all lost.

In this way, the archival record, by its very existence, speaks in a distressed mode that testifies as much to failure as to power. The very conditions of our knowing about such events are tied to the agency of the mutineers. While they did not achieve their ambitions of freedom and Irish riches, they changed the Danish empire. This book feeds off the anxieties such a change provoked and the knowledge it produced, and also feeds off this future-oriented state of fantasies and fears linked to uncertainties over conflicted, recalcitrant pasts in continual renegotiation. The retelling of the discordant history of the *Havmanden* is possible because it was reproduced here as a form of wavering colonial knowledge intended to exorcise Company rule of the spectre of such subaltern agency. Thus, attempts at writing the fragmented histories of subaltern classes and listening to their tongues hinges on amplifying the reverberations of worlds found primarily in the dissonances of the colonial authorities' uneasy self-fashioning as it appears in the archives of their productive anxieties.

It seems almost ironic that the condition of our knowing so many details about the mutiny on the *Havmanden* is so closely linked to the feverish imaginations of the Company, as so much of the history of the *Havmanden* (and with it the early Danish Atlantic) enabled by these sources is, itself, about the imagination. If anything, this book testifies to the storied character of empire-building. So much in the project of building this small Atlantic empire hinged on fantasy. In the context of this book, we might say that the notion of the scattered Scandinavian empire of Denmark-Norway emulating their larger rivals and becoming a genuine player in the colonial race was an ill-fated illusion. So was the hope entertained by men like Iversen and his Company employers of regaining control of St Thomas in the first years of the 1680s by re-peopling it with Danes. In the Company correspondence from the years leading up to the mutiny, we sense how its office on the Copenhagen Stock Exchange resounded with plans and imaginations. The plan of the ship itself – a four-legged voyage that would solve all the problems of the colony by bringing a total of about 450 colonial workers (convicts, indentured and enslaved) to the colony – echoes such reveries, being out of sync with the reality of constant ill success that had marred Company voyages up to this point in their history. As is sometimes hinted in their own writing and their fears of these indomitable bodies, they knew that social reality could intrude upon the realization of such visions. But perhaps even their worst fears did not match what actually happened on 20 January 1683. Instead of a ship returning with a hold full of goods, they received a story told by their assistant, Braad. His narrative was designed to provide the directors with knowledge of how their dream had been denied, but was also an attempt at self-fashioning: a story of loyalty amidst misfortune designed to clear himself of any suspicions that might naturally arise simply on account of his return. This story represents what the Company leaders knew about the causes of the failure of their venture, and in turn it is our gateway to exploring the social world of the ship and how stories circulated there. It tells (often implicitly) of a ship of rumours. Thus, while Braad constructed a recognizable plot with a simple causal logic out of the messy relations onboard ship, his stories contained complex echoes revealing how the state of fantasy in the Company office had been mirrored by a state of distressed storytelling below deck – one that echoes a larger history of coercion in the seventeenth-century Atlantic. Thus, the history of this early modern empire has stories at every level – each with their own logic and often out of tune with each other. Even the pirates who filled the void left on St Thomas by the mutiny were driven by words and legends.

Thus, attempts at storytelling provide the condition of our knowing other practices of storytelling. Yet despite the fact that empires were ripe with stories, some voices have been granted fuller import than others. The dominance of the trend of postcolonialism over the past thirty years or so, and its indebtedness to Foucauldian discourse analysis, has meant that the stories of elites have been interrogated, their ambivalences pondered endlessly and their power to shape colonial reality alternately asserted and questioned. Considering that the analysis of discourse becomes much easier if we have something to analyze, this gravitational pull towards the words of those with power over others (as a consequence: archival representation) is only logical. However, this book has been much more heavily indebted to the far rarer attempts to actually investigate the discourses of lower-class subjects, and not only what was said *about* them.

One might argue that this attempt has been foolish from the outset. That it is, ultimately, impossible. The coerced labourers of empire usually appear to us as silent, and even when they do speak in the records they most often speak in a language that is not theirs – exemplified, for instance, by Gulliksen's letter. This realization is utterly unsurprising to the point of being trivial. In light of the widely recognized fact that the words of subalterns have rarely made it into the archives as these were complicit with and even constitutive of the power relations of colonialism, it is only to be expected that in order for us (as historians) to make it all the way to the lower deck, we need to put our own imaginations at work. Some might argue that such imaginations have been stressed too greatly here. In the end, however, we cannot listen in on the worlds of convicts and sailors without taking a leap of interpretation. Telling the story of events like the mutiny is a game of constructing a whole that cannot be directly verified by reference to the records, but whose plausibility is, nonetheless, underscored by how such a whole can help account for the multitude of traces that *are* in the records. As an academically trained historian, this state of uncertainty makes even me a little uneasy, but I believe nonetheless that it is necessary for us to get a fuller understanding of the processes that made the world what it is today. Thus, despite the archives' effacements and the epistemological violence this entails, subalterns spoke and in enabling actions their words had the power to alter empires. If we do not take the necessary interpretative leap and allow for attempts at reconstruction through radical contextualization of (often minuscule) fragments of discourse, we will fail to understand the dynamics of empire and how they were shaped by the agency of those who, on the surface, appear voiceless. I have tried to make this interpretation as transparent as possible, and to allow for as much complexity to the lower deck discourses as possible in order to avoid the temptation of projecting a too-unified identity upon the coerced labourers of empire. Yet if this book still reads as a manifest for being speculative, I would remark, like Natalie Zemon Davis recently did, that 'being speculative is better than to not do it at all'.[12]

The importance of making such leaps is only stressed by how some of the most important recent attempts at writing global histories 'from below' have repeatedly alluded to the importance of rumours and stories told by the workers of empire. In their attempts at writing Atlantic and global histories from this perspective by looking at how lower-class subjects challenged empire, historians have often come across rumour and storytelling.[13] However, a recurrent theme in such encounters is that our attempts at listening in are frustrated by the state of the archives. In their own ways, the chapters of this book have been attempts at wrestling free of this archival constraint, whether by slow meditation on the words echoing in those rare elite accounts in which such dissonances resound (for reasons that can be historicized), or by contextualizing such acts to the rare lower-class writings that *do* exist and which might be read as indicators of how such actors made sense of their world and their options within it. Thus, this book has been an attempt to restore the full importance to the voices of those men and women whose labours built and shaped empires.

As we try to reconstruct such voices we begin to sense the complexity that defined everyday relations in colonies, on board ships and on the inside of prisons. In the case of the mutiny on the *Havmanden,* a multitude of different factors played into the formation of a site of discourse among the convicts, indentured servants and sailors on the lower deck. Retelling the story of communities like this one means engaging with many different narrative threads, resulting, perhaps, in what might be perceived as a loss of clarity and even explanatory force. The three models outlined in the introduction all help us conceive of elements in the complex tangle developing below deck, although I have engaged mostly with the last one, the class-struggle model, owing to its much-needed stress of the social dynamics of such acts. The mutiny on the *Havmanden,* however, owed both to material distress, a failure of authoritarian performance, social antagonisms and more, all playing out against a backdrop of a highly coercive project of building an Atlantic empire through forced labour. This complexity expressed itself in the rumours and stories told by the actors themselves, incorporating bits and pieces of knowledge and binding their speakers together, just out of earshot of their superiors. Adding to the difficulty, the trajectory of the *Havmanden* forces us to see such hidden sites of discourse as highly dynamic, making the story told here one of constant shifts and intense precariousness in which structural forces and what, for lack of a better term, we might call 'contingencies', both do their work. There was more than one set of antagonisms on the ship, and there were relationships that defied them altogether. The most dramatic shift was that of the chief mutineers against their fellow rebels in the weeks after 20 January 1683. It shows how even those relations that formed in order to enable resistance against unjust power and coercion, proved dangerously porous as power shifted on board. To put it bluntly, as we conceive of the voices of history from below and attempt to reconstruct the processes they expressed, we are confronted with something that does not add up to a set of fixed relations or a single world. As evolving soundscapes, ships (as well as colonies and prisons) were dissonant. This fundamental instability does not necessarily take away from the necessity of exploring colonial history through the prism of social history or opposition, but highlights how the formations of solidarities and communities need to be conceived as a fragile process. In a sense, this reminder to study the processes of collective resistance makes such acts (mutiny, collective desertion, prison break etc.) all the more remarkable. While they often were successful only momentarily, they nevertheless defied so many factors working to introduce difference among its subjects.

We should embrace the confusion induced in us, as social historians, by such complexity and context-dependency. Not only does it mirror the frustrations of elites facing the difficult task of building an empire off of the labours of unruly subalterns, but even the uncertainty that subalterns themselves faced as they took centre stage in colonial history. To them, the future looked as murky as the past does to us.

Notes

Abbreviations used in notes:
CO: Colonial Office.
NA: National Archives, Kew.
RA: Rigsarkivet, Copenhagen.
WIGC: West India and Guinea Company (Vestindisk-Guineisk Kompagni).

Introduction

1 Erik Gøbel, ed., *Jens Mortensen Sveigaards ostindiske rejsebeskrivelse 1665–1684* (Copenhagen: Maritim Kontakt, 2005), 262. All translations are my own, except when otherwise noted.

2 Ibid.

3 *Extraordinaire Maanedlige Relationer*, July 1683 (Copenhagen: Daniel Paulli, 1683).

4 Ibid.

5 Jan von Gent, *Dette er en grundelig Beretning om det Vest-Indiske Skib Hafmanden* (Copenhagen, 1683).

6 Johan Bartram Ernst, *Tage-Register über Des Allerdurchlauchstigsten Groß-mächtigsten Königs und Herrn, K.n. Christian des Fünften, Königs zu Dennemarck Norwegen* (Copenhagen, 1701), 170–71.

7 Erik Pontoppidan, *Annales Ecclesiæ Danicæ Diplomatici* (Copenhagen, 1741–52), 4:618–19; Erik Pontoppidan, *Origines Hafnienses* (Copenhagen, 1760), 426–28; Ludvig Holberg, *Dannmarks og Norges Beskrivelse* (Copenhagen; Jørgen Høpffner, 1729), 487–88; C. E. Secher, *Danmark i ældre og nyere Tid* (Copenhagen: B. Pio, 1874), 1:314–15; Oluf Nielsen, *Kjøbenhavn i Aarene 1660–1699* (Copenhagen: Gad, 1899), 398–99; Kay Larsen, 'Fregatten "Havmandens" togt til Vestindien', *Vikingen*, 1925, 17–27; Jens Olav Bro-Jørgensen, *Vore Gamle Tropokolonier: Dansk Vestindien indtil 1755*, 2. ed. (Copenhagen: Fremad, 1966), 100–105; Kåre Lauring, *Slaverne Dansede og holdte sig lystige: En Fortælling om den danske slavehandel* (Copenhagen: Gyldendal, 2014), 86–90.

8 See also Mark M. Smith, *Listening to Nineteenth-Century America* (Chapel Hill: The University of North Carolina Press, 2001), 47–66; Richard Cullen Rath, *How Early America Sounded* (Ithaca: Cornell University Press, 2003), 6.

9   Magdalena Naum and Jonas Nordin, eds, *Scandinavian Colonialism and the Rise of Modernity* (New York: Springer, 2013).

10 See, for instance, Neville A. T. Hall, *Slave Society in the Danish West Indies: St. Thomas, St. John and St. Croix* (Mona, Cave Hill and St. Augustine: The University of the West Indies Press, 1992); Gunvor Simonsen, *Slave Stories: Gender, Representation, and the Court in the Danish West Indies, 1780s–1820s* (Unpublished PhD thesis, European University Institute, Florence, 2007); Louise Sebro, *Mellem afrikaner og kreol: Etnisk identitet og social navigation i Dansk Vestindien 1730–1770* (Lund: Lund University, 2010); Jeppe Mulich, 'Microregionalism and intercolonial relations: the case of the Danish West Indies, 1730–1830', *Journal of Global History* 8, no. 1 (2013): 72–94.

11 Niklas Thode Jensen, *For the Health of The Enslaved: Slaves, Medicine, and Power in the Danish West Indies, 1803–1848* (Copenhagen: Museum Tusculanum, 2012), 27.

12 Fr. Stuckenberg, *Fængselsvæsenet i Danmark: En historisk skildring* (Copenhagen, G.E.C. Gad, 1893–96); Olaf Olsen, *Christian 4.s. tugt- og børnehus* (Copenhagen: Wormianum, 1978); Peter Agerbo Jensen, 'Christian IV's tugt- og børnehus: Social institution eller merkantilistisk foretagende?', *Kulturstudier* 2, (2012): 6–27.

13 Ole Feldbæk and Ole Justesen, *Kolonierne i Asien og Afrika* (Copenhagen: Politikens Forlag, 1680), 312–28.

14 Bro-Jørgensen, *Tropekolonier*, 11–27.

15 In a recent article published after the manuscript of this book was completed, Mirjam Louise Hviid has explored the institution of indenture at length in the early Danish Atlantic. She argues that it was heavily inspired by British practices. She also argues that the indentured were often recruited among inmates of the prison workhouse in Copenhagen and that they were often perceived as identical with the convicts. Based on a small sample, she argues that convicts came from highly diverse backgrounds. However, my own work in the archives clearly indicates that the majority of the convicts were either rural or urban labourers or soldiers. She briefly notes the role of the mutiny in shaping conceptions of convict labour. Mirjam Louise Hviid, 'Indentured servitude and convict labour in the Danish-Norwegian West Indies, 1671–1755', *Scandinavian Journal of History* 41, no. 4–5 (2016): 541–64.

16 The charter is reprinted in Ole Feldbæk, *Danske Handelskompagnier 1616–1843* (Copenhagen: Selskabet for Udgivelse af Kilder til Dansk Historie, 1986), 365–80.

17 Evelyn P. Jennings, 'Introduction', in *Building the Atlantic Empires: Unfree Labor and Imperial States in the Political Economy of Capitalism, ca. 1500–1914,* ed. John Donoghue and Evelyn P. Jennings (Leiden: Brill, 2016), 1–24 (quote from 2).

18 This basic link between punishment and labour market was famously explored by Georg Rusche and Otto Kirchheimer in *Punishment and Social Structure* (New York: Russell and Russell, 1968. Org. 1939). Christian G. De Vito and Alex Lichtenstein

have recently stressed the need for perceiving of the uses of convict labour in relation to 'an integrated labour market'. Christian G. De Vito and Alex Lichtenstein, 'Writing a Global History of Convict Labour', *International Review of Social History* 58 (2013): 292.

19 Timothy Coates: 'European forced labor in the early modern era', in *The Cambridge World History of Slavery*, eds David Eltis and Stanley Engerman (Cambridge: Cambridge University Press, 2011), 3:631–49; Clare Anderson and Hamish Maxwell-Stewart, 'Convict Labour and the Western Empires, 1415–1954', in *The Routledge History of Western Empires,* eds Robert Aldrich and Kirsten McKenzie (London: Routledge, 2014), 102–17.

20 Coates argues: 'The Portuguese developed their system of penal exile from a Roman model, in use in the Mediterranean in the fifteenth century (notably by Venice on Crete). In turn, this Portuguese system, which incorporated orphan girls, prostitutes, and other marginal figures as colonizers, supplied a blueprint for other European powers'. Timothy Coates, *Convicts and Orphans: Forced and State-Sponsored Colonizers in the Portuguese Empire 1550–1755* (Stanford: Stanford University Press, 2001), 4.

21 Roger Ekirch, *Bound for America: The Transportation of British Convicts to the Colonies, 1718–1775* (Oxford: Clarendon Press, 1987); Peter Rushton and Gwenda Morgan, *Eighteenth-Century Criminal Transportation: The Formation of the Criminal Atlantic* (New York: Palgrave, 2004); Peter Rushton and Gwenda Morgan, *Banishment in the Early Atlantic World: Convicts, Rebels and Slaves* (London: Bloomsbury, 2013); Hamish Maxwell-Stewart, 'Convict Labour Extraction and Transportation from Britain and Ireland, 1615–1870', in *Global Convict Labour*, eds Christian G. De Vito and Alex Lichtenstein (Leiden: Brill, 2015), 168–96; Lauren Benton, *A Search for Sovereignty: Law and Geography in European Empires, 1400–1900* (Cambridge: Cambridge University Press, 2010), 162–76. At least four mutinies happened on board ships transporting convicts to North America in the decade after the Transportation Act. See Tim Hitchcock and Robert Shoemaker, *London Lives: Poverty, Crime and the Making of a Modern City* (Cambridge: Cambridge University Press, 2015), 81–2.

22 Frederik Ekengren, Magdalena Naum and Ulla Isabel Zagal-Mach Wolfe, 'Sweden in the Delaware Valley: Everyday Life and Material Culture in New Sweden', in *Scandinavian Colonialism and the Rise of Modernity*, eds Magdalena Naum and Jonas M. Nordin (New York: Springer, 2013), 169–87.

23 Kerry Ward, *Networks of Empire: Forced migration in the Dutch East India Company* (Cambridge: Cambridge University Press, 2009).

24 Peter N. Moogk, 'Reluctant Exiles: Emigrants from France in Canada before 1760', *The William and Mary Quarterly* 46, no. 3 (1989): 463–505. See also the forthcoming PhD thesis by Yevan Terrien (Pittsburgh University).

25 Ruth Pike, *Penal Servitude in Early Modern Spain* (Madison: The University of Wisconsin Press, 1983); Stephanie Mawson, 'Rebellion and Mutiny in the Mariana Islands, 1680–1690', *Journal of Pacific History* 50, no. 2 (2015): 128–48.

26 Hall, *Slave*, 6.

27 Copybook, fol. 9 and 12, 34, WIGC, RA.

28 Ibid., fol. 10.

29 Ibid., fol. 3–5.

30 Minutes, p. 37, 14, WIGC, RA.

31 Copybook, fol. 19, 34, WIGC, RA.

32 Minutes, p. 33, 14, WIGC, RA.

33 Ibid., p. 17; Copybook, fol. 25, 34, WIGC, RA.

34 Minutes, p. 13, 14, WIGC, RA.

35 Copybook, fol. 22, 34, WIGC, RA.

36 While they operated under a different flag, Dutch merchants were heavily involved in the Brandenburg Company.

37 Gunnar Olsen, *Vore Gamle Tropekolonier: Ostindien 1616–1732* (Copenhagen: Forlaget Fremad, 1967), 195.

38 Simon Braad's journal, 181, WIGC, RA. (hereafter cited as 'Braad's journal')

39 Ibid., 9 November 1682.

40 A rival for this title is the mutiny against Bartholomew Sharp discussed at length in Chapter 6.

41 Thus, it works squarely within the 'evidential paradigm' proposed by Carlo Ginzburg in *Clues, Myths, and the Historical Method*, trans. John and Anne Tedeschi (Baltimore: The Johns Hopkins University Press, 1989), 96–125 and 156–64.

42 A fourth model was put forward by naval historian N.A.M. Rodger. He sees mutinies as a way to air grievances, often about clearly expressed issues such as pay or food, that was to some extent tolerated and even listened to by naval authorities. Such mutinies were a form of negotiation, aimed at righting a wrong, rather than taking over the ship. Such forms of mutiny are touched upon in Chapter 4. However, this fits poorly with the events on the *Havmanden*. N.A.M. Rodger, *The Wooden World: An Anatomy of the Georgian Navy* (London: Collins, 1986), 237–44.

43 The fullest of their accounts is that found in historian Kay Larsen's article 'Fregatten "Havmandens" togt til Vestindien', *Vikingen*, 1925: 17–27. Much of his narrative of the mutiny, however, has no base in sources. Larsen was apparently unaware of Braad's journal and largely based his account on the second mate's short printed narrative. He seems to have filled the gaps with what he supposed might have happened. Ultimately, the mutiny was explained by the depraved minds and empty stomachs of those involved. Propping up his interpretation, Larsen drew some seedy details from a letter written by the Swedish official Sten Arvesen, who (along with Braad) helped salvage the goods from the abandoned ship. More importantly, he

initially helped arrest a group of prisoners held by the mutineer-captain, convict Jokum Gulliksen. In his letter, Arvesen wrote how the captain 'has forced the previous captain's wife to have sex with him'. This, he wrote, happened even though the woman had given birth only a few days earlier. See Sten Arvesen to Frederik Merker, 2 April 1683, 192, WIGC, RA. This was a complete fabrication, which has an interesting story of its own. The captain's wife had not been on board. Rather, Arvesen might have heard a similar story about the governor's wife who was on the ship and indeed gave birth there, although this had happened in late November. However, if an act of rape had actually transpired, Braad's narrative would surely have mentioned this event or at least implied it. It would also have been raised during Braad's interrogation. Indeed, Braad's answers reveal that he and the wife of the governor were friends, so he would have known. Of course, the sentence passed on the mutineers (which Larsen did use as a source) would have mentioned it as well. It painstakingly detailed what each mutineer had done to merit punishment. So why did Arvesen write it? The most likely source of the rumour was in fact Gulliksen's prisoners whom Arvesen had brought from the ship and locked up in Marstrand; men who, as we shall see, had good reason for sullying Gulliksen's name as he was actively trying to make them into scapegoats to save his own neck. Despite such a likely origin, Larsen comfortably asserted that after the mutiny 'an orgy erupted and the governor's wife and other of the women were mercilessly defiled'. He was not alone in drawing such conclusions. In his short biography of Governor Iversen, Larsen's contemporary F.R. Krarup portrayed the governor as a colonial hero and accepted the veracity of the reported rape as well. See, Fr. Krarup, *Jørgen Iversen (Dyppel)* (Copenhagen: Bibliotheca Wegenariana, 1891). This lurid, but utterly unreliable piece of information, is even reproduced in the newest, similarly flawed, account of the mutiny that is briefly included in Kåre Lauring's 2014 monograph on the Danish slave trade. See Lauring, *Slaverne*, 87. The appeal of such a detail lies in the way it comports with a model of explanation which argues that acts of crime come down to the depravity of those who commit them.

44 Greg Dening, *Mr Bligh's Bad Language: Passion, Power and Theatre on the Bounty* (Cambridge: Cambridge University Press, 1992), 83.

45 Ibid., 83.

46 Ibid., 27.

47 A recent study of a mutiny that follows Dening's logic of interpretation (although without referencing it) is found in Nigel Worden, '"Below the Line the Devil Reigns": Death and Dissent aboard a VOC Vessel', *South African Historical Journal* 61, no. 4 (2009): 702–30.

48 Ultimately, this means that they are conceived as fully in sync with order until that order breaks; with ritual creating hegemony, lower-class actors do not act on their own. Yet as James C. Scott has argued, the assumption of the hegemonic character of

the dominant ideology is a common fallacy in so many studies of domination; hegemony cannot be empirically verified, as the subjects that order is imposed upon will always have very material reasons to act in accordance with the script that is imposed. Thus, the historical record is full of subjects acting in accordance to hegemonic logics, but we simply cannot know if they did so because they had internalized it, become subject to the spell of ceremony suggested by Dening, or because they had very clear motivations for what Scott dubs 'laying it on thick'. James C. Scott, *Domination and the Arts of Resistance: Hidden Transcripts* (Yale: Yale University Press, 1990), 70.

49 Dening, *Bligh's*, 380.

50 Marcus Rediker, *Between the Devil and the Deep Blue Sea: Merchant Seamen, Pirates, and the Anglo-American Maritime World* (Cambridge: Cambridge University Press, 1987).

51 Marcus Rediker and Peter Linebaugh, *The Many-Headed Hydra: The Hidden History of the Revolutionary Atlantic* (London: Verso, 2000); Marcus Rediker, *Villains of All Nations: Atlantic Pirates in the Golden Age* (Boston: Beacon Press, 2004); Marcus Rediker, 'African Origins of the Amistad Rebellion', *International Review of Social History* 58, special issue (2013): 15–34; David Featherstone, 'Counter-Insurgency, Subalternity and Spatial Relations: Interrogating Court-Martial Narratives of the Nore Mutiny of 1797', *South African Historical Journal* 61, no. 4 (2009): 766–87; Niklas Frykman, 'Seamen on Late Eighteenth-Century European Warships', *International Review of Social History* 54 (2009): 67–93; Niklas Frykman, 'The Mutiny on the Hermione: Warfare, Revolution and Treason in the Royal Navy', *Journal of Social History* 44, no. 1 (2010): 159–87; Niklas Frykman, 'Connections between Mutinies in European Navies', *International Review of Social History* 58, special issue (2013): 87–108; Isaac Curtis, 'Masterless People: Maroons, Pirates, and Commoners', in *The Caribbean: A History of the Region and Its Peoples*, eds Stephan Palmié and Francisco A. Scarano (Chicago and London: The University of Chicago Press, 2011); Christopher Magra, 'Anti-Impressment Riots and the Origins of the Age of Revolution', *International Review of Social History* 58, special issue (2013): 131–52; Nicole Ulrich, 'International Radicalism, Local Solidarities: The 1797 British Naval Mutinies in Southern African Waters', *International Review of Social History* 58, special issue (2013): 61–86; John Donoghue, *Fire Under the Ashes: An Atlantic History of the English Revolution* (Chicago: The University of Chicago Press, 2013); Peter Way, 'Militarizing the Atlantic World: Army discipline, coerced labor, and Britain's commercial empire', *Atlantic Studies* 13, no. 3 (2016): 345–69.

52 E.g. Hamish Maxwell-Stewart, *Closing Hell's Gates: The Death of a Convict Station* (Crows Nest: Allen & Unwin, 2008); Clare Anderson, '"The Ferringees are flying— the ship is ours!": The Convict Middle Passage in Colonial South and Southeast Asia, 1790–1860', *The Indian Economic and Social Review* 42, no. 2 (2005: 143–86;

Ian Duffield, 'Cutting Out and Taking Liberties: Australia's Convict Pirates',
International Review of Social History 58, special issue (2013), 197–228; Matthias
van Rossum, '"Amok!" Mutinies and Slaves on Dutch East Indiamen in the 1780s',
International Review of Social History 58, special issue (2013): 109–30.

53 Of course, as always, there is a degree of tension when a model used for explaining
events playing out in one context is transposed to another. Rediker's analysis frames
maritime conflict and shipboard unrest within the larger story of the emergence of
capitalism and class struggle. However, he also posits a continuity between maritime
radicalism and specific English seventeenth-century traditions of political dissent.
This imposes a subtle teleology in which traditions of maritime struggle culminate
in the age of revolutions in which English and American sailors played integral
parts, and in which cascades of mutinies shook the British, French and Dutch
navies. Thus, maritime resistance in the early modern Atlantic world foreshadowed
genuine political mobilization at the beginning of the modern world. Yet whereas
his frame of the emergence of capitalism translates easily to other empires, even
to small ones such as the Danish, the latter narrative of continuity does not. The
mutiny on the *Havmanden* had no discernible ties to the radicals of the English
Revolution and, most importantly, it did not foreshadow the coming of popular
radicalism at the dawn of the nineteenth century. While the 1790s were a turbulent
time in Copenhagen as well, and while maritime workers played an important part
in such unrest, Denmark did not see truly revolutionary large-scale mobilization
until much later. Thus, this part of the larger narrative somewhat collapses when
applied to Denmark. For more on the riots in the 1790s see Bent Blüdnikow,
'Folkelig uro i København 1789–1820', *Fortid og Nutid,* (1986): 1–54.

54 Rediker, 'African', 28.

55 Examples of Atlantic and maritime microhistories include Randy Sparks, *The Two
Princes of Calabar: An Eighteenth-Century Atlantic Odyssey* (Cambridge MA:
Harvard University Press, 2004); Jenny Shaw, *Everyday Life in the Early English
Caribbean: Irish, Africans, and the Construction of Difference* (Athens: The University
of Georgia Press, 2013). A microhistory of the North Sea region and its maritime
social groups is found in Jelle van Lottum and Sølvi Sogner, 'Magnus og Barbara:
Mikrohistorie i Nordsjø-regionen på 1600-tallet', *Historisk tidsskrift* 85 (2006):
377–401.

56 Thus, the complexity revealed on the close scale means that the narrative loses some
of the clean-cut character of larger-scale syntheses. Scott has argued that historians
possess an urge to condense history, and a 'desire for clean narratives'. This imposes a
perspective that he likens to the way a television broadcast distorts a game of sports,
making it 'seem deceptively easy to viewers'. Indeed, one of the first realizations upon
studying the struggles of lower-class actors on a close scale is just how incredibly
difficult any sort of resistance was and how many factors worked against it. As we

will see in the story of the *Havmanden*, there were a plethora of factors and contingencies challenging attempts to subvert power structures, some of which (such as the elements) could even be decisive. In this way, one of the reasons for working on a close scale is to avoid too much condensation and to restore some of the 'blinding speed and complexity of the game as the players experience it'. James C. Scott, *Two Cheers for Anarchism* (Princeton: Princeton University Press, 2012), 136–41.

57 I must thank one of my anonymous peer reviewers for this analogy.

58 Ian Duffield and James Bradley, eds, *Representing Convicts: New Perspectives on Convict Forced Labour Migration* (London: Leicester University Press, 1997), 4. In the context of Australia, the question of convict voice has been discussed at some length, often with a clear theoretical nod to subaltern studies. See also, Hamish Maxwell-Stewart, 'The Search for the Convict Voice', *Tasmanian Historical Studies*, 6:1 (1998), 75–89; Lucy Frost and Hamish Maxwell-Stewart, *Chain-Letters: Narrating Convict Lives* (Melbourne: Melbourne University Press, 2001); Nathan Garvey, 'The Convict Voice and British Print Culture: The Case of "Mellish's Book of Botany Bay"', *Australian Historical Studies* 44, no. 3 (2013): 423–37.

59 While we might posit a conceptual difference (for instance, rumour is often conceived of as anonymous, but storytelling as the narration of experiences was not) between these two acts, the sources rarely allow us to distinguish them in practice.

60 Francis Bacon, *The Major Works* (Oxford: Oxford University Press, 2002), 374.

61 As argued in a recent volume on sound histories, 'Sound's ambiguity and indeterminacy reside in part in the differing particular contexts of listeners'. Daniel Bender, Duane J. Corpis and Daniel J. Walkowitz, 'Editors' Introduction', *Radical History Review* 121, no. 1 (2015): 2. See also Evan Kutlzer, 'Captive Audiences: Sound, Silence, and Listening in Civil War Prisons', *Journal of Social History* 48, no. 2 (2014): 239–63; Sophia Rosenfeld, 'On Being Heard: A Case for Paying Attention to the Historical Ear', *American Historical Review* 116, no. 2 (2011): 316–34.

62 Jane Kamensky, *Governing the Tongue: The Politics of Speech in Early New England* (New York: Oxford University Press, 1997).

63 This entails a risk, as it is never completely certain whether words recorded are there because they *were* said or because they are befitting of what the writers found a certain subject *should* say. I have dared many guesses in this regard and have tried to make my reasoning as transparent as possible.

64 Several studies have discussed issues of speech and language in Atlantic colonial empires. E.g. Kamensky, *Governing*; Sandra Gustafson, *Eloquence is Power: Oratory and Performance in Early America* (Chapel Hill: University of North Carolina Press, 2000); Terri Snyder, *Brabbling Women: Disorderly Speech and the Law in Early Virginia* (Ithaca: Cornell University Press, 2003); Javier Villa-Flores, *Dangerous Speech: A Social History of Blasphemy in Colonial Mexico* (Tucson: The University

of Arizona Press, 2006); Miles Ogborn, 'The power of speech: orality, oaths and evidence in the British Atlantic World, 1650–1800', *Transactions of the Institute of British Geographers* 36 (2011): 109–25.

65 The role of speech in voyage narratives has been explored by Carl Thompson, *The Suffering Traveller and the Romantic Imagination* (Oxford: Clarendon Press, 2007); Richard Frohock, *Buccaneers and Privateers: The Story of the English Sea Rover, 1675–1725* (Newark: University of Delaware Press, 2012); Johan Heinsen, '"Nothing but Noyse": Political complexities of English Maritime and Colonial Soundscapes', *Radical History Review* 121, no. 1 (2015): 106–22.

66 Marcus Rediker, *Outlaws of the Atlantic: Sailors, Pirates, and Motley Crews in the Age of Sail* (London: Verso, 2014), 9–29.

67 Nils Trosner, *Tordenskjolds matros: Dagbok ført af en norsk matros paa den dansk-norske flaate* (Oslo: Gyldendalske Bokhandel, 1923), 5.

68 In the context of Atlantic history, rumour has often played a part in the histories of uprisings of enslaved workers in the late eighteenth/early nineteenth century. The maritime angle has been explored by Julius S. Scott, who conceived of the free port of St Thomas as a hub in regional news circulation. See his article 'Crisscrossing Empire: Ships, Sailors, and Resistance in the Lesser Antilles in the Eighteenth Century', in *The Lesser Antilles in the Age of European Expansion*, eds Robert L. Paquette (Gainesville: University Press of Florida, 1996), 128–44. See also, Karwan Fatah-Black, 'Orangism, Patriotism, and Slavery in Curaçao, 1795–1796', *International Review of Social History* 58, special issue (2013), 35–60.

69 Walter Benjamin, *Illuminations* (London: Collins, 1973), 100.

70 Brian J. Rouleau, 'Dead Men Do Tell Tales: Folklore, Fraternity, and the Forecastle', *Early American Studies* 5, no. 1 (2007): 30–52.

71 Robert Darnton, *The Great Cat Massacre: And Other Episodes in French Cultural History* (New York: Basic Books, 1984), 96–9.

72 Scott, *Domination*, 145.

73 For a theoretical exploration of the open-ended character of such conversational narrative, see Elinor Ochs and Lisa Capps, *Living Narrative: Creating Lives in Everyday Storytelling* (Cambridge MA: Harvard University Press, 2001), chap. 1.

74 Scott, *Domination*.

75 Frederick Cooper and Ann Laura Stoler, 'Between Metropole and Colony: Rethinking a Research Agenda', in *Tensions of Empire: Colonial Encounters in a Bourgeois World*, eds Frederick Cooper and Ann Laura Stoler (Berkeley, Los Angeles and London: University of California Press, 1997), 1–58 (esp. 21).

76 For an insightful discussion of Benjamin's concept, see Joan W. Scott, 'Storytelling', *History and Theory*, 50 (2011): 203–9.

77 Benjamin, *Illuminations*, 87.

78 Rediker, *Outlaws*, 13.

79 David M. Hopkin, 'Storytelling, fairytales and autobiography: some observations on eighteenth- and nineteenth-century French soldiers' and sailors' memoirs', *Social History* 29, no. 2 (2004): 186–98 (quote from 187).

80 Ibid.

81 Scott, *Domination*, 144. Scott seems to think of rumour and storytelling as two sides of the same coin. The most important work in the context of rumour as a response to uncertainty remains Ranajit Guha, *Elementary Aspects of Peasant Insurgency in Colonial India* (Delhi: Oxford University Press, 1983). See also Anjan Ghosh, 'The Role of Rumour in History Writing', *History Compass* 6, no. 5 (2008): 1235–43.

82 In her brilliant and highly experimental attempt at reconstructing enslaved Africans' experiences of the Middle Passage, Stephanie Smallwood has discussed the role of uncertainty and how it was met by interpretation and rumour. Stephanie Smallwood, *Saltwater Slavery: A Middle Passage from Africa to American Diaspora* (Cambridge MA: Harvard University Press, 2008), 122–52. Another case study in which the double state of boredom and uncertainty produced subversive speech acts is explored by Stephanie Mawson in her examination of the mutinies among soldiers in the Spanish Pacific in the 1680s. Mawson, 'Rebellion', 138–46.

83 Benjamin, *Illuminations*, 86 and 108.

84 Aristotle, *Poetikken*, trans. Niels Henningsen (Frederiksberg: Det Lille Forlag, 2004), 81.

85 Ibid.

86 Hopkin, 'Storytelling', 197. See also David Hopkin, *Voices of the People in Nineteenth-Century France* (Cambridge: Cambridge University Press, 2012), chap. 2.

87 Ibid.

88 Michel-Rolph Trouillot, *Silencing the Past: Power and the Production of History* (Boston: Beacon Press, 1995), 26.

89 Part of this argument has already been presented in Johan Heinsen, 'Dissonance in the Danish Atlantic: speech, violence, mutiny, 1672–1683', *Atlantic Studies* 13, no. 2. (2016): 187–205.

90 Part of this story has been explored in Johan Heinsen, 'Sørøveriets indbildte fællesskaber: Taler og tunger på sørøverskibets dæk, ca. 1680', *Temp* 9 (2014): 43–67.

1 The Promises of a Seller-of-souls

1 Simon Braad's interrogation, April 1683, 181, WIGC, RA. (hereafter cited as 'Braad's interrogation')

2 Iversen to Oliger Pauli, 19 November 1682, 192, WIGC, RA.

3 Braad's journal, 19 January 1683; Sentence, 20 June 1683, 181, WIGC, RA; von Gent, *Grundelig*.

4 Braad's journal, 19 January 1683.

5 The directors seem to have had great faith in Braad, who according to a secret order was third in line for the task of governor of St Thomas in the case of death. He was only behind the lieutenant Christopher Heins, already stationed at St Thomas. Copybook, fol. 38, 34, WIGC, RA. Jens Peder Skou, 'Braads saga', *Personalhistorisk tidsskrift*, no. 1 (1997): 75–99.

6 Krarup, *Jørgen Iversen.*

7 He was integral to the plan of the voyage. See minutes, p. 58, 14, WICG, RA; Book of participants' resolutions, 31 March 1682, 6, WIGC, RA.

8 Krarup, *Jørgen Iversen,* 27.

9 Braad's journal, 3 December 1682.

10 Ibid., 19 January 1683.

11 Ibid.

12 On threats as 'catalysts' of mutinies see Rediker, 'African', 29.

13 Braad's journal, 20 January 1683.

14 Copybook, fol. 18, 34, WIGC, RA.

15 Ibid.; Minutes, p. 41, 14, WIGC, RA; Feldbæk, *Danske*, 365–80.

16 Copybook, fol. 18, 34, WIGC, RA.

17 Minutes, p. 1, 484, WIGC, RA.

18 Ibid. On oaths in colonial empires see Ogborn, 'Power of Speech'.

19 Minutes, p. 1–2, 484, WIGC, RA. In 1670, Iversen published a short book of prayers. See Jørgen Iwersen, *Fiire Sparetjmers Fructer* (Copenhagen, 1670). The priest on the 1671–72 voyage, Kjeld Jensen, had published a prayer book specifically for seafarers called *Goed-Haffn* (Copenhagen: Jørgen Lamprecht 1670). Undoubtedly, these books were read on board to prevent illicit speech.

20 Copybook of letters, p. 7, 41, WIGC, RA.

21 Ibid., p. 68, 41.

22 Copybook of letters, p. 328, 41, WIGC, RA. Stories about unfreedom in Northern Africa circulated widely in seventeenth- and eighteenth-century Denmark. For more see Martin Rheinheimer, 'From Amrum to Algiers and Back: The Reintegration of a Renegade in the Eighteenth Century', *Central European History* 36, no. 2 (2003): 209–33. Such comparisons on the part of subalterns themselves also took place elsewhere. Rebellious soldiers tasked with heavy labour on Guam in the Spanish Pacific were overheard making the exact same comparison in 1681. Mawson, 'Mutiny', 143.

23 Copybook of letters, p. 212, 42, WIGC, RA.

24 Bro-Jørgensen, *Tropekolonier*, 56.

25 See Memorandum, 'Fortegnelse huad det folck som döde paa henreysen til St Thomas hafuer kost Compagniet', 1682, 138, WIGC, RA.

26 Copybook, fol. 13–4, 34, WIGC, RA.

27 Minutes, p. 31–3, 484, WIGC, RA.

28 Memorandum, 'Memorie om Pieter Jansens forhold her paa St Thomas', n.d., 77, WIGC, RA.

29 Iversen to the company directors, 25 January 1680, 77, WIGC, RA.

30 Minutes, p. 22–3, 484, WIGC, RA.

31 Ibid., p. 25–7. The notion that alcohol attributes to the formation of 'hidden transcripts' has been explored by Scott. His argument is that in situations of domination subordinate groups will carve out hidden spheres in which they can voice those opinions that would otherwise cost them dearly. Such 'hidden transcripts' mark a sort of virtual sphere, or as Scott puts it a 'fantasy' of resistance in which subordinates can act out their dreams of insubordination in speech without running the risk of reciprocal violence. These practices risk spilling into the public transcript (the discourse presided over by authorities) on occasions when the ability to control oneself was, for various reasons, lessened. The intensity and importance of such moments, thus relied on the fact that they broke a silence that both dominant and subordinate groups had much vested in. Scott, *Domination*, 40–1.

32 Memorandum, 'Memorie ang. drukkenskab', n.d., vol. 30, 539, WIGC, RA.

33 Iversen to the Company directors, 25 January 1680, 77, WIGC, RA.

34 Minutes, p. 31–2, 484, WIGC, RA.

35 Iversen to the Company directors, 25 January 1680, 77, WIGC, RA.

36 Esmit lamented how everyone who had complained of Iversen had been labelled a 'rogue and a traitor'. Excerpt of letter from Esmit to the Company directors, 19 September 1680, 78, WIGC, RA.

37 Iversen to the Company directors, 25 January 1680, 77, WIGC, RA.

38 Iversen's journal, 5 July to 20 September, 495, WIGC, RA.

39 Iversen to the Company directors, 25 January 1680, 77, WIGC, RA.

40 Iversen to the Company directors, 16 May 1680, 77, WIGC, RA.

41 At one point, when gathered in the fort for protection against the French, Jansen had reportedly asked if the people were 'imprisoned people'. Iversen to the directors, 16 May 1680, 77, WIGC, RA. In a different letter, Iversen tells the directors how he heard the master Claes Bording saying that Jansen had attempted to raise a mutiny against him during a voyage from Curaçao to Tobago. Iversen to the directors, 16 May 1680, 77, WIGC, RA.

42 Krarup, *Jørgen Iversen*, 23.

43 Iversen to the Company directors, 16 May, 4 June, 18 June and 20 June 1680, 77, WIGC, RA. See also Memorandum, 26 June 1680, 77, WIGC, RA.

44 Iversen to the company directors, 12 December 1680, 77, WIGC, RA.

45 Excerpt of letter from Esmit to the Company directors, 5 July 1681, 78, WIGC, RA.

46 The attestations themselves are found in 78, WIGC, RA. Compared with Iversen's letters, they are brief.

47 The letters have been used in Danish historiography when discussing the tensions in the colony. E.g. Krarup, *Jørgen Iversen* and Bro-Jørgensen, *Tropekolonier*, 90–5.

48 Iversen to the Company directors, 15 September 1681, 78, WIGC, RA.

49 Ibid.; Iversen to the Company directors, 12 October 1681, 78, WIGC, RA.

50 Iversen to the Company directors, 15 September 1681, 78, WIGC, RA.

51 The Company had agreed to the plan only as a temporary measure. Minutes, p. 278, 12, WIGC, RA. Esmit's policy seems to have attracted foreign planters. See Excerpt of Rasmus Pedersen's letter to Iversen, 6 October 1681, 78, WIGC, RA.

52 Iversen to the Company directors, 15 September 1681 and 12 October 1681, 78, WIGC, RA.

53 Bro-Jørgensen was the first to notice this. See Bro-Jørgensen, *Tropekolonier*, 92–3.

54 Memorandum, 'Memorie ang. drukkenskab', vol. 30, 539, WIGC, RA.

55 Iversen to the Company directors, 12 October 1681, 78, WIGC, RA.

56 Attestations against Iversen, 78, WIGC, RA.

57 Iversen to the Company directors, 15 September 1681 and 12 October 1681, 78, WIGC, RA.

58 Ibid.; Minutes, p. 5, 484, WIGC, RA.

59 Copybook of letters, p. 25–6, 41, WIGC, RA.

60 Tyge Krogh, 'Bødlens og natmandens uærlighed', *Historisk Tidsskrift* 94, no. 1 (1994): 30–57.

61 Why Iversen would not want a black man beating a white is unclear. His successors used enslaved Africans as executioners – a practice that was not uncommon in the Caribbean.

62 Iversen to the company directors, 12 October 1681, 78, WIGC, RA.

63 Ibid.

64 Ibid.

65 Ibid.

66 Ibid.

67 Iversen to the company directors, 15 September 1681, 78, WIGC, RA.

68 Ibid.

69 Ibid. A later governor, Gabriel Milan, confirmed that Iversen had worked his own and the Company enslaved so 'brutally' that they had been permanently injured. Gabriel Milan to the Company directors, 26 July 1685, 89, WIGC, RA.

70 Enclosed documents to the letter from Iversen to the Company directors, 19 May 1680, 77, WIGC, RA.

71 For more on slave rebellions in Barbados see Jason T. Sharples, 'Discovering Slave Conspiracies: New Fears of Rebellion and Old Paradigms of Plotting in Seventeenth-Century Barbados', *American Historical Review* 120, no. 3 (2015): 811–47.

72 For a discussion of perceptions on slave suicides see Terri Snyder, 'Suicide, Slavery, and Memory in North America', *Journal of American History* 97, no. 1 (2010): 39–62; Smallwood, *Saltwater*, 179–80; Marcus Rediker, *The Slave Ship: A Human History* (London: John Murray, 2007), 288–91.

73 Vincent Brown, 'Spiritual Terror and Sacred Authority in Jamaican Slave Society', *Slavery and Abolition* 24, no. 1 (2003): 24–53.

74 Iversen to the Company directors, 15 September 1681, 78, WIGC, RA.

75 Krarup, *Jørgen Iversen*; Bro-Jørgensen, *Tropekolonier*, 90–2.

76 Erik Gøbel, *A Guide to Sources for the History of the Danish West Indies (U.S. Virgin Islands), 1671–1917* (Odense: University of Southern Denmark, 2002), 165.

77 Minutes, p. 2–8 and 65–6, 14, WIGC, RA.

78 Miles Ogborn, *Indian Ink: Script and Print in the Making of the East India Company* (Chicago: The University of Chicago Press, 2007).

79 It is hinted at already in Hans Jonsen to Oliger Pauli, 8 October 1681, 78, WIGC, RA.

80 Copybook, fol. 35–6, 34, WIGC, RA.

81 Copybook of letters, p. 16–7, 41, WIGC, RA.

82 Instruction for Iversen, 29 October 1682, 27, WIGC, RA.

83 Krarup, *Jørgen Iversen*, 15.

84 Bro-Jørgensen, *Tropekolonier*, 97; Ove Hornby, *Kolonierne i Vestindien* (Copenhagen: Politikens Forlag, 1980), 46–7.

85 Erling Sandmo, *Voldssamfunnets undergang: Om disiplineringen av Norge på 1600-tallet* (Oslo: Universitetsforlaget 2002), 136–43.

86 Tyge Krogh, *Oplysningstiden og det magiske: Henrettelser og korporlige straffe i 1700-tallets første halvdel* (Copenhagen: Samlerens forlag, 2000), 342–48 and 592.

87 In some ways, the analogy goes even further. In his attempt at defining what makes a 'slave', sociologist Orlando Patterson has argued that being outside of the game of honour and reputation was a key constituting feature in slavery itself. This further highlights the likeness of these two categories of labourers. Orlando Patterson, *Slavery and Social Death: A Comparative Study* (Cambridge: Harvard University Press 1982), 5–6; see also 44–6.

88 See, for instance, Moth's dictionary from 1686. Accessed online at www.mothsordbog.dk on 8 January 2016.

89 Ludvig Holberg, *Introduction Til Naturens- Og Folke-Rettens Kundskab, Uddragen Af de fornemste Juristers besynderlig Grotii Pufendorfs og Thomasii Skrifter* (Copenhagen: Johan Kruse, 1716), 2:110.

90 Memorandum, 'Fortegnelse huad det folck som döde paa henreysen til St Thomas hafuer kost Compagniet', 138, WIGC, RA.

91 Johan Lorents to the Company Directors, 19 December 1689, 510, WIGC, RA.

92 J. L. Carstens, 'Beskrivelse om Alle de Danske, Americanske eller West-Jndiske Ey-Lande', *Danske Magazin* 8, no. 3 (1970), 173–268 (esp. 237).

93 There were men on board who knew the full extent of the attestations against Iversen – among them Captain Blom and merchant Niels Lassen, who had both been at St Thomas at the time of their writing and who had even signed some of the milder accusations. They are, however, unlikely to have shared such stories with the convicts.

94 Minutes, p. 13, 14, WIGC, RA.

95 Braad's journal, 20 January 1683, 181, WIGC, RA.

96 Or perhaps, 'Hertz' does not signify 'heart' but 'fire' (from the old German 'Herd' meaning fireplace) possibly making it 'may the Devil take you into the fire'.

97 Ibid.; Braad's interrogation, 'hvorledes det henger samen ...?'.

98 Braad's interrogation, 'Om hand selv saadan have seet og hørt ...?'

99 Braad's journal, 20 January 1683.

100 Ibid.

101 von Gent, *Grundelig*. Von Gent was himself on the quarterdeck during the altercation between Biermand and Blom and claimed that the furious boatswain's mate had also threatened to throw him overboard.

102 Braad's journal, 20 January 1683.

103 J. R. Bruijn, 'Seamen in Dutch Ports: *c.* 1700–*c.* 1914', *The Mariner's Mirror: The journal of the Society of Nautical Research* 65, no. 4 (1979): 327–37 (quote from 332).

104 C. R. Boxer, *The Dutch Seaborne Empire 1600–1800* (London: Hutchinson & Co., 1965), 81.

105 Bruijn, 'Seamen', 331.

106 Matthias van Rossum, '"Working for the Devil": Desertion in the Eurasian Empire of the VOC', in *Desertion in the Early Modern World: A Comparative History*, eds Matthias van Rossum and Jeanette Kamp (London: Bloomsbury, 2016), 127–160 (140).

107 Hans Mesler, 'Journal paa Reisen fra Kiøbenhavs til Trankebar', NKS 769 kvart, Manuscript collection, The Royal Library, Copenhagen, fol. 29.

108 Census paper, 'Mandtall Paa hans Kongelige May=ts Orlaag skib Engelen, Mandskabsruller for Niels Juels eskadre', nd., 2, Admiralitetet, RA.

109 Copybook, fol. 15, 34, WIGC, RA. See also, minutes, p. 44, 14, WIGC, RA.

110 Braad's interrogation, 'Om hand selv saadan have set og hørt?'

111 Rediker and Linebaugh, *Many-Headed Hydra*.

112 Copybook, fol. 13, 34, WIGC, RA; Minutes, p. 41, 14, WIGC, RA. There are seventeen contracts signed by indentured servants in Box 27, WIGC, RA.

2 Echoes

1 Jan Blom's order, 29 October 1682, 27, WIGC, RA.

2 Braad's journal, 20 January 1683; von Gent, *Grundelig*.

3 Braad's journal, 20 January 1683; von Gent, *Grundelig*.

4 Journal fragment running from 6 to 18 November 1682, 192, WIGC, RA.

5 Braad's journal, 20 November 1682.

6   In 1804, an officer wrote how it was necessary for him to hide his anxieties during storms so as not to discourage his crew. See Ida Christine Jørgensen, 'Identiteter i flåden – en undersøgelse af verdens – og selvopfattelsen hos danske søfolk i perioden 1670–1820', *Sjæk'len* (2014): 23.

7   Johan Heinsen, *Intet andet end støj* (PhD thesis, Aalborg University, 2013).

8   Johan Petri Cortemünde, *Dagbog fra en ostindiefart 1672–75*, trans. Henning Henningsen (Kronborg: Handels- og Søfartsmuseet, 1953), 111.

9   Hans Mesler, 'Journal paa Reisen fra Kiøbenhavs til Trankebar', NKS 769 kvart, Manuscript collection, The Royal Library, Copenhagen, fol. 6.

10 Ibid., fol. 24. A similar critique is found in Jon Olafsson, *Life of the Icelander Jón Ólafsson, Traveller to India: Volume II* (London: The Hakluyt Society, 1931), 214–16.

11 Braad's journal, 21 November 1682.

12 Ibid., 19–23 December 1682.

13 These calculations were done by Iversen. Braad's interrogation, 'Hvorledes de blev spiiset …?'

14 Braad's journal, 23 December 1683.

15 Memorandum, 'Fortegnelse, hvis til dend resolverede Vdreedning requireris', n.d., 192, WIGC, RA.

16 Braad's journal, 2 December 1683.

17 Ibid., 19 November 1682. In an order for Iversen, Peis was described as a cooper and an able seaman. Order for Iversen, 3 November 1682, 192, WIGC, RA.

18 Braad's journal, 23 December 1683.

19 Ibid.

20 Braad's interrogation, 'Hvad Gourerneuren, der ved giorde?'

21 Sandmo, *Voldssamfunnets*, 129–30.

22 Aristotle, *The Politics* (London: Penguin, 1981), 1253b.

23 Dening, *Bligh's*, 132.

24 Braad's journal, 28 December 1682.

25 Ibid. 30 December 1682.

26 Around half of all Danish slave ships had a stay in a Norwegian or, less commonly, a Swedish harbour. See Erik Gøbel, 'Danish Shipping Along the Triangular Route, 1671–1802: voyages and conditions on board', *Scandinavian Journal of History* 36, no. 2 (2011): 135–55 (here 138).

27 Braad's journal, 1–2 January 1683.

28 Ibid. There were several specialized prayer books available to Danish seafarers at this point. In one of them Braad could have found the following lines of instruction for countering the noise with loud religious sound: 'in our deepest fears we scream, cry and shout to you, oh God, hurry to come to our rescue, this water is getting to our souls, and none can be saved, without you alone.' D. Daniel Cram, *Christelige Skibsfart* (Copenhagen, 1677), 48.

29 Braad's journal, 3 January 1683.

30 Ibid., 4–11 January 1683.

31 Ibid., 11–13 January 1683.

32 Ibid., 14–18 January 1683.

33 Braad's interrogation, 'Om hand og saa hafde giort æd?' See also Braad's journal, 20 January 1683.

34 Memorandum, 'Forteignelse huad det folck som döde paa henreysen til St. Thomas hafuer kost Compagniet', n.d. (1682), 138, WIGC, RA.

35 von Gent, *Grundelig.*

36 Jørgen Iversen to Oliger Paulli, 19 November 1682, 192, WIGC, RA.

37 T. A. Topsøe-Jensen and Emil Marquard, *Officerer i den dansk-norske søetat 1660– 1814 og den danske søetat 1814–1932: Første bind* (Copenhagen: H. Hagerup, 1935), 151.

38 Hans Jonsen to Oliger Paulli, 28 October 1680, 77, WIGC, RA.

39 Bastian Pedersen Calundborg to Oliger Paulli, 16 November 1680, 77, WIGC, RA.

40 Hans Jonsen to the company directors, 29 May 1681, 77, WIGC, RA; Hans Jonsen to Oliger Paulli, 6 June 1681, 77, WIGC, RA; Memorandum, 'Designation paa compagniens folck', 1680, 191, WIGC, RA.

41 Complaint, 'Hans Tidsen Raus klagemaal at Capt: Blom hafuer slaget hans broder forderfuet', 78, WIGC, RA; Memorandum, 'Designation paa compagniens folck', 1680, 191, WIGC, RA.

42 Hans Jonsen to the company directors, 4 May 1681, 77, WIGC, RA.

43 Hans Jonsen to the company directors, 29 May 1681, 77, WIGC, RA; Hans Jonsen to Oliger Paulli, 6 June 1681, 77, WIGC, RA.

44 Bastian Pedersen Calundborg to the Company directors, 3 June 1681, 77, WIGC, RA.

45 Ibid.

46 The company directors to Hans Jonsen, 15 November 1681, 42, WIGC, RA.

47 Ann Laura Stoler, *Along the Archival Grain* (Princeton: Princeton University Press 2008), 41. See also Arlette Farge, *The Allure of the Archives* (New Haven: Yale University Press, 2013), 29.

48 Braad's journal, 21 January 1683.

49 Henrik Christiansen, *Orlogsflådens skibe gennem 500 år* (Copenhagen: Statens Forsvarshistoriske Museum, 2010), 1:143.

50 Jørgen Barfod, *Niels Juels flåde 1660–1720* (Copenhagen: Marinehistorisk Selskab, 1997), 46, 51, and 65.

51 Braad's journal, 20 January 1683.

52 Scott, *Domination*, 82–85. Scott seems to think of the type of total institutions explored by Goffman and Foucault.

53 Order for Kay Jessen, 7 April 1688, 510, WIGC, RA.

54 Frederik Christian von Haven, *Min Sundheds Forliis: Frederik Christian von Havens Rejsejournal fra Den Arabiske Rejse 1760–1763* (Copenhagen: Forlaget Vandkunsten, 2005), 75–6.

55 Hans Mesler, 'Journal paa Reisen fra Kiøbenhavs til Trankebar', NKS 769 kvart, Manuscript collection, The Royal Library, Copenhagen, fol. 24.

56 Braad's journal, 26 November 1682.

57 Rediker, *Between*, 165–69.

58 Alain Cabantous, *Blasphemy: Impious Speech in the West from the Seventeenth to the Nineteenth Century* (New York: Columbia University Press, 2002), 84–5.

59 Villa-Flores, *Dangerous Speech*, 58; Nigel Penn, 'The Voyage Out: Peter Kolb and VOC Voyages to the Cape', in *Many Middle Passages: Forced Migration and the Making of the Modern World,* eds Emma Christopher, Cassandra Pybus and Marcus Rediker, (Berkeley: University of California Press, 2007), 72–91.

60 Cortemünde, *Dagbog*, 103.

61 Gøbel, *Sveigaards*, 140.

62 The common sailor Nils Trosner, whose diary is dealt with at length in Chapter 4 related several stories of warning about blaspheming. Cursing was potentially ruinous, he implied. Trosner, *Tordenskiolds,* 150.

63 David Hopkin has argued that stories served a similar function, as it allowed soldiers and sailors to 'sound out the opinion of their comrades through the reaction of their audience, while all the time masking their own intentions behind the fiction of the tale'. Hopkin, 'Storytelling', 197.

64 Braad's journal, 3 December 1682.

65 Hans Mesler, 'Journal paa Reisen fra Kiøbenhavs til Trankebar', NKS 769 kvart, Manuscript collection, The Royal Library, Copenhagen, fol. 9. Cortemunde repeatedly describes how sailors got their hands on brandy and drank to excess, despite being punished by the last time and again. Cortemunde, *Dagbog*, 54–8.

66 Braad's journal, 24 December 1682.

67 Ibid., 7 February 1683.

68 Brandon LaBelle, *Acoustic Territories: Sound Culture and Everyday Life* (London: Continuum International Publishing, 2010), xvii.

69 Braad's journal, 24 February 1683.

70 Ibid., 26 February 1683.

71 Ibid., 20 January 1683.

72 Moth's dictionary. Accessed online (17 November 2015). http://mothsordbog.dk/ordbog?select=Knur,c&query=knur.

73 Braad's journal, 20 January 1683, 181, WIGC, RA.

74 Ibid.

75 von Gent, *Grundelig*, 20 January 1683.

76 Braad's interrogation, 'Hvem flere der blev myrt?'

77   The death of the company's assistant clerk Johan Mohr is, however, difficult to
      ascribe to Blom. Mohr might simply have interfered at the wrong moment when
      the mutineers broke into the cabins. He was thrown through the cabin window
      alive. Braad's journal, 20 January 1683, 181, WIGC, RA.
78   Scott, *Domination*, 38.
79   Ibid. 41–2.
80   Braad's journal, 5 December 1682.
81   See for instance, Gøbel, *Sveigaards*, 42.
82   Braad's journal, 20 January, 11 February and 24 February 1683.
83   Lionel Wafer, *A New Voyage and Description of the Isthmus of America: Reprinted
      from the original of 1699* (Cleveland: The Burrows Brothers Company, 1903), 186–87.
84   Rouleau, 'Dead Men', 53.
85   Braad's journal, 21 January 1683.
86   Worden, 'Below', 728.
87   Kåre Lauring, *Rejsen til Madagascar* (Copenhagen: Gyldendal, 1987), 45–97.
88   Karwan Fatah-Black, 'Desertion by Sailors, Slaves and Soldiers in the Dutch
      Atlantic, *c.* 1600–1800', in *Desertion in the Early Modern World: A Comparative
      History*, eds Matthias van Rossum and Jeanette Kamp (London: Bloomsbury, 2016),
      97–126 (esp. 111).
89   Braad's journal, 20 January 1683.
90   Ibid., 26 February 1683.
91   Ibid.; Sentence, 20 June 1683, 181, WIGC, RA.
92   Braad's interrogation, 'Om Bierman og hans följe hafde Gevæhr?'
93   Braad's journal, 26 February 1683.
94   Ibid.
95   Rediker, 'African', 28.
96   In one of the many inventories of salvaged goods, a mention appears of 'four
      convict irons with chains to have around their waists'. There were four convicts
      among the chief rebels. Inventory, 20 June 1683, 192, WIGC, RA. Of course, we do
      not know if the rest of the convicts wearing chains were also delivered from their
      bondage hardware. In a similar, but later, inventory of more salvaged goods,
      ninety-five 'fetters' are mentioned, though it is possible that these might have
      been shipped to be used in the intended slave voyage. Inventory, 9 July 1685, 366,
      WIGC, RA.
97   Copybook 1682, 14 January 1682, 241, Admiralitetet, RA.
98   Court minutes, fol. 77, vol. 1682, 2, Underadmiralitetsretten, Admiralitetet, RA.
99   Copybook 1682, 18 September 1682, 241, Admiralitetet, RA; Court minutes, fol. 77,
      vol. 1682, 2, Underadmiralitetsretten, Admiralitetet, RA.
100   Court minutes, fol. 44, vol. 1682, 2, Underadmiralitetsretten, Admiralitetet, RA.
101   Court minutes, fol. 21, 44 and 77, ibid.

102 Joen Jakob Seerup, *Søetaten i 1700-tallet: Organisation, personel og dagligdag* (PhD-thesis: University of Copenhagen, 2010), 138–44.

103 Church records for Holmen's Church, 1653–1697, consulted at http://www.sa.dk/content/dk/ao-forside/find_kirkeboger# (1 December 2014).

104 Copybook 1682, 18 September 1682, 241, Admiralitetet, RA.

105 The Original is in box 496, Søkrigskancelliet (søetaten), RA. Copies are in box 51, Søkrigskancelliet (søetaten), RA and Copybook 1682, 20 Oktober 1682, 241, Admiralitetet, RA.

106 The Admiralty to the king, 2 October 1682, 496, Søkrigskancelliet (søetaten), RA.

107 Hamish Maxwell-Stewart, '"Those Lads Contrived a Plan": Attempts at Mutiny on Australia-Bound Convict Vessels', *International Review of Social History* 58, special issue (2013): 188.

108 Rediker, 'African', 15–34. See also, Ulrich, 'British', 73; Frykman, 'Connections', 103.

109 Georg Nørregaard, *Vore Gamle Tropekolonier: Guldkysten* (Copenhagen: Forlaget Fremad, 1968), 89–91; Lauring, *Slaverne*, 84–6.

110 This also seems to have deterred investments in the Company, whose participants were seemingly unwilling to adventure their money. See for instance, Letter copybook, p. 347, 41, WIGC, RA. Justesen has calculated that this loss amounted to the company's entire capital. Feldbæk and Justesen, *Kolonierne*, 329.

111 Complaint against Captain Ove Ovesen, n.d., 78, WIGC, RA.

112 Journal, 18–20 December 1680, 4D Havmanden 1680, 4D–6M, Skibsjournaler, Marineministeriet, RA.

113 Ibid., 8–9 February 1681.

114 Magnus Pranger to the Company directors, 7 April 1681, 78, WIGC, RA.

115 Journal, 1–3 May 1681, 4D Havmanden 1680, 4D–6M, Skibsjournaler, Marineministeriet, RA.

116 Hans Lykke *et al.* to the company directors, 3 May 1681, printed in *Danish Sources for the History of Ghana 1657–1754*, ed. Ole Justesen (Copenhagen: Det Kongelige Danske Videnskabernes Selskab), 1:66.

117 Hans Lykke and Jacob van Tetz to the Directors, 12 May 1681, printed in Justesen, *Sources*, 1:67.

118 Journal excerpt, 'Extract udaf protocollen hvorledis om ded antagne folck er resolveret', n.d., 191, WIGC, RA.

119 Jean Barbot, *Barbot on Guinea* (London: Hakluyt Society, 1992), 2:398–410.

120 Andreas Jacobsen to the Directors, printed in Justesen, *Sources,* 1:63.

121 Nørregaard, *Tropekolonier*, 91.

122 Interrogation, numbered 19/4, 78, WIGC, RA.

123 Seerup, *Søetaten,* 138–44.

124 Copybook 1682, 18 February 1682, 241, Admiralitetet, RA.

125 Braad's interrogation, 'Hvem de vare, som lagde haand paa dem, og tog dem fangen?'

126 Court minutes, fol. 21, vol. 1682, 2, Underadmiralitetsretten, Admiralitetet, RA.

127 Copybook 1682, 21 March 1682, 241, Admiralitetet, RA.

128 Ibid., 10 April 1682. Another convict whom Gulliksen met was Anthony Loumand, who had been sentenced for attempting to stab someone in the king's castle. He seems to have been a soldier. Ibid, 20 September 1682. If he was Gulliksen's friend as well it would explain why he was among the few who made it back with the *Havmanden*. Loumand was among three convicts from *Trunken* who were not executed upon arriving in Copenhagen in 1683. He was instead sentenced to be placed back on Bremerholmen.

129 Sentence, 20 June 1683, 181, WIGC, RA.

130 Braad's journal, 22 February 1683.

131 Iversen's instruction, 29 October 1682, 27, WIGC, RA.

132 Hopkin, *Voices*, 99–108.

133 Braad's journal, 25 February 1683.

134 Ibid.

135 Ibid., 21 January 1683.

136 Ibid., 20 January 1683.

137 Rediker, *Villains*; Christopher Hill, 'Radical Pirates', in *The Collected Essays of Christopher Hill* (Brighton: The Harvester Press, 1986), 3:161–87; Robert C. Ritchie, *Captain Kidd and the War against the Pirates* (Cambridge and London: Harvard University Press, 1986); Heinsen, 'Sørøveriets', 43–67.

138 Rediker and Linebaugh, *Many-Headed Hydra*, 163.

139 Peter Earle, *The Pirate Wars* (London: Methuen, 2004), 32. For more on Irish piracy, see C. M. Senior, *A Nation of Pirates: English Piracy in Its Heyday* (New York: Crane, Russak & Company, 1976); David Delison Hebb, *Piracy and the English Government, 1616–1642* (Aldershot: Scholar Press, 1994).

140 David J. Starkey, 'Pirates and Markets', in *Bandits at Sea,* ed. C.R. Pennel (New York: New York University Press 2001), 107–126 (esp. 111).

141 Earle, *Pirate Wars*, 30–5.

142 Ibid. 55–67.

143 Scott, *Domination*.

3 Ways of Listening

1 Braad's journal, 20 January 1683; von Gent, *Grundelig*, 1683.

2 von Gent, *Grundelig*, 1683.

3 Braad's journal, 20 January 1683; Braad's interrogation, 'Om Biermand og hans følge hafde Gevæhr?'

4 Ibid., 'Hvad talle hand da førte med bemelte Compag: betienter?'

5 Ibid., 'Hvorledes det forholt sig med Compagniens betienter ...'

6 Ibid., 'Hvad talle hand da førte med bemelte Compag: betienter?'

7 Braad's journal, 20 January 1683.

8 Braad's interrogation, 'Om Bierman og hans følge hafde Gevæhr?'

9 Ibid., 'Hvad talle hand da førte med bemelte Compag: betienter?'

10 Ibid., 'Hvad Chargier de var og hvem dem skulle beklæde?'; Braad's journal, 20 January 1683; von Gent, *Grundelig*, 1683.

11 Braad's interrogation, 'Hvorledes det forholt sig med Compagniens betienter ...?'

12 Ibid., 'Hvorledis sligt af Folket blev optagen?'

13 Braad's journal, 20 January 1683.

14 Braad's interrogation, 'Om hand og saa hafde giort æd?'; Braad's journal, 20 January 1683.

15 Ibid.

16 Ibid.

17 Anderson, 'The Ferringees are flying', 146–47.

18 Ibid., 181.

19 Minutes, p. 78–79, 14, WIGC, RA.

20 Minutes, p. 177–78, 12, WIGC, RA.

21 Seerup, *Søetaten*, 204.

22 Ship's articles, 193, WIGC, RA.

23 Minutes, p. 79–80, 14, WIGC, RA.

24 Hugo Matthiessen, *Natten: Studier i gammelt byliv* (Copenhagen: Gyldendalske Boghandel, 1914), 85.

25 Ship's articles, 193, WIGC, RA.

26 Ibid.

27 Minutes, p. 79–80, 14, WIGC, RA.

28 Cortemunde, *Dagbog*, 39.

29 In an inventory of salvaged goods from the *Havmanden*, we find a 'broken trumpet'. The sound of the trumpet carried some of the same connotations as salutary cannons. Inventory, 16 June 1685, 366, WICG, RA.

30 Cortemünde, *Dagbog*, 40.

31 Instruction for Blom, 31 October 1682, 27, WIGC, RA.

32 Miles Ogborn, 'Writing Travels: Power, Knowledge and Ritual on the English East India Company's Early Voyages', *Transactions of the Institute of British Geographers, New Series* 27, no. 2 (2002): 155–71 (esp. 164).

33 Journal fragment, 6–19 November 1682, 192, WIGC, RA.

34 Cortemünde, *Dagbog*, 42.

35 On some ships, the messes also had a disciplinary aim. Olafsson describes how each mess had a leader who was to listen for 'obscene speech'. Olafsson, *Life vol. II*, 44.

36 Journal fragment, 6–19 November 1682, 192, WIGC, RA.

37 Dening, *Bligh's*.

38 Scott, *Domination*, 45–46.

39 Ibid., 61–67.

40 Ship's articles, 193, WIGC, RA.

41 For such a conception of the ears of petty officers, see Peter Schiønning, 'Haandbog i Søemandskab', Peter Schiønning's archive, vol. 42, Schiøn 39–46 kvart, Manuscript collection, Royal Library, Copenhagen, p. 1762–81.

42 Such workings can be understood in the terms of what philosopher Jacques Rancière has termed as a distribution of the 'perceptible.' It is 'an order of the visible and the sayable that sees that a particular activity is visible and another is not, that this speech is understood as discourse and another as noise'. Jacques Rancière, *Disagreement: Politics and Philosophy* (Minneapolis: University of Minnesota Press, 1999), 29.

43 Braad's journal, 12 February 1683.

44 Braad's interrogation, 'Hvem egentlig Rebellerne var?'

45 Braad's journal, 26 February 1683.

46 Ibid., 12 February 1683.

47 Ibid., 22 January 1683.

48 Ibid.

49 Minutes, p. 10, 14, WIGC, RA; van Bronckhorst to Oliger Pauli, 3 January 1682, 78, WIGC, RA.

50 Braad's journal, 28 January 1683.

51 Ibid.

52 Ibid., 20 January 1683.

53 Ibid., 7 February 1683.

54 Ibid., 25 January 1683.

55 Ibid., 25 January 1683.

56 Braad's interrogation, 'Hvorfore efter at de bleve fangerne qvit ...?'

57 Braad's journal, 2 February 1683.

58 Ibid., 24 January 1683.

59 In the Admiralty Court records we find a Magdalena, a Birgitte and an Annika, but the court clerk gets a number of other names wrong, so I go with the names given them by Braad.

60 Braad's interrogation, 'Om da alle Compagniens paa de tiider ...?'; Braad's journal, 12 February 1683; Court minutes, fol. 61–62, 2, vol. 1683, Underadmiralitetsretten, Admiralitetet, RA.

61 Instruction for Blom, 31 October 1682, 27, WIGC, RA.

62 Braad's journal, 8 February 1683.

63 Ibid.

64 Symptomatically, von Gent is murky on the matter.

65 Braad's journal, 10–12 February 1683.

66 Braad's interrogation, 'Hvorfore at Niels Lassen og Lars Thøgesen, ikke saavel som hand blev omborde?'

67 Braad's journal, 12 February 1683, 19 February, 22 February, 4 March, 26 March and 1 April 1683; Braad's interrogation, 'Om da alle Compagniens paa de tiider . . .?'; Sentence, 20 June 1683, 181, WIGC, RA.

68 Braad's interrogation, 'Hvorforre skibet ikke gik til Flores igien . . .?'

69 Letter signed by João Valadares Coelho, Santa Cruz, 13 July 1683, 192, WIGC, RA; Letters signed by Captain António de Freitas Henriques, 12 July 1683, 192, WIGC, RA. I have to thank Sara Pinto for the translation.

70 Coates, *Convicts and Orphans*, 186.

71 Ibid., 35.

72 Ibid., 37.

73 Braad's interrogation, 'Hvorfore at Niels Lassen og Lars Thøgesen, ikke saavel som hand blev omborde?'

74 Braad's journal, 22 February 1683.

75 Ibid., 21 and 23 February 1683; Braad's interrogation, 'Hvoforre efter at de blev fangerne quit . . .?'

76 Braad's journal, 23 February 1683; Braad's interrogation, 'Hvem de vare, som lagde haand paa dem, og tog dem fangen?'

77 Braad's interrogation, 'Om de hafde nogen Suspect til de andre skibs folk, og hvorfore de ikke betroede Dem for vel?'

78 Sentence, 20 June 1683, 181, WIGC, RA.

79 Braad's journal, 24 February 1683; Braad's interrogation, 'Der fangerne nu var satt fast, hvad blev da forretagen?'

80 Braad's journal, 23–27 February 1683.

81 Ibid., 25 February 1683.

82 Ibid., 23 March 1683.

83 It is visible on the illustration accompanying Jan von Gent's relation.

84 This detail is provided by C.E. Secher. He had it from a letter written in German by a witness to the execution. However, his lack of references makes it impossible to find said missive. See Secher, *Danmark*, 314–15. The realness of the letter is, however, indisputable, as it is referenced at length (but in a different translation) in Bering Liisberg's otherwise fictional account of the voyage. See H. C. Bering Liisberg, *Kgl. Majestæts Skib "Havmanden": Billeder i historisk ramme fra Christian den V's tid* (Copenhagen: Det Nordiske Forlag, 1900), 187–88.

85 Braad's journal, 25 March 1683.

86 Jokum Gulliksen to the Admiralty, 25 March 1683, 573, Admiralitetet, RA.

87 Natalie Zemon Davis, *Fiction in the Archives* (Stanford: Stanford University Press, 1987).

88 Farge, *Allure*, 30.

89 Braad's journal, 29 March 1683.

90 Sten Arvesen to Frederik Merker, 2 April 1683, 192, WIGC, RA.

91 Journal of the Makrellen, 11–12 April 1683, 6N–7L, Skibsjournaler, Marineministeriet, RA.

4 Jan Hagel's Stories

1 Seerup, *Søetaten*, 206–09.

2 Arni Magnusson, *En Islandsk Eventyrer: Arni Magnussons Optegnelser* (Copenhagen: Gyldendal, 1918), 107.

3 Holberg, *Dannmarks*, 487–88.

4 Pontoppidan, *Annales,* 4:618–19. Pontoppidan crafted his account on the basis of Braad's, but took many liberties with it.

5 Ethnographer Henning Henningsen came closest to escaping this dead end by hinting at a culture of conflict. However, he seems to reason that it had no public manifestation and consequently failed to make a mark in the sources. Henning Henninsen, 'Sømandsliv på langfart og i hjemlige farvande' in *Dagligliv i Danmark: I det syttende og attende århundrede*, ed. Axel Steenberg (Copenhagen: Nyt Nordisk Forlag, 1969), 687–716.

6 Ole Degn and Erik Gøbel, *Dansk Søfarts Historie: 1588–1720* (Copenhagen: Gyldendal, 1997), 153–54.

7 Jelle van Lottum, 'Some aspects of migration in the North Sea region, 1550–1800', in *The Dynamics of Economic Culture in the North Sea- and Baltic Region in the Late Middle Ages and Early Modern Period*, eds Leos Müller and Hanno Brand (Hilversum: Uitgeverij Verloren, 2007), 170–84. Asger Nørlund Christensen, 'Professional Seamen: A Strategic Resource during the Scanian War, 1675–1679', *International Journal of Maritime History* 27, no. 2 (2015): 192–207.

8 Marcel van der Linden, *Workers of the World: Essays toward a Global Labor History* (Leiden: Brill, 2008), 7. For a call against such nationalism in the context of maritime history see Maria Fusaro, 'Afterword,' in *Law Labour and Empire: Comparative Perspectives on Seafarers c. 1500–1800*, eds Maria Fusaro, Bernard Allaire, Richard Blakemore and Tijl Vanneste (Basingstoke: Palgrave, 2015), 304–310.

9 This distinction was also important, however, because of differences in manning and, in turn, the amount and intensity of the labour. Thus, the work in merchant vessels was typically shared among fewer men.

10 Linebaugh and Rediker, *Many-Headed Hydra*, 150.

11 Rediker, *Between*, 92–94.

12 Ibid., 160; Maillana, *Spain's*, 130–31.

13 Henningsen, 'Sømandsliv', 702–08; Rediker, *Between*, 47–8; Frykman, *Wooden*, 22.

14 Matthias van Rossum, 'Claiming their Rights? Indian Sailors under the Dutch East India Company', in Fusaro *et al.*, *Law*, 272–86 (quote from 278)

15 Ship's articles, 193, WIGC, RA.

16 For a Danish example, see Henningsen, 'Sømandsliv', 697.

17 Rediker, *Between*, 218.

18 Ship's articles, 193, WIGC, RA.

19 This thesis has been explored at length by Rouleau, 'Dead Men', 30–62.

20 Frykman et al, 'Mutiny', 11.

21 Hans Mesler, 'Journal paa Reisen fra Kiøbenhavs til Trankebar', NKS 769 kvart, Manuscript collection, The Royal Library, Copenhagen, fol. 91.

22 Peter Schiønning, 'Haandbog i Søemandskab', Peter Schiønning's archive, vol. 42, Schiøn 39–46 kvart, Manuscript collection, Royal Library, Copenhagen, 1762–81.

23 Even in an international context, the successful shipboard insurrection on the *Havmanden* is a rare case. In the 830 voyages transporting convicts to Australia, Hamish-Maxwell Stewart has found only one case in which shipboard unrest ended in a successful mutiny. Stewart, 'Those Lads', 183.

24 Such numbers can be derived from the slave voyages database at www.slavevoyages.org.

25 Johannes Rask, *A Brief and Truthful Description of a Journey to and from Guinea*, trans. Selena Axelrod Winsnes (Legon: Sub-Saharan Publishers, 2008), 71.

26 Georg Nørregaard, *Farefulde Danske Sørejser: Togter til Afrika i det 18. århundrede* (Copenhagen: Forlaget Fremad, 1969), 11–40. Another incident is discussed by Asta Bredsforff, *The Trials and Travels of Willem Leyel: An Account of the Danish East India Company in Tranquebar, 1643–48* (Copenhagen: Museum Tusculanum, 2009), 66.

27 Frykman, 'Seamen', 67.

28 The heightened tensions of the period were first noticed by H.D. Lind, *Nyboder og dets Beboere, især i ældre tid* (Copenhagen: Klewing-Evers, 1882).

29 Notice to the king, 13 May 1682, Sjællandske Tegnelser 1681–1682, Microfilm S-5032, Danske Kancelli, RA.

30 Court minutes, 1 March 1708, Underadmiralitetsprotokoller, 5, Underadmiralitetsretten, Admiralitetet, RA.

31 Court minutes, 9 January 1694, Kommissionsprotokol, 1, Kommissionsdomstole, Admiralitetet, RA; Ibid., 11 April 1691; Court minutes, fol. 122–24, Standretsprotokoller 50, Overadmiralitetsretten, Admiralitetet, RA.

32 Court minutes, October 1729, Justitssager, 7, Overadmiralitetsretten, Admiralitetet, RA.

33 AnnaSara Hammar, *Mellan kaos och kontrol: Social ordning i Svenska flottan 1670–1716* (Lund: Nordic Academic Press, 2014), 66–7.

34 Court minutes, 3 July 1686, Kommissionsprotokol, 1, Kommissionsdomstole, Admiralitetet, RA.

35 Ibid., 11 December 1690.

36 E.g. Court minutes, 7 September 1713, Underadmiralitetsprotokol, 5, Underadmiralitetsretten, Admiralitetet, RA; Resolution in case, 5 March 1727, Justitsekstrakter, 11125, Generalauditøren, RA.

37 E.g. Court minutes, 6 September 1714, Underadmiralitetsprotokol, 5, Underadmiralitetsretten, Admiralitetet, RA.

38 Sentence of Anders Geed and Rasmus Jørgensen, Justitsekstrakter, 11125, Generalauditøren, RA.

39 Ibid., sentence of Haagen Arentsen and Christopher Christensen.

40 ibid., resolution in the case against Daniel Isacksen, 3 March 1727.

41 Court minutes, 24 May 1708, Underadmiralitetsprotokol, 5, Underadmiralitetsretten, Admiralitetet, RA; 5 and 7 January 1693, Kommissionsprotokol, 1, Kommissionsdomstole, Admiralitetet, RA.

42 Eg., Court minutes, 16 May 1709, Underadmiralitetsprotokoller, 5, Underadmiralitetsretten, Admiralitetet, RA.

43 Court minutes 1728, Justitssager 13, Overadmiralitetsretten, Admiralitetet, RA.

44 Court minutes, January 1729, Justitssager, 14, Overadmiralitetsretten, Admiralitetet, RA.

45 Eg. Court minutes, 7 August 1693, Kommissionsprotokol, 1, Kommissionsdomstole, Admiralitetet, RA.

46 Villads Christensen, 'Daglige begivenheder i København 1716–22. Indberetninger fra Politimester Ernst til Kongen', *Historiske Meddelelser om København* 1, no. 7 (1919–20): 325–85 (342).

47 E.g. Minutes of case against Christen Pedersen, Justitssager, 11, Overadmiralitetsretten, Admiralitetet, RA.

48 E.g. Court minutes, 22 January 1691, Kommissionsprotokol, 1, Kommissionsdomstole, Admiralitetet, RA.

49 Rediker, *Between*, 136.

50 Court minutes, 7 September 1692, Kommissionsprotokol, 1, Kommissionsdomstole, Admiralitetet, RA.

51 Ibid., 29 December 1693.

52 Ibid., 2 November 1691.

53 Eg. Court minutes, 11 June 1712, Underadmiralitetsprotokoller, 5, Underadmiralitetsretten, Admiralitetet, RA.

54 Court minutes, 24 October 1709, Underadmiralitetsprotokoller, 5, Underadmiralitetsretten, Admiralitetet, RA.

55 Ibid., 7 February 1715.

56 Sentence of Joen Ellingsen, Justitsekstrakter, 11125, Generalauditøren, RA.

57 Ibid., Sentence of Christen Jensen; Sentence of Abraham Andersen, Justitsekstrakter, 11126, Generalauditøren, RA.

58 Sentence of Jens Giese, Justitsekstrakter, 11125, Generalauditøren, RA.

59 Court minutes, 25 September 1710, Underadmiralitetsprotokoller, 5, Underadmiralitetsretten, Admiralitetet, RA.

60 Admiralty Court sentence, 30 October 1727, Justitsekstrakter, 11125, Generalauditøren, RA.

61 This figure is based on ongoing work in the Admiralty archives in Rigsarkivet, especially Bøger over fangerne på Bremerholmen, 15 and 16, Holmens chef, RA.

62 All three of these writers are known to Danish maritime historians, but have been neglected or used only for harvesting colourful anecdotes. As a contrast, equivalent writings in other languages have been explored at length by scholars wanting to examine the social and cultural histories of the maritime lower classes. For instance, the autobiography of English sailor Edward Barlow is central to Rediker's work and has also been the subject of a detailed case study in Patricia Fumerton, *Unsettled: The Culture of Mobility and the Working Poor in Early Modern England* (Chicago: Chicago University Press, 2006). Her conclusion that Barlow's writing expresses an unsettled subjectivity characteristic of early modern seamen appears largely applicable to the Danish cases as well.

63 Heinsen, 'Nothing', 106–22.

64 For the sake of accessibility, I quote the English translation here.

65 Jon Olafsson, *The Life of the Icelander Jón Ólafsson, Traveller to India: Volume 1* (London: The Hakluyt Society, 1923), 207.

66 Ibid., 197.

67 Magnusson, *Islandsk*, 70–71.

68 E.g. Darnton, *Great Cat Massacre*.

69 Magnusson, *Islandsk*, 76.

70 Olafsson, *Life vol. 1*, 206–207.

71 Olafsson, *Life vol. 2*, 43–45.

72 Ibid., 104.

73 Magnusson, *Islandsk*, 102 and 107.

74 Ibid. 115–16.

75 Ibid., 77.

76 Ibid., 95–6.

77 Olafsson, *Life vol. II*, 157–58.

78 Ibid., 177–78.

79 Ibid., 220–21.

80 E.g. Trosner, *Tordenskiolds*, 8.

81 Ibid.., 68–9.

82 Ibid.

83 Ibid., 110.

84 Ibid., 117.

85 Ibid., 31.

86 Ibid., 5.

87 Ibid., 34.

88 Ibid., 75.

89 Rediker, *Between*, 229–35.

90 Hopkin, 'Storytelling', 194.

5 Birds in Cages

1 Memorandum, 'Fortegnelse huad det folck som döde paa henreysen til St Thomas hafuer kost Compagniet', 138, WIGC, RA.

2 Blom's instructions, 31 October 1682, 27, WIGC, RA.

3 Rediker and Linebaugh, *Many-Headed Hydra*, 61.

4 E.g. Peter Linebaugh, *The London Hanged: Crime and Civil Society in the Eighteenth Century*, 2nd ed. (London: Verso, 2006. Org. 1991), 23.

5 Stephanie Camp, *Closer to Freedom: Enslaved Women and Everyday Resistance in the Plantation South* (Chapel Hill: The University of North Carolina Press, 2004), 7.

6 Pieter Spierenburg, *The Prison Experience: Disciplinary Institutions and Their Inmates in Early Modern Europe* (Amsterdam: Amsterdam University Press, 2007, org. 1991)

7 de Vito and Lichtenstein, 'Writing'.

8 Poul Johannes Jørgensen, *Dansk Rets Historie* (Copenhagen: G.E.C. Gad, 1974), p. 206; Johan Thorsten Sellin, *Slavery and the Penal System* (New York: Elsevier, 1976).

9 Refererede sager oktober 1717, Litra B, Krigskancelliet, RA.

10 All quantitative data stems from a database of convicts created from the naval clerk's archive. This database will eventually be made public. The sources are boxes numbered 1 to 20 in Holmens chef, RA.

11 List of convicts, 29 August 1685, 181, WIGC, RA.

12 Hans Chr. Johansen, *Danish Population History: 1600–1939* (Odense: University Press of Southern Denmark, 2002), 62.

13 Christensen, 'Daglige', 325–85.

14 Court minutes, fol. 33–7, Dombøger, 25, Underadmiralitetsretten, Admiralitetet, RA.

15 Court minutes, fol. 232–36, Dombøger, 26, Underadmiralitetsretten, Admiralitetet, RA.

16 Court minutes, fol. 45–6, Standretsprotokoller, 50, Overadmiralitetsretten, Admiralitetet, RA.

17 Court minutes, fol. 87–97, Dombøger, 15, Underadmiralitetsretten, Admiralitetet, RA.

18 Court minutes, fol. 256–64, ibid.

19 Court minutes, fol. 261, Dombøger, 16, Underadmiralitetsretten, Admiralitetet, RA.

20 Thomas Agostini,'"Deserted His Majesty's Service": Military Runaways, the
   British-American Press, and the Problem of Desertion during the Seven Years' War',
   Journal of Social History 40, no. 4 (2007): 957–85.
21 Entries of Beck and Nieman, Bøger over Bremerholms fanger, 15, Holmens chef, RA.
22 Olafsson, *Life vol. I,* 41–44 and 175–178.
23 The King to Korfits Ulfeldt, 29 March 1640, in *Kong Christian den fjerdes egenhændige
   breve,* eds C.F. Bricka and J.A. Fridericia, (Copenhagen: Rudolph Klein, 1882), 4:319.
24 Olafsson, *Life vol. II,* 174.
25 Christian Larsen Kjær, *Forbryderen Christian Larsen Kjær, hans liv og Levnet,
   Nedskrevet af ham selv i Aaret 1860* (Rudkøbing, 1860), 122.
26 E.g. C. H. Visby, *Fald og Frelse* (Copenhagen: Fred. Høst, 1867).
27 Caspar Peter Rothe, *Søe-Røverens eller den berygtede Fribytter og Caper-Capitain,
   John Norcross Levnet og Trekker* (Copenhagen, 1756).
28 In Britain, the figure of the prison breaker captured the popular imagination in
   the early eighteenth century. It was epitomized in the character of John Sheppard
   analyzed by Linebaugh in *London,* chap. 1, as well as by Hitchcock and Shoemaker,
   London, 92–94. Sheppard and his daring escapes were the subject of a number of
   texts written by others as well as a short self-mythologizing narrative, supposedly
   written by himself with the assistance of Daniel Defoe. Sheppard's story is known to
   have animated other prisoners to emulate his escapes. No equivalent literature exists
   in Denmark, likely because of the harsh censorship at work in absolutist Denmark.
   However, it seems highly likely that oral traditions enabled similar emulation.
29 Lis Ekelund Nielsen and Palle Tolstrup Nielsen, *Danmarks Værste Fængsel: Om
   krudttånsfangerne i Kastellet 1817–47* (Copenhagen: Gyldendal, 2005), 29.
30 Maxwell-Stewart, *Closing,* 169.
31 Ibid., 165–200.
32 Copybook, p. 568–69, 3103–03, Det teologiske Fakultet, Københavns Universitet,
   RA; Krogh, *Oplysningstiden,* 132–35.
33 Minutes, 22 September 1686, 486–487, WIGC, RA.
34 Krogh, *Oplysningstiden,* 119–50.
35 Documents concerning Johan Otto Berchelmann, 1729, Domme over fangerne på
   Bremerholm, 12, Holmens chef, RA.
36 Documents on Gudmund Möller and Atzer Arentsen, 1706, Domme over fangerne
   på Bremerholm, 6, Holmens chef, RA.
37 Court minutes, fol. 248–52, Standretsprotokoller, box 50, Overadmiralitetsretten,
   Admiralitetet, RA.
38 Ibid., fol. 291–92.
39 Sentence of court martial, 27 September 1732, Justitsekstrakter, 11126,
   Generalauditøren, RA.
40 Minutes of court martial, 7 and 24 October 1732, Ibid.

41 Court minutes, fol. 97–98, Standretsprotokoller, box 50, Overadmiralitetsretten, Admiralitetet, RA.

42 Ibid., fol. 135–37.

43 Court minutes, fol. 26–7, Kommissionsprotokol, 1, Kommissionsdomstole, Admiralitetet, RA.

44 Court minutes, fol. 13–6, Dombøger, 24, Underadmiralitetsretten, Admiralitetet, RA.

45 Court minutes, fol. 217–21, Dombøger, 16, Underadmiralitetsretten, Admiralitetet, RA.

46 Entry of Jens Jensen, Bøger over Bremerholms fanger, 15, Holmens chef, RA.

47 Court minutes, fol. 57–9, Standretsprotokoller, 50, Overadmiralitetsretten, Admiralitetet, RA.

48 E.g. ibid., fol. 50.

49 Resolution of court martial, 12 November 1732, Justitsekstrakter, 11126, Generalauditøren, RA.

50 Court minutes, fol. 53, Standretsprotokoller, 50, Overadmiralitetsretten, Admiralitetet, RA.

51 Ibid., fol. 214–15.

52 Ibid., fol. 135–37.

53 Ibid., fol. 237.

54 Ibid., fol. 47.

55 Court documents on Abraham Bølge, Domme over fangerne på Bremerholmen, 10, Holmens chef, RA; Court records, fol. 636–43, Dombøger, 25, Underadmiralitetsretten, RA.

56 Documents on Arnold Osenberg, Domme over fangerne på Bremerholmen, 11, Holmens chef, RA.

57 Court minutes, fol. 191–92, Standretsprotokoller, 50, Overadmiralitetsretten, Admiralitetet, RA.

58 Court minutes, fol. 171–73, Dombøger, 22, Underadmiralitetsretten, Admiralitetet, RA.

59 Larsen's time on the loose is described in Tyge Krogh, 'Tyven', in *Nattens Gerninger*, eds Poul Duedahl and Ulrik Langen (Copenhagen: Gads forlag, 2015), 194–213 (204).

60 Documents of Anders Jensen Amager, 1737, Domme over fangerne på Bremerholmen, 14, Holmen's chef, RA.

61 Michael Sikora, 'Change and continuity in mercenary armies: Central Europe, 1650–1750', in *Fighting for a Living: A Comparative History of Military Labour,* ed. Erik-Jan Zürcher (Amsterdam: Amsterdam University Press, 2013), 201–42 (227).

62 Jeanette Kamp, 'Between Agency and Force: The Dynamics of Desertion in a Military Labour Market, Frankfurt am Main', in *Desertion,* eds Kamp and van Rossum, 49–72; Karsten Skjold Petersen, *Gevorbne krigskarle: Hvervede soldater i Danmark i 1774–1803* (Copenhagen: Museum Tusculanums Forlag, 2002), 120.

63 Court minutes, fol. 69–70, Standretsprotokoller, 50, Overadmiralitetsretten, Admiralitetet, RA.

64 Ibid., fol. 135–37.

65 Statute on deserters, 13 October 1703, printed in Jacob Henric Schou, *Chronologisk Register over de Kongelige Forordninger*, 2. ed. (Copenhagen, 1795), 2:81–83.

66 C.I.H Speerschneider, *Om isforholdene i danske farvande i ældre og nyere tid* (Copenhagen: G.E.C. Gad, 1915).

67 For more on deserters see, Petersen, *Gevorbne*, 141–47.

68 Documents concerning John Nielsen et al, 1729, Domme over fangerne på Bremerholmen, 12, Holmens chef, RA.

69 Ibid., documents concerning Hans Rasmussen and Peder Rasmussen; Sentence of Abraham Andersen, Justitsekstrakter, 11126, Generalauditøren, RA.

70 *Forordning om Fanger at dømmes effter lowen oc Recessen* (Copenhagen: 1673).

71 E.g. Minutes of court martial, 24 October 1732, Justitsekstrakter, 11126, Generalauditøren, RA.

72 Ingeborg Dalgas, *De bremerholmske jernfanger og fangevogtere på fæstningen Christiansø 1725–1735* (Aarhus, 2014), 51–3.

73 Finn Gad, *Grønlands Historie II: 1700–1782* (Copenhagen: Nyt Nordisk Forlag, 1969), 158.

74 Hall, *Slave*, 124–38.

75 Court minutes, 17 October 1673, 484, WIGC, RA.

76 Ibid., 19 October 1672 and 1 November 1675.

77 Testimony of Simon van Ockeren, 3 July 1680, 77, WIGC, RA.

78 Among them was Kresten Mortensen, discussed in chapter one.

79 9 September and 19 October 1672, court minutes, 484, WIGC, RA.

80 Ibid.

81 Ibid., 8 August 1672.

82 Journal, 11 October, 6 November and 26 November 1686, 496, WIGC, RA.

83 Court minutes, 19 October 1672 and 9 September 1677, 484, WIGC, RA. See also, Hall, *Slave*, 126; Jorge L. Chinea, 'A Quest for Freedom: The Immigration of Maritime Maroons into Puerto Rico, 1656–1800', *The Journal of Caribbean History* 31 (1997): 51–87; Hilary Beckles, 'From Land to Sea: Runaway slaves and servants in Barbados, 1630–1720', *Slavery & Abolition* 6, no. 3 (1985): 79–94.

84 Jørgen Iversen to the company directors, 15 September and 12 October 1681, 78, WIGC, RA.

85 Court minutes, 10 June 1674, 484, 484–485, WIGC, RA.

86 Court martial minutes, June 1751, 284, WIGC, RA.

87 Court minutes, 13 August 1686, 486, WIGC, RA; Journal, 30 July to 3 August 1686, 496, WIGC, RA.

88 Court minutes, 13 August 1686, 486, WIGC, RA; Journal, 13 July 1686, 496, WIGC, RA.

89   Jens Pedersen's sentence, 13 August 1685, Domme over fangerne på Bremerholmen, 2, Holmens chef (Søetaten).

90   Documents on Peder Nelausen, ibid.

91   Court minutes, 13 August 1686, 486, WIGC, RA.

92   Journal, 9–13 August 1686, 496, WIGC, RA.

93   Journal, 9 August 1686, 496, WIGC, RA.

94   Christopher Heins to the company directors, 5 October 1686, 89, WIGC, RA.

95   Court minutes, 13–16 August 1686, 486, WIGC RA; Journal, 19–20 August 1686, 496, WIGC, RA. This plan of sale was never realized because diseases killed most of the convicts in question.

96   Court minutes, 22 September 1686, 486, WIGC, RA.

97   Journal, 16 August to 7 September 1686, 496, WIGC, RA.

98   Court minutes, 22 September 1686, 486, WIGC, RA.

99   Journal, 25 September 1686, 496, WIGC, RA.

100 Christopher Heins to the company directors, 5 October 1686, 89, WIGC, RA.

101 Journal, 23 September 1686, 496, WIGC, RA.

102 Court minutes, 22 September 1686, 486, WIGC, RA.

103 Journal, 23 September 1686, 496, WIGC, RA.

104 Sentence of Niels Krog, 21 September 1686, Domme over fangerne på Bremerholm, 1, Holmens chef, RA.

105 List of convicts, 29 August 1685, 181, WIGC, RA.

106 Court minutes, 22 September 1686, 486, WIGC, RA.

107 Ibid.

108 Court minutes, 16 November 1686, 486, WIGC, RA.

109 One might, however, speculate if their overseer tacitly allowed it. He was none other than Hans Wadskye, introduced in Chapter 1. See Journal, 1 February 1687, 496, WIGC, RA. In February 1688, he again angered the governor, as he beat one of the company's enslaved workers so severely that the victim could not work. Ibid, 18 March 1688.

110 Court minutes, 16 November 1686, 486, WIGC, RA.

111 Journal, 5–6 November 1686, 496, WIGC, RA.

112 Court minutes, 16 November 1686, 486, WIGC, RA.

113 Journal, 8 November 1686, vol. 496, 496–498, WIGC, RA.

114 Court minutes, 16 November 1686, 486, WIGC, RA; Journal, 9–11 November 1686, 496, WIGC, RA.

115 Court minutes, 16 November 1686, court minutes, 486, WIGC, RA.

116 Rediker and Linebaugh, *Many-Headed Hydra,* chapter 2.

117 Journal, 19 November 1686, 496, WIGC, RA.

118 Ibid., 6 August 1687.

6 Dissonant Empire

1   Sir William Stapleton to Lords of Trade and Plantations, 30 August 1683, CO 1/52, no. 80, NA.

2   Nuala Zahedieh, 'Trade, Plunder, and Economic Development in Early English Jamaica, 1655–89', *The Economic History Review* 39, no. 2 (1986): 205–22; Starkey, 'Pirates'; Mark Hanna, *Pirate Nests and the Rise of the British Empire, 1570–1740* (Chapel Hill: The University of North Carolina Press, 2015); Janice E. Thomson, *Mercenaries, Pirates and Sovereigns: State-building and Extraterritorial Violence in Early Modern Europe* (Princeton: Princeton University Press, 1994).

3   Rediker, *Between*, 254–87; Rediker and Linebaugh, *Many-Headed*, 143–73.

4   Earle, *Pirate Wars*, 87–108 and 135–55.

5   Niklas Frykman, 'Pirates and Smugglers: Political Economy in the Red Atlantic', in *Mercantilism Reimagined: Political Economy in Early Modern Britain and Its Empire*, eds Philip J. Stern and Carl Wennerlind (Oxford: Oxford University Press 2014), 218–38 (esp. 221); The most famous example is the indentured servant–turned pirate Exquemelin, who escaped the brutalities of the plantations to engage upon a career of maritime crime. See Alexandre O. Exquemelin, *Bucaniers of America: Or, a True Account of the Most Remarkable Assaults Committed of late Years upon the Coasts of The West Indies, by the Bucaniers of Jamaica and Tortuga, Both English and French*, 2. ed. (London: William Crooke, 1684).

6   Sir William Stapleton to the Governor of St Thomas, 15 August 1683, CO 1/52, no. 57, NA. The figure of the enemy of mankind has been discussed in depth by Daniel Heller-Roazen, *The Enemy of All: Piracy and the Law of Nations* (New York: Zone Books, 2009).

7   Jesse Cromwell, '(Ex) Buccaneers and Spanish Subjects on the Campeche Logwood Periphery, 1660–1716', *Itinerario* 33, no. 3 (2009): 43–71; Nicholas Rogers, 'Caribbean Borderland: Empire, Ethnicity, and the Exotic on the Mosquito Coast', *Eighteenth-Century Life* 26, no. 3 (2002): 117–38.

8   See for instance, Earle, *Pirate Wars*, 143–44. The notoriety owes much to C. H. Haring's classic study *The Buccaneers in the West Indies in the XVII Century* (London: Methuen, 1910). Haring described English efforts to rid the Leeward Islands of pirates in the 1680s.

9   I use the term 'microregion' in the sense outlined by Mulich in his article 'Microregionalism', 72–94.

10 Extract of letter from Esmit, May 1682, 169, WIGC, RA.

11 Hans Jonsen to the company directors, 15 July and 8 October 1681, 78, WIGC, RA; Company directors to Nicholas Esmit, 15 November 1681, 42, WIGC, RA.

12 John Cox, 'The Adventures of Capt. Barth. Sharp', in *The Voyages and Adventures of Capt. Barth. Sharp And others,* ed. Philip Ayres (London: Walter Davis 1684), 1–114, (22).

13 Anonymous narrative, fol. 711, Additional manuscripts, 11.410, British Library.

14 Basil Ringrose, *Bucaniers of America. The Second Volume* (London: William Crooke, 1685), 63.

15 Howse and Thrower have provided an overview of the various journals and printed editions. See, Derek Howse and Norman J. W. Thrower: *A Buccaneer's Atlas* (Berkeley: University of California Press, 1992).

16 Heinsen, 'Sørøveriets', 43–67.

17 Ringrose, *Bucaniers*, the preface.

18 Cox, 'Adventures', 25–7; Bartholomew Sharp, 'Captain Sharp's Journal of his Expedition. Written by Himself', in *A Collection of Voyages,* ed. William Hacke (London: James Knapton 1699), 1–55.

19 Anonymous narrative, fol. 681–82, Additional manuscripts, 11.410, British Library. Upon his return to the Caribbean, Coxon entered into the service of the governor of Jamaica, who commissioned him to hunt pirates. In this respect, he faced a mutiny by his men who wanted themselves to go pirating, but he managed to suppress it by personally killing two of the mutineers. Sir Thomas Lynch to Secretary Sir Leoline Jenkins, 6 November 1682, CO 1/49, No. 91, NA.

20 Ringrose, *Bucaniers*, 90.

21 Cox, 'The Adventures', 48–9.

22 Rediker, *Villains.*

23 William Dick, 'A brief account of Captain Sharp, and other his Companions', in *Bucaniers of America*, [Alexandre O. Exquemelin] (London: William Crooke, 1984), 63–84 (76).

24 E.g. Woodes Rogers, *A Cruising Voyage Round the World: First to the South-Seas, Thence To The East-Indies, And Homewards By The Cape Of Good Hope* (London: A. Bell, 1712), 235.

25 E.g. ibid.

26 Sir Richard Hawkins, 'The Observations of Sir Richard Hawkins, Knight, in his Voyage to the South Sea', in *The Hawkins' Voyages During the Reigns of Henry VII, Queen Elizabeth, and James I*, ed. Clements R. Markham (London: The Hakluyt Society, 1878. Org. 1622), 87–329 (quote from 220).

27 Sharp, 'Journal', 46. The irony is apparent, as this was, in fact, not his ship.

28 Rediker, *Villains.*

29 Ritchie, *Captain Kidd*, 25.

30 Sharp, 'Journal', 54; Anonymous narrative, fol. 739, Additional manuscripts, 11.410, British Library.

31 Glyndwr Williams, *The Great South Sea: English Voyages and Encounters 1570–1750* (Yale: Yale University Press, 1997), 83–93.

32 Anonymous narrative, Additional manuscripts, 11.410, British Library.

33 Sharp would eventually end up at St Thomas as well. In the second half of the 1690s, he arrived there to settle down but quickly fell into debt and died in prison in 1702. At one point, the governor tried having him transferred to Bremerholmen. See Johan Lorentz to the company directors, 24 June 1698, 89, WIGC, RA. Before coming to St Thomas, he had roamed the Caribbean, at times acting as a pirate hunter. See Michael Jarvis, *In the Eye of All Trade* (Williamsburg: University of North Carolina Press 2010), 69. See also Westergaard, *Danish West Indies,* 49.

34 Gabriel Milan to the company directors, 26 July 1685, 89 WIGC, RA.

35 As hinted throughout Rediker's analysis of piracy, it was very much a phenomenon driven by storytelling and legend. See, for instance, Rediker, *Villains*, 41–2.

36 Deposition of Richard Richardson, 17 December 1683, CO 1/53, no. 98, NA.

37 Eaton's crew would later form the base of the crews that roamed the Pacific in the middle of the 1680s, some of whom ended up circumnavigating the globe.

38 At this point, Moreton left Bond's men. See the manuscript of Ambrose Cowley entitled 'The voyage of Capt. Cowley, a Papist' in 642 Miscellany, Lambeth Palace Manuscripts, Lambeth Palace Library, London.

39 Deposition of Richard Richardson, 17 December 1683, CO 1/53, no. 98, NA.

40 Deposition of John Thomson, 17 December 1683, CO 1/53, no. 100, NA.

41 Deposition of Richard Richardson, 17 December 1683, CO 1/53, no. 98, NA; Deposition of John Poynting, 17 December 1683, CO 1/53, no. 99, NA.

42 The reasons behind this coup are unclear.

43 Deposition of Richard Richardson, 17 December 1683, CO 1/53, no. 98, NA.

44 Sir Thomas Lynch to Secretary Sir Leoline Jenkins, 6 November 1682, CO 1/49, no. 91, NA.

45 'A Journal of my proceedings of H.M.S. Francis with the Governor of St Thomas's Island'. CO 1/52, no. 40. July 30, 1683.

46 Narrative, 'A true and perfect narrative and relation of all the horrid and villainous murthers, robberies, spoils, and piracies committed as well in the American as the African seas by John Hamlyn', 18 October 1683, CO 1/53, no. 9, NA.

47 Ibid.

48 Stapleton's career has been discussed at some length in Shaw, *Everyday*, 171–73.

49 Sir William Stapleton to Lords of Trade and Plantations, 8 June, 1684, CO 1/54, no. 121, NA.

50 Sir William Stapleton to Lords of Trade and Plantations, 11 November 1682, CO 1/49, no. 95, NA.

51 Ibid.

52 Ibid.

53 Sir William Stapleton to Lords of Trade and Plantations, 15 August 1683, CO 1/52, no. 56, NA.

54 Sir William Stapleton to Lords of Trade and Plantations, 13 January 1684, CO 1/54, no. 5, NA.

55 Sir William Stapleton to Lords of Trade and Plantations, 15 August 1683, CO 1/52, no. 56, NA.

56 Sir William Stapleton to the Governor of St Thomas, 15 August 1683, CO 1/52, no. 57, NA.

57 Sir William Stapleton to Lords of Trade and Plantations, 16 July 1683, CO 1/52, no. 27, NA.

58 'Narrative account of Capt Carlile's burning of the TROMPEUSE', 1683, Gosse Papers, 8, National Maritime Museum, Greenwich; Journal of Carlyle, 'A Journal of my proceedings of H.M.S. Francis', CO 1/52, no. 40, NA.

59 Sir William Stapleton to Lords of Trade and Plantations, 30 August 1683, CO 1/52, no. 80, NA; Sir Thomas Lynch to the Lord President of the Council, June 20, 1684, CO 1/54, no. 132, NA.

60 Earle, *Pirate Wars*, 144.

61 Sir William Stapleton to Lords of Trade and Plantations, 28 October 1684, CO 1/55, no. 57, NA.

62 Memorandum, 'Relation om St Thomas og St Jans Tilstand', 15 May 1686, 366, WIGC, RA.

63 Such tension became especially pronounced during this era, but was in no way singular. See, Ward, *Networks of Empire*, 78.

64 Michel de Certeau, *The Practice of Everyday Life* (Berkeley: University of California Press, 1984).

65 Bro-Jørgensen, *Tropekolonier*, 147–8. For more on the Brandenburg empire see Eberhard Schmitt, 'The Brandenburg Overseas Trading Companies in the 17th Century', in *Companies and Trade*, eds Leonard Blussé and Femme Gaastra (Leiden: Leiden University Press, 1981), 159–78.

66 Thus, at the same time that the use of convicts was abandoned the island began seeing a steady influx of enslaved Africans. See the following URL for details http://slavevoyages.org/tast/database/search.faces?yearFrom=1514&yearTo=1866&mjslptimp= (accessed online 12 December 2016)

67 Bro-Jørgensen, *Tropekolonier*, 156–62.

68 Ibid., 152–53.

69 Ibid., 167.

70 Ibid., 168.

71 Linda Rupert, *Creolization and Contraband: Curacao in the Early Modern Atlantic World* (Athens and London: The University of Georgia Press, 2012).

72 E.g. Victor Enthoven, 'That Abominable Nest of Pirates: St. Eustatius and the North Americans, 1680–1780', *Early American Studies: An Interdisciplinary Journal* 10, no. 2 (2012): 239–301 (248). Michael Jarvis argues that the Dutch presence meant that

St Thomas 'became more an extension of Amsterdam than Copenhagen' (Jarvis,
In the Eye, 167). In his in-depth analysis of the trading networks of merchants
and seafarers at Bermuda, he argues that 'Bermudian mariners appreciated these
Dutch and Danish neutral ports because they offered safe havens and lucrative
markets as well as broader international webs of commercial contact and
information' (ibid., 112–13). Building on the pioneering work of Julius S. Scott,
Jarvis also argues that places such as St Thomas functioned as hubs for the
sharing of information (Ibid., 138.) Another historian, Christian J. Koot, has
argued that the inter-imperial trade at St Thomas spurred anxieties among
local British officials well into the eighteenth century (Christian J. Koot,
*Empire at the Periphery: British Colonists, Anglo-Dutch Trade, and the
Development of the British Atlantic, 1621–1713* (New York and London: New
York University Press, 2011), 195–96.) Thus, even while the piracy problem
mostly abated, St Thomas kept frustrating mercantilist imperatives. See also
Wim Klooster, *Illicit Riches: Dutch trade in the Caribbean 1648–1795* (Leiden:
KITLV Press, 1998).
73 Jean-Baptiste Labat, *The Memoirs of Père Labat 1693–1705*, trans. John Eaden
(London: Frank Cass, 1970), 200–05.
74 William Dampier, *A New Voyage Round the World* (London: James Knapton,
1697), 46.
75 Koot, *Empire at the Periphery*.
76 Hornby, *Kolonierne*, 61–3; Hall, *Slave*, 5–6.
77 Olsen, *Tropekolonier*, 195.
78 Fredrik Hyrum Svensli, '"A Fine Flintlock, a Pair of Ditto Pistols and a Hat with a
Gold Galloon": Danish Political and Commercial Strategies on the Gold Coast in
the Early 18th Century', in *Ports of Globalisation, Places of Creolisation: Nordic
Possessions in the Atlantic World during the Era of the Slave Trade*, ed. Holger Weiss
(Leiden: Brill, 2015), 68–100 (73).
79 Ibid. See also Nørregaard, *Tropekolonier*, 99–100.

Conclusion

1 The Company directors to Copenhagen's chief of police, 4 June 1701, 181,
WIGC, RA.
2 J. L. v Holstein to the Company directors, 14 August 1737, 181, WIGC, RA.
3 The Company directors to J. L. v Holstein, 21 September 1737, 181, WIGC, RA.
4 The Copenhagen poor relief commissioners to the Company directors, 12 February
1738, 181, WIGC, RA.
5 J. L. v Holstein to the Company directors, 4 November 1747, 181, WIGC, RA.

6 The chronology is a little unclear, as a draft for the answer appears to predate the enquiry itself. This suggests that there were more such requests that have, however, not survived.

7 The company directors to J. L. v Holstein, 28 November 1747, 181, WIGC, RA.

8 Ibid.

9 Ibid.

10 Unsigned note, 1746, 181, WIGC, RA.

11 In recent years, scholars have increasingly attempted to historicize the archives themselves, perhaps most notably Trouillot, *Silencing*; Nicholas Dirks, 'Annals of the Archive: Ethnographic Notes on the Sources of History', in *From the Margins: Historical Anthropology and Its Futures*, ed. Brian Keith Axel (Durham: Duke University Press, 2002), 47–65; Antoinette Burton, *Dwelling in the Archive: Women Writing House, Home, and History in Late Colonial India* (New York: Oxford University Press, 2003); Betty Joseph, *Reading the East India Company, 1720–1840: Colonial Currencies of Gender* (Chicago: The University of Chicago Press, 2004); Anjali Arondekar, 'Without a Trace: Sexuality and the Colonial Archive', *Journal of the History of Sexuality* 14, no. 1 (2005): 10–27; Tony Ballantyne, 'Mr Peal's Archive: Mobility and Exchange in Histories of Empire', in *Archive Stories: Facts, Fictions, and the Writing of History*, ed Antoinette Burton (Durham: Duke University Press, 2005), 87–110; Stoler, *Along*; James Epstein, *Scandal of Colonial Rule: Power and Subversion in the British Atlantic during the Age of Revolution* (Cambridge: Cambridge University Press, 2012). Stoler provides a useful overview of the archival turn in colonial history in Stoler, *Along*, 44–51.

12 Jessica Roitman and Karwan Fatah-Black, '"Being speculative is better than to not do it at all": an interview with Natalie Zemon Davis', *Itinerario* 39, no. 1 (2015): 3–15.

13 Rediker has stressed just how much of the knowledge colonial elites possessed actually stemmed from maritime workers. Rediker, *Outlaws*, chap. 1. Even though their voices were distrusted, the entire project of European expansion often hinged on the knowledge sailors produced and transmitted. Another maritime historian, Niklas Frykman, has highlighted the many connections between mutinies in the revolutionary 1790s – connections constituted by the circulation of men, but also of news informed by lower-deck traditions (Frykman, 'Connections'). Echoing an older tradition of seeing black sailors as carriers of rumour in the Caribbean, Karwan Fatah-Black has highlighted how the unrest on Curaçao in those same years was also shaped by news circulated by common sailors (Fatah-Black, 'Orangism', 35–60). Even more recently, Stephanie Mawson has highlighted the importance of rumour in the convict mutinies that marred the Spanish Pacific in the 1680s – mutinies influenced by deteriorating material conditions and fears exacerbated by the fragility of Spanish colonization in the region (a case with many parallels to the one discussed here; see

Mawson, 'Rebellion,' 138–46). Similarly, Tim Hitchcock and Robert Shoemaker, building on the work of Emma Christopher, have noted how a mutiny on board an English transport ship bound for Maryland in 1783 was prompted by rumour that the convicts were instead to be taken to Africa. Hitchcock and Shoemaker, *London*, 372–73. The list of examples continues, demonstrating just how much power, even violent power, subaltern voices carried.

Index

Printed in Great Britain
by Amazon